THE MALTHUSIAN CONTROVERSY

THE MALTHUSIAN CONTROVERSY

by

KENNETH SMITH

M.SC.(ECON.), B.COM., PH.D. (LONDON)

OCTAGON BOOKS

A DIVISION OF FARRAR, STRAUS AND GIROUX

New York 1978

First published 1951

Reprinted 1978
by special arrangement with Routledge & Kegan Paul

OCTAGON BOOKS
A DIVISION OF FARRAR, STRAUS & GIROUX, INC.
19 Union Square West
New York, N.Y. 10003

TO MY WIFE

Library of Congress Cataloging in Publication Data

Smith, Kenneth, 1910-1966.
The Malthusian controversy.

Reprint of the 1951 ed. published by Routledge & K. Paul, London.
Originally presented as the author's thesis, University of London.
Bibliography: p.
Includes index.
1. Malthus, Thomas Robert, 1766-1834. 2. Population. I. Title.
HB863.S6 1978 301.32 78-15727
ISBN 0-374-97510-8

Printed in USA by
Thomson-Shore, Inc.
Dexter, Michigan

1-10-79

CONTENTS

AUTHOR'S NOTE

This work was approved by the University of London as a thesis for the award of the Degree of Doctor of Philosophy.

I should like to place on record my gratitude to Mr. H. L. Beales for suggesting such a vitally interesting subject for a thesis; to Professor D. V. Glass who arranged for its publication; and to Dr. P. Jordan for help and encouragement extending over many years.

My grateful thanks are especially due to my colleague, Mr. E. S. Robinson, who has read the proofs and relieved me of the onerous task of preparing the index.

K. S.

Mid-Essex Technical College and School of Art,
Chelmsford.
1st March, 1951.

BOOK ONE
INTRODUCTORY

CHAPTER ONE

THE ORIGINS OF THE THEORY

THE FIRST ESSAY

'He has not left opinion where he found it; he has advanced or given it a wrong bias, or thrown a stumbling-block in its way. In a word, his name is not stuck, like so many others, in the firmament of reputation, nobody knows why, inscribed in great letters, and with a transparency of TALENTS, GENIUS, LEARNING blazing round it. It is tantamount to an idea; it is identified with a principle; it means that *the population cannot go on perpetually increasing without pressing on the limits of the means of subsistence, and that a check of some kind or other must, sooner or later, be opposed to it.* This is the essence of the doctrine which Mr. Malthus has been the first to bring into general notice, and, as we think, to establish beyond the fear of contradiction.'[1]

So wrote Hazlitt, one of Malthus's most bitter and most persistent critics, and with a great measure of truth.

When in 1798 an obscure curate of a small Surrey parish,[2] who had frequently argued with his father concerning the merits of the views of Godwin on the perfectibility of mankind, sat down to clarify his thoughts by writing them on paper; and when, finding the subject developing even more convincingly than he had at first expected, he decided to publish his views anonymously, he little guessed that the year of the publication of the *Essay on Population* would thenceforth be taken as a base year in the history of population doctrines. Yet so it was, and,

[1] Hazlitt, *Spirit of the Age*, O.U.P., World's Classics, p. 143.

[2] For biographical details see Bonar, *Malthus and His Work*, 1924; Empson, *Edinburgh Review*, Jan., 1837; Otter's *Memoir*, 1836; Keynes, *Essays in Biography*, 1933.

until comparatively recent times at any rate, views on population could be conveniently classified as pre-Malthusian, Malthusian, anti-Malthusian, and neo-Malthusian.

The *Essay* was avowedly a controversial work, aimed at Condorcet and Godwin. 'I have read some of the speculations on the perfectibility of man and of society, with great pleasure. . . . But I see great, and, to my understanding, unconquerable difficulties in the way to them.'[1] These difficulties were embodied in the principle of population.

The doctrine, in its unqualified form, is comparatively easy to state, and there is a sense in which, despite many qualifications, and subsequent modifications, Malthus adhered tenaciously not only to the original framework, but also to certain specific forms of statement. Yet an impartial study of the various editions of his main work, and of his other cognate writings, leaves the reader often in doubt as to where exactly Malthus is taking his stand. He was often misrepresented, both by his friends and his critics—though not so often by the latter as too fervent admirers would aver—but some responsibility at least rests on his own shoulders. His work is a mixture of dogmatic propositions and diffuse qualifications, not always easily assimilated, and often apparently contradictory. Moreover, a good deal of the criticism was directed as much against the followers of Malthus as against the leader himself. If his disciples misunderstood or misrepresented him, it was as necessary for his contemporaries to attack these misconceptions as it was to attack the more cautious attitude of Malthus himself.

Substantial modifications were made in the theory in the second edition of 1803, and in Professor Cannan's judgment: 'It is in great measure the result of this change between the first and the later editions that the soundest economists will hesitate if asked directly, "What is the principle of population as understood by Malthus?" or "What is the Malthusian theory of population?"'[2] However that may be, the message of the *Essay* of 1798 was clear enough. It startled the attention of Godwin and his followers. It was a 'facer,'[3] brilliantly written and much easier to attack than to refute.

[1] *Essay*, 1798 edn., Royal Economic Society Reprint, p. 7.

[2] *Theories of Production and Distribution*, 1903, p. 134.

[3] Hazlitt, *Spirit of the Age*, p. 144.

Malthus starts by making two postulata: 'First, that food is necessary to the existence of man. Secondly, that the passion between the sexes is necessary, and will remain nearly in its present state.'[1] Having justified his regard for these postulata as fixed laws of nature he proceeds:

'Assuming then, my postulata as granted, I say, that the power of population is indefinitely greater than the power in the earth to produce subsistence for man. Population, when unchecked, increases in a geometrical ratio. Subsistence increases only in an arithmetical ratio. A slight acquaintance with numbers will shew the immensity of the first power in comparison of the second.

'By that law of our nature which makes food necessary to the life of man, the effects of these two unequal powers must be kept equal.

'This implies a strong and constantly operating check on population from the difficulty of subsistence. This difficulty must fall some where; and must necessarily be severely felt by a large portion of mankind' (pp. 13-14).

There is a constant struggle for existence among plants and animals. Man cannot escape from it. 'Among plants and animals its effects are waste of seed, sickness, and premature death. Among mankind, misery and vice (p. 15). This natural inequality of the two powers of population, and of production in the earth . . . appears insurmountable in the way to the perfectibility of society' (p. 16). 'Consequently, if the premises are just, the argument is conclusive against the perfectibility of the mass of mankind' (p. 17).

The period during which population might double itself is deduced from American experience to be twenty-five years. The arithmetical ratio rests on less firm ground. It is a maximum beyond which 'the most enthusiastic speculator' cannot conceive the earth to produce (p. 22). Hence arises the absolute necessity for some checks to the growth of population; and these checks are misery and vice.

'That population cannot increase without the means of subsistence, is a proposition so evident, that it needs no illustration.

'That population does invariably increase, where there are

[1] *Essay*, 1798 edn., p. 11.

the means of subsistence, the history of every people that have ever existed will abundantly prove.

'And, that the superior power of population cannot be checked, without producing misery or vice, the ample portion of these too bitter ingredients in the cup of human life, and the continuance of the physical causes that seem to have produced them, bear too convincing a testimony' (p. 37).

Malthus notes the operation of the preventive check (postponed marriage) in this country, but attributes to it the extension of vice (pp. 63–70). The positive check shows itself in such phenomena as severe distress amongst the lowest orders of society and a high infant mortality.

'The happiness of a country does not depend, absolutely, upon its poverty, or its riches, upon its youth, or its age, upon its being thinly, or fully inhabited, but upon the rapidity with which it is increasing, upon the degree in which the yearly increase of food approaches to the yearly increase of an unrestricted population' (p. 137).

Thus he arrives at the gloomy conclusion that 'famine seems to be the last, the most dreadful resource of nature. The power of population is so superior to the power in the earth to produce subsistence for man, that premature death must in some shape or other visit the human race. The vices of mankind are active and able ministers of depopulation. They are the precursors in the great army of destruction; and often finish the dreadful work themselves. But should they fail in this war of extermination, sickly seasons, epidemics, pestilence, and plague, advance in terrific array, and sweep off their thousands and ten thousands. Should success be still incomplete; gigantic inevitable famine stalks in the rear, and with one mighty blow, levels the population with the food of the world' (pp. 139–140).[1]

Alas for the dreams of Condorcet and Godwin! Wallace had been wrong in supposing that the danger was remote; it was here and now. Godwin was quite wrong too in attributing vice and misery to human institutions which are mere feathers on the surface. Deeper seated causes 'corrupt the springs, and render

[1] There is a gusto about passages like these which, if not denoting approval, implies a sort of sense of fitness. There are many such, and they stung the critics into extravagant expressions which marred the force of their criticism.

turbid the whole stream of human life' (p. 177). The perfect society would be wrecked by the increase of its own numbers without a corresponding increase of food. The institutions of marriage and property would have to be restored, the world would be divided among the living, and fresh children would be born into a world already appropriated. 'These are the unhappy persons who, in the great lottery of life, have drawn a blank' (p. 204).

A society founded on benevolence must degenerate into a 'society divided into a class of proprietors, and a class of labourers, and with self-love for the main-spring of the great machine' (p. 207). If Godwin's system were completely established, 'not thirty years could elapse, before its utter destruction from the simple principle of population' (p. 208).

This is not the place to expand the above summary treatment of the arguments of the first *Essay*, and their bearing on perfectibility will be raised later. Nor is it necessary to dwell on the salient features of the principle as enunciated in 1798: within five years it was to be expanded and transformed. The arguments against Godwin receded into the background; the arguments against the poor laws, already in embryo in 1798, emerged in their full stature by 1803. Nevertheless, if the *Essay* of 1803 is counted as Malthus's main contribution, it was that of 1798 which enabled him to make his mark. It is worth while, therefore, before passing on to our main task, to pause and inquire why this work was so successful.

SOME EARLY VIEWS—RALEIGH AND BACON

It was not that the doctrine was original. In the first edition Malthus acknowledges the work of Hume, Adam Smith, and Wallace. In the edition of 1803 he notes how much more had been done previously than he had hitherto thought, mentioning particularly Montesquieu, Dr. Franklin, Sir James Steuart, Arthur Young, and Townsend. Nevertheless it is possible to agree with the *Quarterly Review*:

'Though not original, these opinions were, however, brought forward by him in so striking and authoritative a manner, with the advantages of a polished style and eloquent language, a tone of philosophical inquiry, and the justificatory evidence of statistical details, as to attract far more attention than they had previously obtained, and irrevocably couple the name of Malthus with the theory they comprehend.'[1]

Almost every age has had something to say on the question of population, usually from a political, national, or religious angle, but before Malthus no one had treated this aspect of the subject on such an ample scale.[2]

In Italy Botero, in his book *Ragione di Stato*, was the first to bring out clearly the relation between population and the means of subsistence, between the generative power of mankind and the nutritive power of the State—a stage which was only reached much later in England.[3]

Sir Walter Raleigh, in his *Historie of the World*, 1652, argued that population would have grown beyond the possibility of subsistence but for the checks of war and pestilence. War is the necessary and logical outcome of population pressure, he asserts, and the alternative course of sending out emigrants supplied with the necessaries of life is not likely to be carried out by powerful nations when, by making war on their neighbours, they can force on them this unpleasant task.

'Suffice it, that when any country is overlaid by the multitude which live upon it, there is a natural necessity compelling it to disburden itself, and lay the load upon others, by right or wrong; for (to omit the danger of pestilence, often visiting them which live in throngs) there is no misery that urgeth men so violently unto desperate courses and contempt of death, as the torments and threats of famine: wherefore the war that is grounded upon this general remediless necessity may be termed the general and remediless, or necessary war.'[4]

Not that colonization really weakens the home population. It is 'like a tree from whom plants have been taken to fill whole orchards.[5] If Edward III had succeeded in conquering France, it could have been peopled with English without noticeably

[1] *Quarterly Review*, April, 1831, p. 99.

[2] Nitti, *Population and the Social System*, p. 6.

[3] See Nitti, op. cit., p. 7; Bonar, *Theories of Population from Raleigh to Arthur Young*; Stangeland, *Pre-Malthusian Doctrines of Population*.

[4] *Works of Sir Walter Ralegh*, Oxford, 1829; *Discourse of War in General*, p. 256.

[5] Raleigh, op. cit., p. 258.

emptying this island.[1] What then has become of this potential multitude?

'Surely, they died not of old age, nor went out of the world by the ordinary ways of nature; but famine and contagious distempers, the sword, the halter, and a thousand mischiefs have consumed them. Yea of many of them perhaps children were never born; for they that want means to nourish children will abstain from marriage; or (which is all one) they cast away their bodies upon rich old women; or otherwise make unequal or unhealthy matches for gain; or because of poverty they think it a blessing, which in nature is a curse, to have their wives barren.'[2]

The answer thus given is thoroughly Malthusian: they perished by vice and misery, the positive or preventive checks.

War is at basis an economic phenomenon. 'Princes, excusing their drawing the sword by devised pretences of necessity, speak often more truly than they are aware.' The natural cause of remediless war is 'want of room upon the earth.'[3]

Francis Bacon, Raleigh's contemporary, had also definite ideas on the subject of population, and, although he favoured an increasing population, he advocated certain conditions and precautions. 'Generally, it is to be foreseene, that the Population of a Kingdome, (especially if it be not mowen downe by warrs) doe not exceed, the Stock of the Kingdome, which should maintaine them.'[4]

The aim should not be numbers alone, but productive numbers. The principal objective of any state is to have a 'Race of Military Men,'[5] but states that aim at greatness should beware of multiplying their nobility and gentlemen too fast.[6] 'For that maketh the Common Subject, grow to be a Peasant, and Base Swaine, driven out of Heart, and in effect but the *Gentlemans* Labourer.'[7]

Bacon saw clearly the danger of over-population, and the

[1] Cf. Franklin, *Observations concerning the Increase of Mankind, Peopling of Countries, &c.*, 1751 (McCulloch's Reprint, p. 171). Referred to by Malthus.

[2] Raleigh, op. cit., pp. 258–259.

[3] Id., p. 259.

[4] Essay on *Seditions and Troubles* (Wright's edn. 1865), p. 59.

[5] *Of the True Greatnesse of Kingdomes and Estates*, p. 121.

[6] *Of Seditions and Troubles*, p. 59.

[7] *Of the True Greatnesse of Kingdomes etc.*, p. 122.

necessity of emigration when population exceeded the means of subsistence.

'Looke when the World hath fewest *Barbarous Peoples*, but such as commonly will not marry or generate, except they know meanes to live; (As it is almost every where at this day, except *Tartary*) there is no Danger of Inundations of People: But when there be great *Shoales of People* which go on to populate, without foreseeing Meanes of Life and Sustentation, it is of Necessity, that once in an Age or two, they discharge a Portion of their People upon other Nations.'[1]

Elsewhere he gives his views on colonization, in particular deprecating colonizing by means of transported men.[2]

GRAUNT AND PETTY

Raleigh and Bacon hinted at the Malthusian theory, but their views were little more than hints; there was no systematic treatment. It was not until Graunt published his celebrated book that adequate demographic foundations began to be laid upon which a safer structure could be erected.

From the middle of the sixteenth to the middle of the eighteenth century opinion was dominated by the ideas of the Mercantile system. Governments required men and money; consequently the views of population writers generally were in favour of expansion. Indeed many governments made positive attempts to stimulate an increase in the number of their subjects. Direct encouragements were given to marriage, fecundity was encouraged by the granting of rewards for large families, celibacy was visited with various disabilities, and punishment of illegitimacy was modified or removed, hospitals being provided for foundlings.[3]

In the year 1662 Captain John Graunt published that striking book *Natural and Political Observations upon the Bills of Mortality*. Graunt was 'an opulent merchant of London, of great weight and consideration in the city.'[4] His work is a careful and painstaking analysis of the London Bills of Mortality, together with a

[1] *Of Vicissitude of Things*, p. 236. [2] *Of Plantations*, p. 139.

[3] Stangeland, *Pre-Malthusian Doctrines of Population*, 1904, Chapter IV.

[4] *Economic Writings of Sir Wm. Petty* (Ed. C. H. Hull, 1899), quoted on p. xxxv.

series of illuminating deductions. Graunt, an 'ordinary man, who did an extraordinary deed,'[1] was the founder of Demography, and his work became a model for subsequent inquirers.

According to Hull his four chief statistical discoveries were as follows: the regularity of certain social phenomena which appear to depend upon chance, the excess of the male over the female births and the approximate numerical equality of the sexes, the high rate of mortality in the early years of life, and the excess of the urban over the rural death rate.[2] Graunt's influence on subsequent writers is sufficiently obvious.

His great contemporary, Sir William Petty, lies even closer to our subject, and Malthus's debt to him is specifically acknowledged. In various Essays on Political Arithmetick Petty brings to the measure of number as many facts as possible. From our point of view, possibly the most notable remarks are to be found in *Another Essay on Political Arithmetick, concerning the Growth of the City of London, etc.*, 1682. He deduces from the figures of mortality that London has doubled its population in approximately forty years.

In estimating the rate at which the population of the whole country doubles he has more difficulty. There are good observations which work out at a doubling in about 1,200 years; other good observations show an increase ten times as great. There is also a third 'Natural possibility.'[3] This gives a birth rate of 125—four times as much as in London, and three times as much as in the country.

[1] Bonar, *Theories of Population from Raleigh to Arthur Young*, p. 68.

[2] Hull, op. cit., p. lxxvi.

[3] Hull (Vol. II), p. 462: 'For that by some late Observations, the Teeming Females between 15 and 44, are about 180 of the said 600, and the Males of between 18 and 59, are about 180 also, and that every Teeming Woman can bear a Child once in two Years; from all which it is plain, that the Births may be 90. (and abating 15 for Sickness, Young Abortions, and Natural Barrenness) there may remain 75 Births, which is an Eighth of the People; which by some Observations we have found to be but a two and thirtieth part, or but a quarter of what is thus shewn to be Naturally possible. Now, according to this Reckoning, if the Births may be 75 of 600, and the Burials but 15, then the Annual Increase of the People will be 60; and so the said 600 People may double in 10 Years, which differs yet more from 1200 above-mentioned.'

Petty thus arrives at possible doubling periods ranging from ten years to twelve hundred, but resolves the difficulty by striking a kind of average which results in a figure of '360 Years for the time of doubling (including some Allowance for Wars, Plagues, and Famine, the Effects thereof, though they be Terrible at the Times and Places where they happen, yet in a period of 360 Years, is no great Matter in the whole Nation).'[1] Even at this rate of doubling the 320 millions then on the earth would increase within 2,000 years so as to give 'one Head for every two Acres of land in the Habitable part of the Earth. And then, according to the Prediction of the Scriptures, there must be Wars and great Slaughter.'[2]

Turning his attention to the Ancient World, Petty finds that no fixed period of doubling will fit the facts. A doubling in 150 years, apparently the most suitable, means that there were only 512 souls in the whole world in the time of Moses. A less number, such as 100 years, would have made the world over-peopled 700 years ago. He therefore abandons the attempt to find a single doubling period, and rectifies his doctrine 'by making many Numbers in Continuall Proportion.' The periods of doubling range from 10 years at the time of the Flood to 1,200 years in his own day, and give intermediate results apparently to his satisfaction. It is noteworthy that this notion of successive doublings, which so overlays and mystifies the whole subject, gives in his case a geometrical progression for the number of people in successive periods; but the periods themselves are varied in an attempt to square with the facts.[3]

Petty had none of Malthus's dread of increase in population. Fewness of people was the real poverty.

'If the people be so few, as that they can live, *Ex sponte Creatis*, or with little labour, such as is Grazing, &c. they become wholly without Art.[4] . . . and one Man by Art may do as much work, as many without it; viz one Man with a Mill can grind as much Corn, as twenty can pound in a Mortar.'[5]

Improvements in the division of labour and economies of government would enable the growing population to be sustained.

[1] Hull, op. cit., Vol. II, p. 463.
[2] Id., p. 464.
[3] Id., Table, p. 468.
[4] Hull, op. cit., Vol. I, p. 34.
[5] Id., p. 249.

SIR MATTHEW HALE

Another notable contemporary of both Petty and Graunt was Sir Matthew Hale, whose work, *The Primitive Origination of Mankind*, published in 1677, a year after the death of the author, contains a thorough examination of the growth of population in the earth. His object being to prove that mankind had a beginning, he proposes the following inquiries:

'1. Whether according to the ordinary course and procedure of Nature in the Generations of Mankind, there be not a gradual and considerable Increase of Mankind upon the face of the Earth, unless some collateral Emergency or Occurrence interrupt or correct that Increase.

'2. What Correctives there may be supposed that may check and restrain that Increase of Mankind, that otherwise according to the ordinary course of Nature would have obtained in the World.

'3. Whether those Correctives or collateral Occurrences which have been, or may be supposed to have been in the World, have so far prevailed, as totally to stop that Increase of Mankind, which upon a Natural account, without the intervention of such Correctives would have obtained.

'4. Whether notwithstanding all these Correctives of the Increase or Excesses of Generations, yet if still the numbers of Mankind have increased, it be not a sufficient argument to satisfie a reasonable Man that Mankind had an Inception, and that within such a period or compass of Duration as is not of a vast or prodigious Excess' (pp. 203–204).

Without the intervention of some accidental correctives mankind must increase. Births in the ordinary course exceed natural deaths. Taking the procreative period at twenty years, it is possible for twenty children to be born of one woman, but the average may be taken at less than a third, say six. Owing to the high death rate in early years, he assumes that only two of these six will reach maturity, which gives him, after the performance of a suitable calculation, an increase in geometrical proportion in a period of thirty-four years.[1]

[1] The calculation occurs on p. 205 and appears to be wrong. If a woman rears only two children to maturity the phenomena are those of a stationary population. Like Cain, the children appear to have got their wives from the land of Nod.

He appeals to experience and observation and quotes Graunt with approval, refusing to 'decline that light or evidence that this little Book affords in this matter' (p. 205). These observations give a greater demonstration of the increase of mankind 'than a hundred notional arguments' (p. 206). Hence it is clear that mankind does and must necessarily increase.

What then are the correctives to this multiplication? The natural increase of animals is much greater than that of man, and Hale discusses the checks to the increase of various animals, birds and fish, noting that equilibrium is preserved. Turning to man he finds the following correctives: 1. Plagues and Epidemical Diseases: 2. Famines: 3. Wars and Internecions: 4. Floods and Inundations: 5. Conflagrations (p. 212).

After a survey of various plagues, he reaches the conclusion that they are 'a great Corrective of the Redundance and Increase of Mankind' (p. 213). Famines have not been so serious of recent times owing to improvements in agriculture, the supplies obtainable from other countries by sea, and the seasonable weather and fruitful seasons which have prevailed. Nevertheless in former times they were grievous and destroyed multitudes. Ordinarily famine and plague went together, and both were the usual consequence of war, on which subject, like Raleigh, he anticipated the Malthusian view.

'And although Wars are in a great measure accidental, or at least proceed in a great measure from the Wills of Men . . . yet it seems, that abstracting from all these Occasions, Wars seem to be in a manner a Natural Consequence of the over-plenitude and redundancy of the Number of Men in the World: And so by a kind of congruity and consequence, morally necessary when the World grows too full of Inhabitants, that there is not room one by another; or that the common Supplies which the World should afford to Mankind begin to be too few, too strait, or too narrow for the Numbers of Men; that natural propension of Self-love, and natural principle of Self-preservation will necessarily break out into Wars and Internecions, to make room for those that find themselves straitned or inconvenienced. . . . And consequently there seems to be no fear of the surcharge of the World with Mankind, because there is this natural and necessary Remedy at hand; the very Redundance itself of Mankind seeming by a natural consecution to yield and subminister this Remedy, for its Reduction and Equation' (pp. 215–216).[1]

But Hale's object is quite different from that of Malthus. He is concerned to prove the inconsistency of an Eternal Succession of generations. Without these checks—plagues, famines, wars, and the like—the earth would long ago have been full. God uses these methods both to accomplish his ends and to punish man (p. 226). Nevertheless famines are never universal. The defects of one country are supplied by another, and if ordinary supplies fail, man is ingenious and adaptable. Plagues have certain allays—many escape by flight, some 'by Physick and some by their Age and Complexion' (p. 227). They do not last long, they are local, rarely consume more than half the inhabitants, and there is quick recovery. As to wars, man is normally sociable, and the more destructive civil wars are rare.

'Therefore I do affirm, That notwithstanding all these Ordinary and Extraordinary Occurrences that have afflicted Mankind, as shortness of Life, divers Casualties and common Diseases, loss of Men by Navigation, the Intemperance and Luxury of Mankind, the Weaknesses and destructive Sicknesses incident especially to Infancy, Childhood, and Youth, Abortions voluntary or accidental, and all those ordinary Casualties incident to our nature. And notwithstanding also those great and vast Consumptions by Famine, by Pestilence, by strange and Epidemical Diseases, by Wars and Battels, Sea-fights, Internecions, Massacres and Persecutions, Earthquakes, Floods, Inundations, Conflagrations, or what other extraordinary or terrible and universal Accidents that have happened to Mankind in any or all the Ages past since the Flood of *Noah*; Mankind hath notwithstanding all these increased and grown fuller, the Generations of Mankind have exceeded their Decays' pp. (229–230).[2]

But the problems of Sir Matthew Hale were not those of 1798, and the whole of his careful survey fizzles out in the tame conclusion that, since this growth has probably persisted through all time, therefore mankind has not been eternal!

[1] The similarity of this passage (and many others) to the views and even expressions of Malthus is remarkable.

[2] Hale's enumeration of positive and preventive checks is, if anything, more comprehensive than that of Malthus. His influence on Malthus, however, was probably indirect. Townsend is much closer.

AN AMERICAN VIEW—DR. FRANKLIN

Passing now to the middle of the next century, we come to a group of writers to whom Malthus acknowledges a specific debt: Franklin, Hume, and Wallace.

The relevant work of Dr. Franklin is entitled *Observations Concerning the Increase of Mankind, Peopling of Countries, &c.*, and was written in Pennsylvania in 1751.[1] People, he writes, increase in proportion to the number of their marriages, which depend upon the ease and convenience of supporting a family. 'When families can be easily supported, more persons marry, and earlier in life' (p. 165).

Luxury delays marriage in cities, where deaths exceed births, and the case is similar in fully-settled countries, where the competition of landless labourers brings about low wages, difficulty in supporting a family, and consequently postponement of marriage.

Europe is fully settled and cannot increase much, but America is in a different position. Being inhabited by hunters, it has a low population density, and large tracts of land are easily obtainable. Land being available in abundance, men are not afraid to marry, since there will be ample means for their children.

'Hence marriages in America are more general, and more generally early, than in Europe. And if it is reckoned there, that there is but one marriage *per annum* among 100 persons, perhaps we may here reckon two; and if in Europe, they have but four births to a marriage, (many of their marriages being late) we may here reckon eight, of which, if one-half grow up, and our marriages are made, reckoning one with another, at twenty years of age, our people must at least be doubled every twenty years' (pp. 166–167).

North America will require many ages to settle fully, and labour will never be cheap. Privileges to the married may hasten the filling process 'but cannot increase a people beyond the means provided for their subsistence' (p. 170). Exports of manufactures strengthen the home country and weaken the foreigner, but home luxuries should never become common.

[1] Quotations are taken from *A Select Collection of Scarce and Valuable Economical Tracts* (McCulloch, 1859).

Importation of foreigners does not lead to an increasing population, for, if they are more frugal and industrious, they will drive out the natives.

Franklin has great faith in the impulse to and the power of reproduction.

'There is, in short, no bound to the prolific nature of plants or animals, but what is made by their crowding and interfering with each other's means of subsistence. Was the face of the earth vacant of other plants, it might be gradually sowed and overspread with one kind only, as, for instance, with fennel: and were it empty of other inhabitants, it might, in a few ages, be replenished from one nation only, as, for instance, with Englishmen.[1] Thus there are supposed to be now upwards of one million of English souls in North America (though it is thought scarce 80,000 have been brought over sea), and yet perhaps there is not one the fewer in Britain, but rather many more, on account of the employment the colonies afford to manufacturers at home. This million doubling, suppose but once in twenty-five years, will, in another century, be more than the people of England, and the greatest number of Englishmen will be on this side the water. . . . In fine, a nation well regulated is like a polypus: take away a limb, its place is soon supplied: cut it in two, and each deficient part shall speedily grow out of the part remaining. Thus, if you have room and subsistence enough, as you may, by dividing, make ten polypuses out of one, you may, of one, make ten nations, equally populous and powerful; or, rather, increase the nation tenfold in numbers and strength' (pp. 171–172).

The expression of the principle of population is becoming more particular, clearer and more certain.

THE HUME–WALLACE CONTROVERSY

At about the same time Hume and Wallace were engaged in a controversy as to the relative populousness of modern and ancient nations with Wallace on the side of the ancients, and Hume on the side of the moderns.

Hume's Essay, *Of the Populousness of Ancient Nations*, appeared

[1] Franklin's hypotheses which are expressed with some caution are taken over by Malthus (1806 edn., p. 3) with the words: 'This is incontrovertibly true.'

in 1752.[1] In one brief paragraph he gives us the raw material which later, in the hands of Malthus, was to be developed with such telling effect.

'For as there is in all men, both male and female, a desire and power of generation, more active than is ever universally exerted, the restraints, which they lie under, must proceed from some difficulties in their situation, which it belongs to a wise legislature carefully to observe and remove. Almost every man who thinks he can maintain a family will have one; and the human species, at this rate of propagation, would more than double every generation. How fast do mankind multiply in every colony or new settlement; where it is an easy matter to provide for a family; and where men are nowise straitened or confined, as in long established governments? History tells us frequently of plagues, which have swept away the third or fourth part of a people: Yet in a generation or two, the destruction was not perceived; and the society had again acquired their former number. The lands which were cultivated, the houses built, the commodities raised, the riches acquired, enabled the people, who escaped, immediately to marry, and to rear families, which supplied the place of those who had perished. And for a like reason, every wise, just, and mild government, by rendering the condition of its subjects easy and secure, will always abound most in people, as well as in commodities and riches. A country, indeed, whose climate and soil are fitted for vines, will naturally be more populous than one which produces corn only, and that more populous than one which is only fitted for pasturage. In general, warm climates, as the necessities of the inhabitants are there fewer, and vegetation more powerful, are likely to be most populous: But if everything else be equal, it seems natural to expect, that, wherever there are most happiness and virtue, and the wisest institutions, there will also be most people.' (pp. 383–384).

Here we have all the ingredients of the Malthusian theory: in fact, Malthusianism in a nutshell. There is even the germ of the application to Godwin's theory of political justice and human perfectibility.

'The prolific virtue of men, were it to act in its full extent, with-

[1] Quotations from *Essays Moral, Political, and Literary* by David Hume (edn. Green and Grose, 1898), Vol. I.

out that restraint which poverty and necessity imposes on it, would double the number every generation: And nothing surely can give it more liberty, than such small commonwealths, and such an equality of fortune among the citizens' (p. 398).

Nevertheless, like Hale and Franklin, Hume, although enunciating the Malthusian premises, failed to draw the Malthusian conclusions. His argument with Wallace was no doubt part of the debate on the idea of progress. But Hume and Wallace were sailing the tributaries; the controversy had not yet reached the main stream.

* * *

Wallace's book, *A Dissertation on the Numbers of Mankind, In Ancient and Modern Times*, was first published in 1753,[1] although it had been read before the Philosophical Society of Edinburgh several years before.

He tabulates the growth of a hypothetical population in which each marriage produces four children who live to reproductive age. At the end of 37 periods of 33⅓ years each there will be a population of 412,316,860,416.

This figure is inconsistent with experience of the world and is therefore inadmissible. Clearly, however, each marriage must produce one couple, otherwise population growth would be impossible.

'Every couple, therefore, produces more than one, but fewer than two couples, at a medium; and it is easy to institute a calculation according to any assumed hypothesis' (p. 8).

'It is not owing to the want of prolific virtue, but to the distressed circumstances of mankind, that every generation does not more than double themselves; for this would be the case, if every man were married at the age of puberty, and could sufficiently provide for a family (p. 8 n.) . . . but . . . though mankind do not actually propagate according to either the rule in our tables, or any other constant rule; yet tables of this nature are not entirely useless, but may serve to shew how much the increase of mankind is prevented by the various causes which confine their number within such narrow limits' (p. 9 n.).

Wallace estimates the population of the world at not more than 1,000 millions, which suggests that the world must have

[1] References are to the 1809 edn.

been more populous in the past than it is now, as, according to the table, there must have been 1,610 millions in the 966th year of the world. But it must not be assumed that mankind has multiplied regularly. Indeed it is almost certain that growth of population is irregular. The reasons for the paucity of inhabitants and the irregularity of growth are many: some physical and independent of mankind; others moral, depending on the affections, passions and institutions of men.

Some physical causes are more constant, like temperatures, barrenness of soil, or unfavourable climate; others are more variable, like the inclemency of particular seasons, plagues, famines, and earthquakes. But these natural causes can be prevented, or mitigated to some extent, by the skill and industry of men, or by wholesome laws and institutions.

Moral causes, arising from the vices and passions of men, are more serious. Such causes are wars, great poverty, corrupt institutions whether religious or civil, intemperance, debauchery, irregular amours, idleness, luxury, and 'whatever either prevents marriage, or weakens the generating faculties of men, or renders them either negligent or incapable of educating their children, and of cultivating the earth to advantage. It is chiefly to such destructive causes we must ascribe the small number of men. Indeed had it not been for the errors and the vices of mankind, and for the defects of government and of education, the earth must have been much better peopled, perhaps might have been overstocked, many ages ago: and as these causes operate more or less strongly, the earth will be better or worse peopled, at different times' (p. 13).[1]

Wallace then examines the factors making for population density. A tract of land devoted to hunting, fishing, or pastoral pursuits cannot achieve the density of population which would be possible under agriculture.

'In every country, there shall always be found a greater number of inhabitants, *cæteris paribus*, in proportion to the plenty of provisions it affords, as plenty will always encourage the generality of the people to marry' (p. 15).

Climates and soils make a great difference, independently of the best culture or constitutions, but nevertheless numbers are

[1] Wallace must be regarded as having anticipated Malthus in the most important of his conclusions.

directly affected by political maxims and institutions concerning land. Equal division means that the land will be well supplied with people. In particular, inducements to marriage and every encouragement for agriculture are desirable; but if, in spite of the best culture, the land will not support the whole people, reliance must be placed on the export of manufactures.

In addition to the *Dissertation*, Wallace published a further work in 1761 entitled, *Various Prospects of Mankind, Nature and Providence*, in which he completely anticipated the Malthusian argument against perfectibility. Having delineated in *Prospect* 2 the model of a perfect government, he turns in *Prospect* 4 to the cause which must inevitably bring it down in ruins.

A perfect government is 'inconsistent with the present frame of nature, and with a limited extent of earth' (p. 114).

'Under a perfect government, the inconveniences of having a family would be so intirely removed, children would be so well taken care of, and every thing become so favourable to populousness, that though some sickly seasons or dreadful plagues in particular climates might cut off multitudes, yet in general, mankind would encrease so prodigiously, that the earth would at last be overstocked, and become unable to support its numerous inhabitants' (p. 114).

How long the best culture might delay the evil day is impossible and unnecessary to determine. Clearly it cannot be delayed indefinitely. Even if some mysterious way of feeding the multitudes were discovered there would not be room for their bodies on the earth!

'Now since philosophers may as soon attempt to make mankind immortal, as to support the animal frame without food; it is equally certain, that limits are set to the fertility of the earth. . . . It would be impossible, therefore, to support the great numbers of men who would be raised up under a perfect government; the earth would be overstocked at last . . .' (p. 116).

He then visualizes the harassed rulers casting round for some way of restricting the population, toying with the idea of creating vestals, celibates, eunuchs, with child exposure by lot, or legally inflicted death at a certain age. Disagreement about these measures would lead to war, and the utopia would collapse in a state of anarchy. Consequently jealous and selfish politicians need not feel alarmed at such visionary schemes.

'There is too powerful a charm which works secretly in favour of such politicians, which will for ever defeat all attempts to establish a perfect government. There is no need of miracles for this purpose. The vices of mankind are sufficient. And we need not doubt but providence will make use of them, for preventing the establishment of governments which are by no means suitable to the present circumstances of the earth' (pp. 124–125).

A limited earth, a limited degree of fertility, and the continual increase of mankind: these are the determinants. Malthus had only to add the ratios!

SÜSSMILCH—*DIE GÖTTLICHE ORDNUNG*

Meanwhile in Germany there had appeared an outstanding book by Süssmilch, a theologian and a member of the Berlin Academy of Sciences, entitled *Die Göttliche Ordnung*. In this work Süssmilch aimed at a complete and scientific treatment of the whole subject, and he showed that apparently accidental phenomena, when considered over a sufficiently long period of time, presented regularly recurring features. From a study of the available statistics and a comparison of most European countries, he concludes that a surplus of births over deaths is found everywhere, larger in some countries than in others according to local conditions. Thus the whole human race is increasing, and growth will cease only when the births and deaths are equal in number.

It is obvious that population cannot grow indefinitely, as the earth can only feed a certain number of people, but growth will cease of its own accord. Later marriages and fewer births will bring about an equilibrium between the birth and death rates, and, if fertility does not diminish, then the death rate will rise. However, mankind being what it is, numbers are sure to be kept down by strife and bloodshed. He concludes these observations by reflecting on the divine foresight which fulfils its purposes in spite of the vicissitudes of mankind. All has been long foreseen, and whatever happens, nothing will prevail against the eternal principle that men will multiply on the earth.[1]

If there were no preponderance of births over deaths, nations

[1] Fourth edn., 1775, p. 270.

could not recover from plagues and other acts of God, apart from wars. Prussia lost almost two-fifths of its population in the plague of 1710, and yet the balance was restored within thirty years. Indeed Prussia is a case in point, for, although it has been at war, off and on, for two hundred years, it is unchallenged in population supremacy. It could lose a million of its population every five years, and still continue to flourish, and has in fact sent many colonists to America and elsewhere.

He pays particular attention to the rate of increase, and the period in which populations might be expected to double themselves. Clearly such periods depend on the relative preponderance of births over deaths, and he enlists the aid of his colleague Euler, the mathematician, to calculate a number of tables based on various hypotheses.

With a quite average surplus of births, ten deaths to thirteen births, doubling could occur in eighty-three to eighty-four years,[1] and since in all Prussian states this is the normal rate, the population of the next hundred years is predictable in the absence of a major war. Doubling could be speeded up by an increased surplus of births, and figures for the mark of Brandenburg, which between 1698 and 1712 had seventeen births to ten deaths, would have resulted in a doubling by 1740, had the rate of increase not slackened by a return to the ratio 13:10, which ratio, or something very near it, appears to be a general average.

He makes several calculations of population growth and shows doublings in different periods, including one as low as $10\frac{7}{10}$ years,[2] at the same time denying that such a general fertility is universally possible. Such a rate could occur locally but not generally. He then proceeds to draw up a table showing the phenomenal potential increase of mankind before the Flood, the purpose for which the calculation was made.

His general position is that population has a strong tendency to increase, and this tendency is part of the Divine Order for the purpose of peopling the earth and repairing the ravages of the great natural checks: pestilence, war, starvation, floods, and earthquakes. But there are also artificial checks such as polygamy, celibacy, eunuchism, and the absence of soldiers at war. He regards agriculture and industry as the two most important elements in national life, and a peasant's land should be neither

[1] Op. cit., Table, p. 280.
[2] Id., p. 288.

too large nor too small, nor should the price of necessaries be so high as to prevent marriage.

Unlike Malthus, Süssmilch favoured a large population. He regarded luxury as undesirable, and quantity of people as of more importance than a high standard of living. Far from favouring emigration, he thought it the duty of a ruler to keep his people at home, and even to attract foreigners. A man should always consider his ability to support a family, but the state should attempt to remedy adverse conditions, by solicitude for the subject's welfare and the preservation of life.[1]

SIR JAMES STEUART

Malthus's debt to Süssmilch is obvious and is frequently acknowledged by that writer. So too is his obligation to Sir James Steuart (1712–1780), whose contribution to the subject is contained in his *Principles of Political Economy*, 1767.[2]

Animals multiply in proportion to the food available, and the fact that they do not increase more rapidly than is observed would appear to be due to the destruction of the surplus through lack of food (pp. 18–19). Man would be similarly limited if he did not cultivate the land, and, even then, his power of increase exceeds what is required.

'The generative faculty resembles a spring with a loaded weight, which always exerts itself in proportion to the diminution of resistance: when food has remained some time without augmentation or diminution, generation will carry numbers as high as possible; if then food come to be diminished, the spring is overpowered; the force of it becomes less than nothing. Inhabitants will diminish, at least, in proportion to the overcharge. If upon the other hand, food be increased, the spring which stood at o, will begin to exert itself in proportion as the resistance diminishes; people will begin to be better fed; they

[1] For further accounts of Süssmilch and his work reference may be made to Stangeland, *Pre-Malthusian Doctrines of Population*, 1904, pp. 213–223; and to Bonar, *Theories of Population from Raleigh to Arthur Young*, Chapter V.

[2] Malthus writes (2nd edn., p. 15): 'Sir James Steuart very justly compares the generative faculty to a spring loaded with a variable weight . . . which would of course produce exactly that kind of oscillation which has been mentioned. In the first book of his Political Economy, he has explained many parts of the subject of population very ably.'

will multiply, and in proportion as they increase in numbers, the food will become scarce again' (p. 20).

Nothing is easier than to marry, and marriages are common among the lower orders, but 'as in order to reap, it is not sufficient to plough and sow, so in order to bring up children it is not sufficient to marry.' Consequently, since numbers must always be limited by the food produced, the fertility of the climate and the industry of the inhabitants, the best size for the population is that which is compatible with full employment.

PRICE, WALES, AND HOWLETT

Hume and Wallace had debated whether population was greater in modern than in ancient times. Three writers, Dr. Richard Price, Rev. John Howlett, and William Wales, now turned their attention to the question whether the population of England and Wales had increased or decreased since the Revolution.

Price's view was that the population had declined.[1] His deductions were made from the number of houses declared in the taxation returns taken in conjunction with estimates of the average size of families in many places. As a result of such calculations he declared that the population had fallen by nearly a quarter since the Revolution, and this decline he attributed to the increase in the army and navy, a devouring capital, three long and destructive Continental wars, emigration, particularly to the East and West Indies, the engrossing of farms, the high price of provisions, but above all to the increase of luxury and of public taxes and debts (p. 29). He noted, however, that the decline was in some degree peculiar to this country, whereas in North America there had been for many years an increase at a rate scarcely ever before known to mankind.

This *Essay* provoked two replies: one from Wales and the second from Howlett. Wales[2] did not question the logic of Price's calculation, but regarded his data as inadequate. In attempting to collect better figures, however, he encountered great difficulties, including religious opposition to anything

[1] *An Essay on the Population of England, From the Revolution to the Present Time*, 2nd edn., 1780.

[2] *An Inquiry into the Present State of Population in England and Wales; etc.*, 1781.

savouring of a census. From his own experience he suggested that a reduction in the death rate pointed to an increase in healthiness, and finally concluded that the numbers in London compared with those of the Revolution as 10 to 9 nearly (p. 68).

Enclosures had increased employment, particularly if they were of waste lands. Engrossing, though injurious to certain individuals, was advantageous to the state. Leaving all property to the eldest son was detrimental to population growth, as also were marriage between persons of disproportionate ages and the extravagance of women. Wales favoured the taking of a census, although it might put heart into England's enemies if they found her less numerous than they had supposed.

Howlett's view[1] was that the population had increased, a presumption which was supported by appearances, and he rebutted Price's contentions in detail. Of interest from our point of view is his opinion that the engrossing schemes, by increasing the labouring poor, were responsible not only for the growth of parish rates, but also for the increase of population.

'It is allowed, on every hand, that early and general marriage is of all things most conducive to this desirable purpose. But amongst whom does this most universally take place? Is it not among the lower and labouring part of mankind? Go into any country town, village, or parish, and who are the unmarried? Who are the maids and batchelors between the ages of twenty and fifty? Are they not of the middle and higher ranks? . . . The marriages among the lower classes of society are to those among the middle and higher orders, in the proportion of nearly nine to one' (pp. 27–28). And this, although the working classes only outnumber the others by three to one. What then is the reason?

'These latter have a certain pride of station; a shame and fear of descending beneath it; a superior, perhaps, a false, refinement of thought; a luxury and delicacy of habit; a tenderness of body and mind, which rendering formidable the prospect of poverty, and thereby checking the impulses of nature, frequently prevent matrimonial connections. The former, on the contrary, having none of these impediments to surmount, readily obey the

[1] *An Examination of Dr. Price's Essay on the Population of England and Wales; and the Doctrine of an Increased Population in this Kingdom, established by Facts*, by the Rev. John Howlett, A.B.

suggestions of natural constitution, and embrace the first opportunity of an inseparable union with some one of the other sex.... Let the worst happen that may, it will be nothing more than what they have been enured to in their earlier years' (pp. 28–29).

Unlike Malthus, however, he favoured an increase of people, and believed, in opposition to Price, that the population had increased by one-third since the Revolution, and one-sixth during the last twenty years.

ADAM SMITH, PALEY, AND ARTHUR YOUNG

Of the other precursors referred to by Malthus mention must be made of Adam Smith, Arthur Young, Archdeacon Paley, and more especially the Rev. Joseph Townsend.

Although Adam Smith[1] did not make a systematic treatment of the subject of population, Malthus frequently quotes him. It cannot be said, however, that it is possible to put together a distinctive theory of population from Adam Smith's scattered fragments, consequently Malthus's debt to him is less direct than to many other writers.

Paley's views are contained in his *Principles of Moral and Political Philosophy*, 1785. He believes that the improvement of population ought to be the first aim of any country. Both animal and human fecundity provide for an indefinite multiplication, and under favourable conditions of subsistence populations have doubled themselves in twenty years. Wars, earthquakes, famines, and pestilences have only temporary effects, and there is a natural tendency in the human species towards a continual increase of numbers. What then occurs to check this growth? The answer is that the population of a country must stop when the country can maintain no more, that is when the inhabitants are already so numerous as to exhaust all the provision which the soil can be made to produce. This check is seldom the real one in practice, because numbers rarely in any country arrive at or even approach this limit. Therefore population is restricted, not by the amount of food which could be produced, but by what actually is produced.

[1] For a fuller discussion of the views of Adam Smith, Paley, and Arthur Young see Stangeland (op. cit.) and Bonar, *Theories of Population from Raleigh to Arthur Young*.

Arthur Young has much to say on the subject scattered in various works. He repudiates the notion that mere growth of population is a test of national prosperity. It is not the numbers but the working population which counts. France is a typical example of an over-populated country, and he attributes this state of affairs to the excessive division of the land into small portions. Advocacy of increase must go with adequate attention to the need for the provision of full employment.

JOSEPH TOWNSEND

Joseph Townsend puts the case even more strongly against those who are continually crying out for population. His views are contained in *A Dissertation on the Poor Laws*, by a Well-Wisher to Mankind,[1] published in 1786, and *A Journey Through Spain in the Years 1786 and 1787*, published in 1791.[2]

Commenting on the former work, McCulloch writes:

'The statements given in it, in reference to the island of Juan Fernandez, afford as perfect an illustration as can well be imagined of the balance between population and food, and of their influence on each other. They are not so much a foreshadowing of Malthus's theory, as the theory itself. And only required to have been presented in a more detailed and systematic manner to have anticipated the *Essay on Population*.'[3]

Since it is possible to concur in this judgment, we will examine Townsend's views in more detail.

He opens his *Dissertation* with an attack on the poor laws, and descants on the virtues of hunger as a motive force. The poor laws, so beautiful in theory, promote the evil they seek to remedy. 'There never was greater distress among the poor: there never was more money collected for their relief' (p. 400). Wretchedness has increased in proportion to the efforts made to relieve it.

'Hope and fear are the springs of industry. It is the part of a good politician to strengthen these: but our laws weaken the one and destroy the other (p. 403).... The poor know little of the motives which stimulate the higher ranks to action—pride, honour, and ambition. In general it is only hunger which can

[1] References are to McCulloch's Reprint, 1859.

[2] References are to the 2nd edn., 1792.

[3] McCulloch (op. cit.), p. xx.

spur and goad them on to labour; yet our laws have said they shall never hunger.' The laws have also said that they shall work, but this is a troublesome and violent method, 'whereas hunger is not only a peaceable, silent, unremitted pressure, but, as the most natural motive to industry and labour, it calls forth the most powerful exertions (p. 404).... Their hopes and fears should centre in themselves: they should have no hope but from their own sobriety, diligence, fidelity, and from the well-earnt friendship of their employers' (p. 406).

Laws compelling employers to find work for the poor destroy the relation of master and servant. The master has no redress for bad work; he has lost the power of dismissal.

'The wisest legislator will never be able to devise a more equitable, a more effectual, or in any respect a more suitable punishment, than hunger is for a disobedient servant. Hunger will tame the fiercest animals, it will teach decency and civility, obedience and subjection, to the most brutish, the most obstinate, and the most perverse' (pp. 407–408).[1]

All agree that the poor are seldom diligent, except when labour is cheap, and corn is dear. High wages cause high prices, and high prices in turn cause higher wages, thus discouraging the growth of manufactures.

'It seems to be a law of nature, that the poor should be to a certain degree improvident, that there may always be some to fulfil the most servile, the most sordid, and the most ignoble offices in the community. The stock of human happiness is thereby much increased, whilst the more delicate are not only relieved from drudgery, and freed from those occasional employments which would make them miserable, but are left at liberty, without interruption, to pursue those callings which are suited to their various dispositions, and most useful to the state' (p. 415).

The poor soon get accustomed to their lot, and the armies would soon be short of soldiers if sobriety and diligence

[1] Cf. Malthus's proposed treatment of the man who marries without the prospect of supporting a family, 1806 edn., Vol. II, pp. 397–398. 'Though to marry, in this case, is in my opinion clearly an immoral act, yet it is not one which society can justly take upon itself to prevent or punish. . . . When nature will govern and punish for us, it is a very miserable ambition to wish to snatch the rod from her hands, and draw upon ourselves the odium of executioner. To the punishment therefore of nature he should be left, the punishment of want.'

universally prevailed. How otherwise would the poor be persuaded to face the horrors of battle? 'There must be a degree of pressure, and that which is attended with the least violence will be the best' (p. 415).

A fixed, certain and constant provision for the poor makes them less compliant 'with those demands, which the community is obliged to make on the most indigent of its members.' The poor laws are absurd. They say that no man, however indolent, improvident or vicious, shall suffer want, but in the progress of society some must want: the only question to decide is who?

Townsend then recounts the famous story of John Fernando, who placed two goats, a male and a female, on Juan Fernandes, where they multiplied rapidly owing to the plenty of subsistence till they had filled the whole island.

'In advancing to this period they were strangers to misery and want, and seemed to glory in their numbers: but from this unhappy moment they began to suffer hunger; yet continuing for a time to increase their numbers, had they been endued with reason, they must have apprehended the extremity of famine. In this situation, the weakest first gave way, and plenty was again restored. Thus they fluctuated between happiness and misery, and either suffered want or rejoiced in abundance, according as their numbers were diminished or increased; never at a stay, yet nearly balancing at all times their quantity of food.' Epidemics provided temporary relief until the island was again full. 'Thus, what might have been considered as misfortunes, proved a source of comfort; and, to them at least, partial evil was universal good' (p. 417).[1]

To extirpate the goats a greyhound dog and bitch were introduced to the island, and they in turn increased rapidly in numbers, and the goats decreased as expected.

'Had they been totally destroyed, the dogs likewise must have perished. But as many of the goats retired to the craggy rocks, where the dogs could never follow them, descending only for short intervals to feed with fear and circumspection in the vallies, few of these, besides the careless and the rash, became a prey; and none but the most watchful, strong, and active of the dogs could get a sufficiency of food. Thus a new kind of balance was established. The weakest of both species were among the first

[1] Cf. Malthus, 3rd edn., Vol. I, pp. 22–24.

to pay the debt of nature; the most active and vigorous preserved their lives. It is the quantity of food which regulates the numbers of the human species' (p. 418).[1]

Community of goods would lead to general weakness in human societies. Cattle breeding and agriculture add to the world's resources.

'But is it not clear, that when all that is fertile has been cultivated to the highest pitch of industry, the progress must of necessity be stopped, and that when the human species shall have multiplied in proportion to this increase of food, it can proceed no further? . . . Nations may for a time increase their numbers beyond the due proportion of their food, but they will in the same proportion destroy the ease and comfort of the affluent, and, without any possible advantage, give universality to that misery and want, which had been only partial' (p. 419).

If an equal division of property were made in England the same inequality we now observe would soon reappear; only there would be more general distress, and more would die than if poverty found its proper channel. When a country is far advanced in population, only two remedies remain: 'None must marry, but they who can maintain a family, or else all who are in distress must emigrate' (p. 423). The only other alternative is child exposure.

'There is an appetite, which is and should be urgent, but which, if left to operate without restraint, would multiply the human species before provision could be made for their support. Some check, some balance is therefore absolutely needful, and hunger is the proper balance; hunger, not as directly felt, or feared by the individual for himself, but as foreseen and feared for his immediate offspring. Were it not for this the equilibrium would not be preserved so near as it is at present in the world, between the numbers of people and the quantity of food' (pp. 423–424).

Even when all cannot marry, it should be left to every man's

[1] Cf. Darwin, *Origin of Species*, Ch. III. 'Hence, as more individuals are produced than can possibly survive, there must in every case be a struggle for existence, either one individual with another of the same species, or with the individuals of distinct species, or with the physical conditions of life. It is the doctrine of Malthus applied with manifold force to the whole animal and vegetable kingdoms.' It is noteworthy that the doctrine was expressed more clearly and earlier than Malthus by Townsend.

discretion, to the balance of his appetites. If men insist on marrying, the only resource left is emigration. The chief check to population has been the lack of houses,[1] but shame and reproach have also played their part in checking recourse to the poor laws (p. 430).

Lack of space prevents detailed consideration of the remedies proposed. Relief should be limited and precarious. Unless the degree of pressure is increased, the poor will never learn frugality. The tax should be reduced in nine years to one-tenth its present proportions. It would be better still if it were entirely abolished.

Townsend's ideas on population are also scattered in the three volumes of his *Journey Through Spain.* If the population of North America doubles in twenty-five years while that of Europe takes five hundred years, what are the reasons? He enumerates eight, viz., want of food, diseases, want of commerce, war in all its forms, celibacy, emigration, want of land, and want of habitations. Remove these obstacles and population will advance. There is one general principle:

'Increase the quantity of food, or where that is limited, prescribe bounds to population. In a fully peopled country, to say, that no one shall suffer want is absurd. Could you supply their wants, you would soon double their numbers, and advance your population *ad infinitum*, which is contrary to the supposition. It is indeed possible to banish hunger, and to supply that want at the expence of another; but then you must determine the proportion that shall marry, because you will have no other way to limit the number of your people. No human efforts will get rid of this dilemma; nor will men ever find a method, either more natural, or better in any respect, than to leave one appetite to regulate another' (Vol. II, p. 391).[2]

[1] Cf. Malthus, *A Letter to Samuel Whitbread, Esq., M.P., on his proposed bill for the amendment of the Poor Laws*, 2nd edn., 1807, p. 16.

[2] See also *Journey through Spain*, Vol. I, pp. 382–383, and Vol. III, p. 107.

CHAPTER TWO

THE THEORY IS LAUNCHED

THE WIND IS FAVOURABLE

MALTHUS'S book then was not original. The ideas in which he dealt had been current for many years. The completeness with which he had been anticipated by Wallace and Townsend is astonishing; yet Malthus took these ideas in 1798, wove them into an Essay, and captured the mind of a generation. Books have their fortunes as well as men. Thus, while the paradox of Wallace remained a philosophical speculation, advanced against a hypothesis of his own contriving; and while the work of Townsend, though well enough known, made little enough impression, the success of Malthus was immediate.

Much of the credit must go to the *Essay* itself. It was brilliantly written in an easy, graceful style; quite different from the treatise of 1803. It contained an interesting paradox, which, if not new, was presented with a clearer application and a greater degree of emphasis. Ideas, long floating here and there in the works of his predecessors, were brought together in a striking synthesis.

Nevertheless, much of the success of the book must also be attributed to the opportune circumstances surrounding its appearance. It was a reply to Godwin. That alone, if the book possessed any merit at all, was sufficient to bring it to general notice, for Godwin had made an immense reputation with his *Political Justice*. In particular he had won the allegiance of the young intellectuals.

'Nothing less satisfied them than political anarchy, abolition of private property, absolute reign of reason, universal benevolence and joyful devotion to social duty and justice. And he supplied it to them in two quarto volumes for three guineas.'[1]

Godwin's book appeared in 1793 and embodied the doctrines of the French Revolution, 'but it had a vigour of its own, and was no mere translation.'[2] It reached its third edition by 1798, the *Enquirer* having meanwhile appeared in 1797. These doctrines Malthus attacked with such success that, slowly at first, and then almost completely, Godwin's authority waned, leaving Malthus the acknowledged leader and apostle of the new philosophy.

There is a captivating simplicity about the central doctrine of the *Essay on Population*, and once the mind has surrendered to the charms of the ratios, they tend to dominate the whole outlook. They give an air of profundity and accuracy to what is *prima facie* plausible. They are much easier to state than to refute. Moreover they seemed to be so applicable to the troubled nineties and to England in particular that it is not remarkable that they received an attentive hearing.

The French Revolution had not lived up to the illusions it had created in the minds of the progressives. The political climate was troubled and uncertain; already the shadow of the Napoleonic Wars was beginning to creep over England. The mood of optimism gave way to one of pessimism; alarmed, disordered and confused. For minds which had lost their bearings it was gratifying to have their course restored. Man had tried to do too much. He had been too enthusiastic in the cause of progress. His well-meant efforts had disordered the laws of nature which are the laws of God. Malthus offered a scientific pessimism, which, gloomy and fatalistic as it was towards the hopes of the working classes, absolved the ruling classes from the need to make 'futile' efforts on their behalf.

If its political implications were timely, its economic message was no less appropriate to the age. The poverty of the labourers was becoming menacing in its proportions. Writer after writer had made proposals for the improvement or abolition of the poor laws. Malthus coolly and calmly and reasonably lays the poverty of the land at the door of God. It is almost blasphemy to argue.

[1] Beer, *History of British Socialism*, Vol. I, p. 114.

[2] Bonar, *Malthus and His Work*, p. 28.

He was a countryman well acquainted with the distress among the labouring classes. He was also aware in a limited sense of the importance of diminishing returns in the application of labour and capital to a fixed area of land. And, although he was not able to formulate this doctrine in a way which was subsequently acceptable, the enunciation of the arithmetical ratio served his purpose equally well, if not better.

The danger of over-population was felt to be real. England was at war and comparatively isolated. The means of transport were defective and rudimentary in the extreme. The industrial revolution was in its teething stage. Under these circumstances the argument of a limited earth and a limited fertility came home with especial force to the inhabitants of a small island, able only with difficulty to draw on outside sources for subsistence.

The argument of limited fertility was particularly appropriate. Since 1794 there had been a series of poor harvests. The price of wheat, which was 55*s.* 7*d.*[1] in January 1795, rose to 77*s.* 2*d.* in July of that year. The spring and summer of 1795 were unfavourable and prices reached the enormous figure of 108*s.* 4*d.* in August, declining, however, to 76*s.* 9*d.* by October. One of the consequences of this dearth was the 'self-denying ordinance' entered into by members of both Houses of Parliament whereby they undertook to reduce their consumption of wheat by one-third. The suffering reached its height in the spring of 1796, when the average price of wheat was 100*s.*, but an abundant harvest in 1796, supplemented by a substantial importation, brought prices down to about 50*s.* in the summer of 1797.

In 1799 a 'dry, harsh and ungenial spring' was succeeded by a cold wet summer in which crops suffered enormously. At the end of the year the price of wheat stood at 94*s.* 2*d.*, and by June 1800 reached the crippling figure of 134*s.* 5*d.* The price of other provisions had risen too to considerable heights. The early promise of the year 1800 soon changed to a threat of renewed scarcity so that in December 1800 a price of 133*s.* was recorded for wheat, and in spite of encouragements to importation, economy and other measures, prices continued to advance progressively, wheat reaching 156*s.* 2*d.* in March 1801.

Price increases of this order imperatively demanded an increase of wages or dearth would have given way to famine.

[1] Figures from Tooke, *History of Prices*, Vol. I, Part IV, Chapters 2 and 3.

Increases did in fact take place in 1795 and 1796 and again in 1801, but as Smart commented: 'The labourer had little chance of maintaining any standard of living when the quartern loaf one year was 9*d*. and another 18*d*.'[1]

Arthur Young estimated that a person living in Suffolk would have to pay £1 6*s*. 5*d*. for goods which formerly cost 5*s*., leaving a deficiency of 11*s*. 5*d*. per week even if wages had risen to 9*s*. per week in 1801, and had been supplemented by a contribution of 6*s*. from parish rates.[2]

Whitbread had proposed regulating wages by the price of provisions in 1795, and the justices of Speenhamland had actually initiated a system of sliding scale allowances, afterwards to spread to many other parts of the country.

In the midst of all this confusion, unrest and uncertainty the *Essay* of Malthus appeared and commanded a ready hearing. There was an obvious disproportion between mouths and food, which the existing chaotic system of poor laws seemed powerless to remedy, and which none of the proposed schemes seemed likely to remove. Then came the voice of the prophet Malthus, proclaiming the laws of God, and parodying the earlier utterance: 'The poor always ye have with you.'[3]

He was accused of sophistry by more than one of his critics. His doctrine was certainly a convenient one for rulers who were alarmed at a growing poverty, a growing poor rate, and a growing unrest.

'It was not an uncomfortable doctrine for statesmen,' wrote Ravenstone, 'not one they would be disposed to visit with too much severity of criticism, which represented the happiness of a people as the work of its government, which made their wealth and their comforts to flow from the wisdom of their rulers, but taught that misery and want were the mere inflictions of Providence: evils inevitably inherent in our nature, which could not be relieved, no not even mitigated by any institutions of men.'[4]

Or as J. M. Keynes said at the Centenary Commemoration of the death of Malthus:

[1] Smart, *Economic Annals*, p. 8.

[2] Id., p. 8.

[3] John xii. 8.

[4] Piercy Ravenstone, *A Few Doubts as to the correctness of some opinions generally entertained on the subjects of Population and Political Economy*, pp. 9–10.

'The work begun by Malthus and completed by Ricardo did, in fact, provide an immensely powerful intellectual foundation to justify the *status quo*, to ward off experiments, to damp enthusiasm, and to keep us all in order.'[1]

The times then were propitious. The French Revolution had alarmed even its sympathizers by its excesses, and a reaction had already started. Harassed rulers, confronted with the insoluble problem of poverty and destitution, were given a formula which made these evils the inevitable result of natural laws against which they would struggle in vain. The poor, and the poor alone, could solve the problem of poverty.

THE SECOND EDITION

When in 1803 Malthus published his second edition, he already had a considerable reputation; but the book was in no sense a reprint. It retained a substantial basis of the old, but was differently arranged, was supplemented by a considerable collection of statistical material, and differed a great deal in emphasis. The criticism of Godwin still remained, but the attack on the poor laws, which was secondary in the *Essay* of 1798, had now usurped the position of the attack on perfectibility.

One of the chief differences, however, is the inclusion of a new check, not strictly covered by either vice or misery, namely 'Moral Restraint.' In this way he hopes to soften some of the harshest conclusions of the first *Essay*. We shall have occasion frequently to refer to these points in subsequent pages: our present interest is the reason for the changes.

Successful as the first effort had been, far more successful indeed than he could possibly have hoped, it became clear to Malthus that, to be more than a speculative hypothesis, his book would require much more support in the shape of historical and statistical data. He therefore occupied the intervening years by a wider reading of the existing authorities, supplemented, during the temporary peace, by a tour of certain Continental countries. As a result of this research, the whole form of the book was recast; even its title was altered, and the appearance of the whole work was completely changed. So much so that the superficial and substantial alterations tend to conceal from the casual reader

[1] *Economic Journal*, June 1935.

those fundamental similarities in thought and treatment which still remain, and are far more important than the obvious changes.

It is probable that a letter from Godwin to Malthus in 1798 had something to do with the introduction of the check of moral restraint. The letter is lost and only Malthus's reply remains, but it is clear that Godwin had suggested prudence as a solution to the supposed difficulty arising from the law of population.[1] Malthus rejected this solution for a communistic society, but accepted prudential foresight as a potential check in a society where private property prevailed.

GODWIN'S FIRST REPLY

In addition to this missing letter to Malthus, Godwin also replied to him in public in his *Thoughts Occasioned by the Perusal of Dr. Parr's Spital Sermon.* The sermon was preached in 1800; Godwin's reply was published in 1801.

This reply, so different in tone and content from his later work of 1820, illustrates the interest which Malthus's work had already aroused, and the impression it had made. Godwin, it is clear, underestimated its strength and its effects. He applauds both Malthus's strain of argument and liberality of mind. Malthus has made an unquestionable addition to the theory of political economy and it is a pleasure to have furnished the incentive to such a treatise.[2]

In 1801 Godwin has no misgivings. Accustomed as he was becoming to abuse, he welcomes the restrained and dignified tone of Malthus's argument. He accepts the geometrical ratio as an explanation of the growth of population. He concedes the inadequacy of the food supply to keep pace with such a rate of growth. He accepts the need for checks, which for Malthus are vice and misery, or the fear of misery. But from the tone of the

[1] Kegan Paul, *William Godwin: his friends and contemporaries*, 1876, Vol. I, p. 323.

[2] How differently he bemoans in 1820: 'I have, instead of contributing as I desired to the improvement of society, become, very unintentionally, the occasion of placing a bar upon all improvements to come, and bringing into discredit all improvements that are past.' Godwin, *Of Population*, 1820, p. vi.

concessions one feels that he is giving away the early tricks because he knows that later he will bring out the trumps and aces.

Admitting Malthus's foundations, he feels nevertheless obliged to repel his conclusions. There is a constant need for a check, and the old notion that celibacy is dishonourable and large families desirable has been exploded; but the danger of the new doctrine is clear.

'Every generous attempt for any important melioration of the condition of mankind, is here at stake. The advocates of old establishments and old abuses, could not have found a doctrine, more to their heart's content, more effectual to shut out all reform and improvement for ever' (p. 63).

Godwin sensed the danger, but he underestimated the strength of the hold which the doctrine would obtain. It is difficult otherwise to believe that he would have made such handsome concessions to his new opponent if he had believed that the Malthusian argument would capture the minds of thinkers and statesmen in the way it actually did. The application of the principle of population to England had impressed men's minds, but Godwin pleads for a broader outlook. 'One of the greatest evils which can infest political disquisition, is the imagination that what takes place in the spot and period in which we live, is essential to the general regulation and well-being of mankind' (p. 63).[1]

Various expedients such as child exposure would be preferable to the positive checks of vice and misery, but there is no need to have recourse to these.

'It is right . . . that . . . we should hypothetically take into the account, the resources of the human mind; the inventions and discoveries with which almost every period of literature and refinement is pregnant, rendering familiar and obvious to every understanding, what previously to such discoveries presumption and ignorance had pronounced to be impossible; and the vast multitude of such discoveries which may be expected, before we arrive at the chance of making experiment of a state of equality and universal benevolence' (p. 67).

[1] There is a sense in which Malthus's views are essentially class-conscious and insular. Many of his critics escaped such limitations, e.g. Godwin, Gray (*Happiness of States*, p. 486), and Thompson (*Inquiry into the Principles of the Distribution of Wealth*, p. 536).

Even when population had reached the utmost limits of advance, marriage would still be permissible, and probably four children would be needed to keep up the population. Hence the checks are not really so alarming, tremendous and urgent as they at first appear to be. The general doctrine of population appears to be so obvious that it tends to 'hurry away the mind, and take from us all power of expostulation and distinction' (p. 70). But in fact the terrific consequences predicted have not been felt in any country or in any age. Its operation has been silent, graduated and unremarked. Yet it is no new phenomenon, and in all old settled countries the pressure on subsistence has been constantly felt.

What are the checks in England? High infant mortality due to neglect and improper food: this is the chief of the positive checks. 'Another check upon increasing population which operates very powerfully and extensively in the country we inhabit, is that sentiment, whether virtue, prudence or pride, which continually restrains the universality and frequent repetition of the marriage contract' (p. 72). Early marriages are uncommon. Few men in England marry without repeatedly contemplating whether they can support a family; many classes such as clerks never marry at all. Late marriages mean fewer offspring, and if this prudential check does not operate among the lower classes it is because their plight is so desperate that conditions of prudence are almost entirely absent.

Applying these arguments to the state of society envisaged in *Political Justice*, where equality, virtue, and benevolence prevail, will there be less prudence and honourable pride than exist at present? It is true that the consequences of a large family will not come home so coarsely to each man's individual interest; the burden of extra children would fall on the community. But men do not reason so in such a society. The higher men rise above poverty and a life of expedients, the more decent, sober, and prudent will be their sentiments. Moreover, if the doctrines of the *Essay on Population* are true, they will be well known and their evil effects prevented. Admitting the basis of Malthus's work as unassailable, his conclusions are insufficient.

'If I look to the future, I cannot so despair of the virtues of man to submit to the most obvious rules of prudence, or of the faculties of man to strike out remedies as yet unknown, as to convince me that we ought to sit down for ever contented with all the oppression, abuses and inequality, which we now find fastened on the necks, and withering the hearts, of so great a portion of our species' (pp. 76–77).

A CHANGE OF EMPHASIS

In the second *Essay* Malthus too, though still opposed to the equalitarian doctrines of Godwin, became the apostle of the doctrine of prudence, or to be more exact of moral restraint. The general basis of the doctrine of population is restated in a couple of chapters. The rest of the book consists of illustrations and applications, interspersed with occasional exhortations, somewhat more appropriate to the pulpit than to a treatise on political economy.

There is a constant tendency in all animated life to increase beyond the nourishment prepared for it. Plants and animals cannot escape this law. They have no doubts about providing for their offspring. Wherever they can increase they do until checked by want of room or nourishment.

'The effects of this check on man are more complicated. Impelled to the increase of his species by an equally powerful instinct, reason interrupts his career, and asks him whether he may not bring beings into the world, for whom he cannot provide the means of support.'[1]

If he attends to this suggestion the result is frequently vice: if not then the result is misery.

'This difficulty must fall somewhere; and must necessarily be severely felt in some or other of the various forms of misery, or the fear of misery, by a large portion of mankind.'[2]

So far then we have the checks—vice, misery, and the fear of misery.

Before, however, going on to the illustrative part of the work, which forms such a distinctive feature of the second and subsequent editions, Malthus proceeds as before to deduce, enunciate and establish the geometrical and arithmetical ratios of the first edition. Population must be checked: the only question that really remains is by what method? The ultimate check is famine, but clearly famines are rare in old established countries.

[1] *Essay*, 1803 edn., p. 3. [2] Id., p. 3.

They are rendered unnecessary by the strength of the immediate checks included in the comprehensive classification of vice and misery.

So we have the same classification as before, the positive and the preventive checks, which had been clearly laid down in the first *Essay*, but Malthus does not let the matter rest there, for he introduces a new classification, or at least one that has the appearance of novelty.

'On examining these obstacles to the increase of population which I have classed under the heads of preventive, and positive checks, it will appear that they are all resolvable into moral restraint, vice, and misery.'[1]

We must now determine how far this new classification adds to an understanding of or provides a solution to the problem.

Moral restraint is rigidly defined as the 'restraint from marriage which is not followed by irregular gratifications.' It has nothing to do with motive. The sole difference between the prudential check and moral restraint is the obligation to abstain from sexual intercourse in the latter case.[2] Malthus allows that moral restraint produces temporary unhappiness. It might therefore almost be comprehended in the term 'misery'. Moreover the prudental check is clearly included both under the headings of 'fear of misery' and also of 'vice'. So that, although the fresh classification appears to be novel, it contains all the old ingredients. It is not so much the basis of the theory that has changed as the emphasis.

In fact the category of moral restraint remains a dead letter.[3] It belongs to the sermon, not to the political economy, and it is difficult not to sympathize with those critics who regarded it as a

[1] Op. cit., p. 11.

[2] 'It is our duty to defer marriage till we can feed our children, and . . . it is also our duty not to indulge ourselves in vicious gratifications; but I have never said that I expected either, much less both of these duties to be completely fulfilled. In this, and a number of other cases, it may happen, that the violation of one of two duties will enable a man to perform the other with greater facility; but if they be really both duties, and both practicable, no power *on earth* can absolve a man from the guilt of violating either' (*Essay*, 3rd edn., 1806, Appendix, p. 538).

[3] '. . . knowing that some checks to population must exist, I have not the slightest hesitation in saying, that the prudential check to marriage is better than premature mortality' (id., p. 538).

stick to beat the poor.[1] Malthus had no faith in its efficacy. Indeed it is difficult to see how anyone, who believed that an enlightened communistic society such as Godwin envisaged would breed itself to destruction, could have much hope that the ignorant poor of the early nineteenth century would fare any better.

Far away, at the end of the book, he returns to the topic. The vices of the poor are not only sexual. Squalid and hopeless poverty spells even greater degradation.[2] It leads to attacks on property![3] Consequently an attempt, even if it prove abortive, at moral restraint, though it degenerate into the preventive check, is better than the positive check. So we see the philosopher, in spite of his new classification, standing nearly where he stood before. The effective checks are vice, misery, and the fear of misery. Moral restraint remains the ideal, but the practical philosophy is that vice is preferable to misery.

This is not the place to follow Malthus through all the illustrations, applications and qualifications of his theory. They will be adequately covered later. Suffice it to say that the second *Essay* was aimed at the poor. Their poverty was irremediable save by themselves. Only prudence could save them, and prudence meant delayed marriage. Did they fly in the face of the laws of nature, to the punishment of nature they should be left. They should be doomed to starvation by the abolition of the poor laws.

This was the creed which provoked the terrific controversy which is the subject of this work, and an examination of which brooks no further delay.

[1] For details of Malthus's views on the poor laws and his proposals for their abolition, reference may be made to Book IV, Chapter III (post).

[2] *Essay*, 1803 edn., pp. 512–513. [3] Id., pp. 513–514.

BOOK TWO

THE DEVELOPMENT OF THE CONTROVERSY

CHAPTER ONE

THE EARLIER CRITICS – 1803 to 1815

SOME GENERAL CONSIDERATIONS

MALTHUS was a much-abused man; but so too was Godwin: and when Godwin complained to Mackintosh of some of his expressions, Mackintosh was wise enough to reply:

'You published opinions which you believed to be true and most salutary, but which I had from the first thought mistakes of a most dangerous tendency. You did your duty in making public your opinions. I do mine by attempting to refute them; and one of my chief means of confutation is the display of those bad consequences which I think likely to flow from them. I, however, allow that I should have confined those epithets, which I apply to denote pernicious consequences, merely to doctrines. Though these epithets, when they are applied by me to men, are never intended to convey any aspersion upon the moral or intellectual character of individuals, but merely to describe them as the promulgators of opinions which I think false and pernicious, yet I admit that I should not in any way have applied the epithets to *men*.'[1]

Much of the abuse of Malthus was of this nature. It was unwise, but it did him more good than harm, for obloquy is a poor form of argument. Nevertheless, to assert, as his supporters did, that in private life he was kind, gentlemanly, and benevolent is no more to the point. The abuse, whether directed against Malthus himself, or, as it more frequently was, against his doctrines, merely indicates the intensity of feeling which was aroused by his writing.

[1] *William Godwin: His Friends and Contemporaries*, Kegan Paul, Vol. I, p. 329.

It were better if the critics had written more temperately—better for them and for their cause; but the fact that many of their attacks were scurrilous is no guarantee that the arguments were unsound. Vituperation was a commonplace in those days, as it is today, and they certainly abused Malthus, as the author of what they believed a monstrous theory, but our concern is, in the main, to dig below the abuse and sift out the argument.

It is also frequently asserted that the critics had not read Malthus; that their criticisms were based, not on anything he himself said, but on what other people thought he said. This is not true. The critics may have erred in certain matters of interpretation, though by no means so often as the supporters of Malthus would suggest. But a detailed study of the following writers shows clearly that they had not only read the *Essay*, but had studied it with considerable care. If at times they attack views which Malthus did not enunciate, but which were deduced with or without his consent from his work, this is quite a legitimate undertaking. They were not only concerned with metaphysical abstractions, but with a doctrine which threatened the rights of the poor. What men thought Malthus said was as important in the eyes of his critics as the very things he did say.[1]

The scarcity of both the first and second editions suggests that they did not have a wide circulation. There must have been a substantial oral tradition prior to 1806, and in the realm of ideas this was of as much importance as the actual printed word.

Moreover, whether it be true or not that Malthus was criticized by those who had never read him, it is a fact that the critics of Malthus have been criticized by those who had read them but cursorily. Isolated passages, wrenched from their context, are given as their considered opinions. Crude extracts from their writings are set alongside the distilled quintessence of the master with obvious results. Malthus's work was a great one, but it is not free from blemish, and it is extraordinarily difficult to criticize for reasons not entirely connected with its soundness.

It has a strong lay-out. Beginning as it does with a few pages of generalized statement of an extremely dogmatic type, it is subsequently reinforced by masses of statistics, historical data, qualifications, and comments on qualifications. So much so that a critic, attacking a clause in the first chapter, is liable to find

[1] Cf. Hazlitt's *Reply*, 1807, p. 121.

himself confronted by an opponent who quotes some remote qualification in the twentieth. There is so much in the *Essay*, relevant and irrelevant, that it is an almost superhuman effort to see the wood for the trees.[1]

There are at least two principles of population.

(1) Population has such enormous potential powers of growth that sooner or later the earth will be filled, and in the absence of checks, very soon indeed.

(2) The disproportion between the rates of growth of population and food is constantly operating, and requires immediate practical steps aimed at restricting the former.

Now these are distinct propositions, and to admit the first, as many of Malthus's critics did, by no means implies or demands assent to the second. Speaking generally, the arguments of the critics were concentrated on disproving the second proposition, which is the really important one, and their work has been belittled by writers who fail to discern a fundamental difference between these two aspects of Malthus's theory, a difference which he himself did not consistently maintain.

In proceeding, therefore, to a searching scrutiny of the mass of contemporary writing on the subject, it is essential, in order to avoid misunderstanding, to set out clearly what the critics really said on this matter, and this alone is a huge task. There were literally hundreds of criticisms, and this section will be confined mainly to those appearing in book form; but the periodicals of the time are strewn with articles, reviews and allusions, often repetitive, though occasionally of importance. Scarcely an issue of the *Quarterly* or *Edinburgh Review* but contains such an article, review or reference. Cobbett entered the fray for round after round. There is so much available on the subject that sheer volume alone has imperatively dictated rigorous selection which has been confined to the principal critics whose views are now presented.

[1] 'The last reason that shall be here adduced for the spread of this notion of the superfecundity of the human race, is the confidence with which it is pronounced and repeated, and the strong facts by which it professes to be demonstrated. The human mind, thus assailed, generally declines the labour of an apparently useless examination, and naturally reposing some degree of trust in the authorities it consults, surrenders itself up to a settled conviction, which it is unwilling afterwards to have disturbed' (Sadler, *Law of Population*, 1830, Vol. I, p. 14).

We have also adopted the method of extensive quotation when paraphrase would have been easy. The task of condensing the voluminous replies into reasonable compass has involved the most careful analysis to avoid misrepresentation and at the same time to preserve the important elements, but our aim has been to show by a chronological development of the controversy the cut-and-thrust of debate, and to this end quotation serves to show the temper and outlook of the different participants. The threads are gathered together in subsequent sections.

CHARLES HALL—THE EFFECTS OF CIVILIZATION

The year 1805 witnessed the appearance of that remarkable book by Charles Hall: *The Effects of Civilization on the People in European States.* Some copies contained an Appendix entitled: *Observations on the Principal Conclusion in Mr. Malthus's Essay on Population.* Copies of this book are rare, although there was a reprint of the *Effects* in the Phœnix Library, dated 1850.

Little is known of his life, and this is a pity, for he must have been a remarkable man[1] His book is a testimony to his intellect, to his learning, and still more to a humanity born of years of bitter experience as a physician to the poor. Much of what he wrote will bear reading even today, and, although our chief concern is with the Appendix, his main position ought to be made clear.

The people are divided into two orders—the rich and the poor, and since the latter are by far the more numerous, it is their state which is of the greater importance. This state is deplorable. They are not sufficiently supplied with the necessaries of life, and live in squalor and hardship.

If a human population can double its numbers in twenty years, then a population of ten million which is stationary must lose 500,000 people a year. The cause of this loss is want of proper and sufficient food and other necessaries, the unwholesomeness of their employments, or some other cause equally attributable to extreme civilization (p. 9). Exact calculation is impossible but 'it seems probable that the deaths of the poor are to those of

[1] For biographical details see *Dictionary of National Biography*; Beer, *History of British Socialism*; Gray, *The Socialist Tradition—Moses to Lenin.*

the rich as two to one, in proportion to the numbers of each' (p. 10).[1]

This great mortality is due to the difference in their supplies of the necessaries of life. In particular does it show itself in infant mortality, and he documents in no half-hearted manner the conditions which make a high infant mortality rate among the poor inevitable.[2] Prudence he dismisses as a check to population. The cause is obvious.

'We see half of the children born, die before they are two years and a half old; and a very great part of the remainder drop off before they are seven. We have, therefore, no occasion to look for other causes' (p. 14).

The employments of the poor are injurious to their health, and certain manufactures are responsible for many early and very painful deaths. The moral and spiritual instruction of the masses is neglected, their minds are uncultivated, their leisure is called idleness because they are too ignorant to know how to use it, their lot is hard and miserable in the extreme. All this he lays at the door of civilization.[3]

The dearness of corn in 1801 was due to real scarcity. The produce of the earth depends on two things: favourable or unfavourable climatic conditions, and the greater or less quantity of labour bestowed on its cultivation. As there are three classes of people: those who work on the land, those employed in trade and manufactures, and those who do nothing, and as the first class provides all the food for the whole of the three classes, it is the paucity of this class which has caused the scarcity (p. 30).

The wealth of the rich is power over the labour of men. Men need not work for any one man, but work for somebody they must (p. 39). The direction of a disproportionate amount of

[1] References are to the 1850 edn. unless otherwise stated.

[2] See especially pp. 11–13.

[3] 'We understand by civilization that manner of living in societies of men, which is opposite to that of those who are called savages; such as are the natives of North America, &c. It consists in the study and knowledge of the sciences, and in the production and enjoyment of the conveniences, elegancies, and luxuries of life. . . . It does not seem to arise from any particular constitution of governments, or to be attributable to the administration of them, but to flow from the natural propensities of mankind' (Section I, p. 1).

labour from agriculture to the production of refined manufactures means that the amount of food is insufficient for the mass of the people. It is an illusion to think that the rich feed the poor, that those who produce nothing feed those who produce everything, and this illusion arises through the intervention of money. The necessaries of life are the joint production of land and labour, and the poor ought to have access to the land.

It is an essential liberty that a man enjoy the fruits of his own labour, but in fact eight-tenths of the people consume only one-eighth of the produce. The mechanism of this deprivation is money.

'The poor cannot eat without money. They cannot get money without labour. Those, therefore, that are in possession of money, or the necessaries of life, have the command of the labour of the poor, by having the power of withholding the necessaries of life from them' (p. 102).

This power is used to direct their labour from the production of necessaries to the production of luxuries.

'The sum, therefore, of the effects of civilization, in most civilized states, is to enable a few of mankind to attain all possible enjoyments both of mind and body, that their nature is susceptible of; but at the expense, and by depriving the bulk of mankind of the necessaries and comforts of life, by which a great proportion of them is destroyed, and the remainder reduced, both corporally and mentally, far below the most savage and barbarous state of man' (p. 170).

And all this is brought about in a seemly manner by specious forms, and with the assistance of the money power.

That in brief is Hall's analytical position in regard to the problem of poverty. It is due to the starving of the land of labour in order to provide luxury for the rich. The remedy is the restoration of labour to the land.

REPLY TO MALTHUS

We turn now from the main work to the Appendix: *Observations on the Principal Conclusion in Mr. Malthus's 'Essay on Population.'* Hall begins by noting the agreement and the difference.

'Mr. Malthus agrees with me in many of my positions, and most of my premises. In particular he thinks with me, that the great scarcity of the necessaries of life, and the evils attending it, are occasioned by the employment of the poor in manufactures, instead of the land; but notwithstanding this, he does not consider civilization as chargeable with any thing on this account, because, as he says, the same want and misery must necessarily happen in every system, and particularly in a state of equality of property; for as the number of the people would increase more than the subsistence would be made to increase, their number would so much exceed the supply the land would afford, whatever the culture of it might be, as, after some interval, to produce a scarcity equal to the present in civilized states' (pp. 325–326).[1]

As Hall points out, he has noticed the theory in his main work.

'It must happen, in the course of time, that the whole world, and every part of it, will be fully peopled; and that the produce of it will be insufficient for the support of the inhabitants, however well-cultivated it may be; but this period must be very remote, and the event cannot be prevented by any human means; we ought not to anticipate the evil by any systems or practices of our own.' (p. 258).[2]

He gives four reasons why he only noticed the position generally.

'1st.—Because I suppose that in any case the period of its arrival is very distant; even although no preventive methods were used.

'2dly.—Because I suppose that by preventive methods it may be removed to a much more distant period, even with regard to the whole world; and with respect to any given nation, that it might be prevented altogether.

'3dly.—Because I suppose, that, if ever it does happen in a state of equality, it will not be attended with evils in any proportion equal to the present.

'4thly.—Because I suppose a part of a nation, especially a small part of it, to have no right to induce a state of want, disease, and mortality, on the other parts of it, exempting itself at the same time from them' (pp. 327–328).[3]

[1] Quotations from Appendix, 1805 edn. [2] 1805 edn.

[3] Here we have a clear separation of the two aspects of the principle of population. Hall accepts the implications of the long-run view and rejects those of the short-run. Elsewhere (Note, p. 344) he inquires shrewdly why in this matter the rich are so solicitous for future generations. Some debts they throw forward to posterity, some they impose on the present generation. In each case they consult their own interests.

Three and a half acres will support five people, and with plenty of labour every acre would support two persons. Thus England will support 140 millions. Allowing for a doubling every 20 years, this gives 80 years reprieve, and, since plenty will only come gradually, there will still be many deaths, which will extend the period of reprieve to 100 years. Happiness for an average of 70,000,000 people for 100 years is not to be despised.

But this period can be protracted to a much greater length by the use of preventive methods, such as colonization, which is the natural method, and the regulation of marriages. To fill all the world by colonization, even if all European nations did it, would take many generations; if only one or a few adopt it, it would be even more successful. In any case: 'Are we not to attempt a thing which we might succeed in, because if all others were to do the same they could not all succeed?' (p. 332).

The other preventive method is the regulation of marriage, and this would be the natural thing in an equalitarian state where everybody was equally affected and equally interested in a solution.

Therefore the solution to the problem is: for England colonization; for the world, restraints on marriage by law. Destruction of the people by want and manufactures is unnecessary. The evils of supra-population under a system of equality would be less than at present, for we acquiesce in the dispensations of Providence with less repugnance than those brought on by man. Even if the people were hungry, their hunger would not be aggravated by the superfluity of others.

'A part of the people, and especially the smaller part, cannot have a right to induce a state of misery and mortality on the great body of the nation. . . . If the rich have a right, by the present degree of luxury, &c. to destroy the people they now destroy, in order to keep the rest down to their present numbers; they may introduce a still greater quantity of luxuries, and that to an indefinite degree, and so destroy and reduce mankind to any number, *ad libitum.* It is allowed that there is at present, and that there always has been since civilization has taken place, land sufficient, if more labour had been bestowed on it, to furnish necessaries of life to its inhabitants, and of course to have prevented this loss of lives; civilization, therefore, is chargeable with anticipating, at least, the evils, and bringing them on the people, long before they would otherwise have been afflicted with them; and consequently has been the occasion of the destruction of all those that have hitherto been destroyed by this cause' (pp. 337–338).

Malthus's view is that the masses can only be kept down by scarcity, want, and disease, and that these must be sufficient to prevent them from rising above the number required. A man, he says, who cannot support his family must be 'doomed to starve.'

'The treatment of this labouring man, I cannot help saying, appears to me not only inhuman to the last degree, but unjust and iniquitous. I will ask, why is he thus treated? Because, it will be answered, he does not produce by his labour sufficient to maintain his family.—But, I say he produces six or eight times as much as his family consumes or requires, but which is taken from him by those who produce nothing. What he is entitled to is, all that his hands have made or produced, the whole fruits of his labour, not that pittance his wages enable him to purchase.[1] That he has produced what I assert, is literally true if he is an husbandman; and, if he is an artificer, the labour which he applies in his trade, would, if it was suffered to be employed on the land, do the same. It is not true that he has *doomed himself*, or that nature has doomed *him, and his family to starve;* that cruel doom is brought on him by the rich' (pp. 340–341).

If any ought to be so treated, it is the rich; but none ought to be so treated. Who marries without adequate provision? Not this or that man, but the whole of the poor.[2] None of them can possibly save an adequate amount while they are single. And for whose benefit do they remain single? 'No restraint can be justly imposed on any, unless they receive all the advantages derived from it' (p. 343).

The rapid tendency in animals to increase is evident, and the

[1] Cf. Hazlitt, *Reply*, p. 322. 'The real funds for the maintenance of labour are the produce of labour. According to Mr. Malthus, they are not the produce itself, but what happens to be left of it, as the husks only and not the corn are given to the swine.'

[2] Cf. Malthus, 1806 edn., Vol. II, 537 n. 'The lowest prospect with which a man can be justified in marrying seems to be, the power, when in health, of earning such wages, as at the average price of corn will maintain the average number of living children to a marriage.' The poor man would be a rare mathematician to solve an equation with so many unknowns—particularly the price of corn and the number of children he was likely to have!

increase of population in Europe has been kept down by infant mortality. 'Mr. Malthus has travelled, it seems, over Europe, to evince the truth of these observations: for my part, I think that when I employed two or three pages in proving them, I did more than was necessary' (p. 343). But to prove that this mortality is necessary is another matter.

'The question at issue is, whether an evil, that may invade mankind at a distant period, in certain possible contingencies, and in different degrees of severity, and which may then be much mitigated, and even wholly removed, can be justly brought on the present generation in its utmost degree of force and malignity, in order to exempt a few from it, and by which exemption they are rendered capable and strongly disposed to add greatly to the evil? This is the question,—it demands an answer' (pp. 343–344).

Under a state of inequality the poor will always be miserable, because, even if their numbers are reduced without a reduction in inequality, the same proportion of them would suffice to raise the necessaries of life for the whole, and there would be the same want among the poor and the same profusion among the rich. The chief point is this: the produce of the land is not what it would be if labour were not diverted from it to support the luxuries of the rich.

Hall's book did not attract much attention, although it was probably read in socialist and kindred circles. The *Effects of Civilization* was indeed thought worthy of a reprint in 1850, but the reply to Malthus does not seem to have cut much ice, although the ideas Hall puts forward appear over and over again in the course of the subsequent controversy.

THOMAS JARROLD—DISSERTATIONS ON MAN

In the following year, Thomas Jarrold,[1] like Hall a doctor, published a book which was certainly well known and frequently quoted by subsequent writers. It was entitled: *Dissertations on Man, Philosophical, Physiological and Political; in answer to Mr.*

[1] Born at Manningtree in Essex in 1770. Educated at Edinburgh where he took the degree of M.D. In 1806 when this book was written he was in practice in Stockport, but soon afterwards he removed to Manchester where he remained till he died. He wrote several other works, among them one on 'Form and Colour in Man,' and another on 'Curvature of the Spine.' The medical portion of the 'Dissertation' (not dealt with here) is sound in view of the time at which he wrote.

Malthus's 'Essay on the Principle of Population.' This reply was by no means a negligible work, for Jarrold had evidently studied the *Essay* with considerable care, and he brings forward a number of searching criticisms.

He examines the theory first in its short-run implications. Malthus does not distinguish between avoidable and unavoidable evils. 'Common diseases and unwholesome seasons are beyond the controul of man . . . but war is a voluntary act' (p. 17). By Malthus's reasoning all deaths are natural. Consequently war is necessary since, if there were no wars, there must be more misery in some other way. Hence those who die by war die by a law of nature.

'It would add considerably to the perspicuity of Mr. M's reasoning, if he had made a distinction between the natural tendency to death, implanted in the constitution, and the acceleration of it by war and other calamities' (p. 18).[1]

For Malthus there is a great gulf fixed between the rich and the poor, the few and the multitude. It underlines all his reasoning, and nowhere more clearly than in the illustration of the feast.[2]

[1] For a fuller treatment of this point see W. F. Lloyd, *Two Lectures on the Checks to Population*, 1832 (Lec. I).

[2] 'A man who is born into a world already possessed, if he cannot get subsistence from his parents on whom he has a just demand, and if the society do not want his labour, has no claim of *right* to the smallest portion of food, and, in fact, has no business to be where he is. At nature's mighty feast there is no vacant cover for him. She tells him to be gone, and will quickly execute her own orders, if he do not work upon the compassion of some of her guests. If these guests get up and make room for him, other intruders immediately appear demanding the same favour. The report of a provision for all that come, fills the hall with numerous claimants. The order and harmony of the feast is disturbed, the plenty that before reigned is changed into scarcity; and the happiness of the guests is destroyed by the spectacle of misery and dependence in every part of the hall, and by the clamorous importunity of those, who are justly enraged at not finding the provision which they had been taught to expect. The guests learn too late their error, in counteracting those strict orders to all intruders, issued by the great mistress of the feast, who, wishing that all her guests should have plenty, and knowing that she could not provide for unlimited numbers, humanely refused to admit fresh comers when her table was already full' (Malthus, 1803 edn., pp. 531–532). This passage was subsequently withdrawn when Malthus 'softened his conclusions.' But the impression remained. Indeed, although the passage was withdrawn, its substance was retained. It was such passages which aroused the ire of his opponents, and caused them to abuse him.

'But at nature's mighty feast, none are bishops, but all are men; there is no distinction; all that are invited are at liberty to partake, and the life of a guest is sacred: to be invited to the same table, implies equality; and to possess life is to possess the invitation. The table is not spread by any set of men, they only pluck the fruit; the Master himself presides, and all he invites are equally welcome. Nor is it the prerogative of one guest to dismiss another from the hall, the Master calls on whom he will to vacate a seat, and his voice is irresistibly heard' (p. 21).

Has all the fruit been gathered? When it has, then will be the time for Mr. Malthus to 'charge his maker with folly.' Until the uncultivated land has been brought under the plough, it is improper to say that the bounty of Providence is not equal to the wants of men. Malthus concentrates entirely upon the quantity of subsistence actually possessed.

'In his estimation, the Indians, thinly scattered over the vast continent of North America, are as completely prevented from increasing in number, by impending scarcity, as the comparatively full peopled empire of China; and the same check which keeps down the population of these countries operates in every other. In other terms, as the present generation has no surplus of food, an increase in the next is impossible' (pp. 27–28).

No nation collects more food than it wants, but men could collect more if they pleased. Malthus has overlooked two fundamentals of production—the need for labour and mutual assistance. Society is built upon the division of labour. Since men must work, society lightens their toil by dividing it: one is a farmer, another a manufacturer. The objective is to order the flow of labour, so that each department is adequately supplied.

On Malthus's plan the necessaries of life are natural productions incapable of being increased in quantity by well-directed labour. But the farmer does not work on these principles. Like the merchant he works for profit; he is governed by the laws of supply and demand; and no new market will be regularly supplied unless there are regular purchasers. On the other hand, a new market will develop new and superior modes of husbandry, and there will be an increase in either the intensity or the extent of cultivation.

'It is reversing the order established in the world, to increase the quantity of subsistence, under an idea that at some future period children will be born to consume it. In place of saying, population increases where subsistence increases, it would be more correct to say, subsistence increases because population increases, but this would be to destroy the doctrine Mr. M. labours with so much pains to establish' (p. 30).

It is the duty of the government to provide for exceptional scarcities by keeping stocks or by importing. Both age and childhood have a claim on the labour of others, 'but it does not concern one generation to abridge the toil of the succeeding, or to live in celibacy lest they should be too numerous. The measure of our labour is not the measure of theirs: as are the wants so must be the exertion to remove them' (p. 34).

If Malthus had said that population presses hard against the cotton or woollen cloth, he would have been laughed at. But the case is similar. 'The world is in as great danger of a scarcity of clothing as of corn, but hitherto the increase in sheep has kept pace with the increase of people' (p. 34). If more corn or cotton were wanted more would be produced. People are indifferent whether they plant cotton, or sow corn, or throw the shuttle. Just as Manchester would take the necessary steps to meet a doubled demand for muslin, so do farmers respond to an increased demand for food. If the demand were instantaneous it could not be supplied, but the increase of population is gradual, and it is anticipated.

Jarrold then considers the checks. Drunkenness and prostitution, he believes, have little effect on numbers. Most other vices and crimes are irrelevant to the problem. Malthus thinks that frequency of marriage is the root of the trouble, and its comparative infrequency one of the most powerful checks in modern Europe. It is also the very bones of the Malthusian theory that in the ordinary way an increase in wages promotes increased births, and a decrease has the reverse effect. Jarrold disputes this, and is nearer the truth.

'Do the poor calculate with nicety? Do they divide, as Mr. M. represents, their daily earnings, which is just enough to support themselves, between four or five others, and shrink from marriage? Is the period of love with them the period of calculation; and the fear of evil believed to be more than an imaginary fear? It would increase their happiness were it so: but the poor are always inconsiderate. Is their climate inhospitable and rude, and their subsistence mean and tasteless, they are not induced to relinquish the hope of finding pleasure in a family. The natural and necessary difficulty of obtaining one description of good, is not a reason with them to abandon another. The fear of poverty is never felt by a poor man, it is the rich who are in bondage to it. A year of bad trade, or a reduction in wages from any cause, may, for a time, suspend a marriage; but habitual poverty, however great, has not this effect; no person, who has never been richer, thinks himself too poor to marry' (pp. 52–53).

A consideration of what are unwholesome occupations leads Jarrold to his next point.[1] If the population of America increases twenty times as fast as the population of Europe, they must live to a greater age.

'What is understood by the operation of vice and misery, is premature death; if the Americans are in a great degree exempt from the causes of premature death, it follows, of course, that they live nearly the full term of human life. . . . Here, then, follows the question,—are the people of America, taken as a whole, longer lived than those of Europe? If they are not, and I know of no statement which represents them as such, Mr. M. may show how widely spread vice and misery are over the surface of the globe, but he cannot prove that their smaller operation in America is the cause of the rapid increase in the population of that country' (pp. 64–65).

Misery is not forced upon the human race. War, famine, pestilence, and unwholesome occupations are not necessary. 'There is no physical cause of war, none of famine, none of pestilence' (p. 68). They either arise out of human folly, or as a result of ignorance. War is the parent of pestilence; improvements in the arts of peace have driven it away. The misery that has disfigured the history of the human race is not the appointment of God. Man himself has been the cause and the instrument of his own destruction. Malthus has proved the existence of misery. He must prove its necessity. Anything less will not answer his purpose.

'In the general view I take of the subject, man has sufficient liberty, sufficient power, to keep down the population of any country to any standard he may please by violence and

[1] Jarrold quotes from his experience that he finds the cotton industry healthy!

bloodshed; but God has not appointed him to that task; he is not an executioner by nature; and the office never becomes him' (p. 73).

It is unnecessary to follow Jarrold on his tour of the countries from which Malthus drew support for his thesis. The relevant portions will be considered elsewhere. One point, however, deserves mention. It is part of the Malthusian argument that plagues do not make a permanent gap in the numbers of a people. The ravages are soon repaired by increased births, and as soon as the numbers are restored the time is ripe for a further stroke. Thus there is a perpetual struggle between vice, misery, and moral restraint on the one hand, and the principle of increase on the other, with peace, happiness, and plenty restored only after pestilence has thinned the land.

Jarrold's comment is worth noting because it is an early instance of a refusal to accept uncritically statements made concerning population figures as though they were homogeneous.

If a plague strikes a town, it will not confine itself to one class. It will make inroads into all sections of the community—grocers, drapers, attorneys, surgeons, clergymen, etc. Those who escape the plague will retain something like the same proportions as they formerly did. 'The loss of two grocers, and their customers, presents no inducement to two young men to marry, that they may occupy their places; the shops, indeed, may be obtained, but the customers are dead' (p. 163). This is borne out by British experience. Growing towns like London and Manchester offer better prospects to the young than York or Norwich which are declining. 'An active people are never too numerous; but indolence has never room enough' (p. 166). Pestilence in fact is indiscriminate and benefits none.[1]

It is tempting to linger in the second part of the book where Jarrold develops his own ideas, but space forbids. He does, however, suggest checks to human increase. Life has certain evils like labour and childbirth. Grief destroys health, and ultimately occasions death. He believes that mind has a great influence over the bodily processes and secretions. 'As the faculties of the mind

[1] The point is interesting but not, of course, conclusive. The poor live in more crowded conditions than the rich and would, therefore, be more liable to catch a disease. Extra thinning of the ranks of the poor would tend to raise wages. Cf. the Black Death.

are unemployed, as the man sinks down towards the animal, he is prolific; as he ascends above them, his fruitfulness decreases' (p. 250).[1] Savages are unprolific because they are fierce, vindictive, and cruel. A prostitute is seldom a mother owing to the influence of her mind, although promiscuous intercourse of itself does not produce sterility if there is no disgrace. Peasants are freest from care and are great propagators, whereas philosophers keep up their line with difficulty. 'Thus we find a large part of the community that does not require the operation of vice, misery, or moral restraint, to prevent its increase; and what is true of the part may be so of the whole' (p. 267).

Malthus has paid insufficient attention to differential class fertility. He has assumed that the American rate of increase is natural to every country. Furthermore he regards the passion between the sexes as a given quantity. 'This may be true, but the resemblance holds good no further: an equality of affection does not ensure an equal number of children' (p. 275). Fecundity depends upon circumstances, as Malthus himself notices in his discussion of native tribes.[2] It varies with respect to different nations, different classes of the same nation, and different times. Greater or less fecundity is not the sport of accidental causes, but part of the economy of nature, and in consequence no country can ever be overpopulated.

Once again Jarrold breaks up the statistical problem of fertility by considering its individual features. Malthus's theory deals with fecundity in the mass. Jarrold advances the following considerations.

'No woman is always susceptible of pregnancy, there must first be a predisposition in the constitution, brought about by the co-operation of many evolutions; these may be interrupted, and many interruptions constitute barrenness; and when not interrupted they require a considerable length of time for their accomplishment. After the birth of one child, nature demands time to prepare for a second; the system must undergo a determined change, and unless this happens, barrenness is the consequence. Pregnancy is not optional; it is not certain. A female, susceptible of pregnancy today, may not be so tomorrow. . . . After child-bearing has commenced, most women are subject to

[1] An interesting hint of the conflict between Individuation and Genesis.

[2] *Essay*, 3rd edn., 1806, p. 37.

very considerable periods of sterility. Some bear a child every seven, others every fourteen years, and others have only one child in a whole life' (p. 291).[1]

Fecundity depends upon a certain assimilation of constitutions. It is 'independent of passion, the principle is different, passion commences earlier and continues longer than the period of fruitfulness' (p. 298).

A government which improves its people and as far as possible suppresses vice and banishes misery will not need the sword to thin the ranks. Rather will it have to guard against a decrease than try to prevent an increase.

'Population cannot advance too fast while knowledge is increasing; nor can it ever extend so far as to need the correction of vice, for the principle is lessened by the emulation consequent on a full population' (p. 313).

THE *ESSAY*—A THIRD EDITION

In the same year, 1806, Malthus published his third edition in two volumes. As he himself states in the advertisement (pp. v–vii), the alterations made do not affect the main principles of the quarto edition. There are some corrections of statistical lapses, a few passages omitted and a few inserted, but broadly speaking the substance of the second edition still stands.

A few of the expressions are softened, a few unhappy similes disappear, but since the conclusions remain, these alterations are of literary rather than social significance. The poor man is now to be doomed to 'suffer,' not to 'starve' (p. 398),[2] but since he is to be deprived of public assistance as before, it is clear that his sufferings will still consist of starvation. There is a minor concession of help during temporary seasons of distress; and there is an Appendix, which replies to certain criticisms, and gives the 'aim and bent of the whole' to those who have not the leisure to read the whole work.

This Appendix reinforces the view that the Malthusian doctrine was become as much an oral tradition as a written one. The third edition seems to have been the first to have had a wide

[1] Cf. Pearl, R., *Natural History of Population*, for modern ideas on such subjects.

[2] Quotations from 3rd edn., 1806, Vol. II.

circulation, and the fourth[1] is plentiful. Prior to this, the gospel probably spread as much by word of mouth as by the printed word. This fact alone justifies the critics in attacking not only the writings of Malthus but also the current views of his doctrines; although, of course, Malthus is entitled to disclaim responsibility for accepting opinions he does not explicitly state, and which do not flow directly from his actual writings.

Thus he says: 'But though the work has excited a degree of public attention much greater than I could have presumed to expect, yet very little has been written to controvert it; and of that little, the greatest part is so full of illiberal declamation, and so entirely destitute of argument, as to be evidently beneath notice. What I have to say therefore at present, will be directed rather more to the objections which have been urged in conversation, than to those which have appeared in print' (p. 505).

As the object of the Appendix is to correct misrepresentations, it is worth some attention if it serves to give a clearer idea of Malthus's ideas. He first justifies his theological basis, and then proceeds to deny that he is an enemy to population.

'I am only an enemy to vice and misery, and consequently to that unfavourable proportion between population and food which produces these evils. But this unfavourable proportion has no necessary connection with the quantity of absolute population which a country may contain. On the contrary, it is more frequently found in countries which are very thinly peopled, than in those which are populous' (p. 508).

He illustrates his point by the stocking of a farm with cattle, although the parallel is only partially apt since the cattle themselves are unable to till the land, whereas additional men in a country presumably add something, if not proportionately, to the produce.

He agrees with the warmest advocates of increase on the desirability of a large and efficient population, but this is not necessarily achieved by a large birth rate, which would merely increase the pressure, and might even result in a smaller number of children reaching the age of puberty. A decrease of mortality is what is to be aimed at, and the best criterion of good government is not the largeness of the proportion of births but the smallness of the proportion who die under the age of puberty. He

[1] Published in 1807.

is therefore surprised to hear that he is considered to be an enemy of inoculation.

His aim is not to check population but to diminish vice and misery, and any checks suggested are solely as a means to achieve this end.

It is worth noting, however, that the object of his book is to show that with every growth of population the need for checks increases, and, as he is inclined to disparage any immediate amelioration on the ground that it is storing up trouble for the future, this protest has a feeble ring.[1] It is a distinction, but not a difference. Indeed in a subsequent passage he falls into a certain confusion, which some of his critics contrived to escape.

'I have said that in the course of some centuries it might contain two or three times as many inhabitants as at present, and yet every person be both better fed and better clothed. . . . It is not a little curious therefore, that it should still continue to be urged against me as an argument, that this country might contain two or three times as many inhabitants; and it is still more curious, that some persons who have allowed the different ratios of increase on which all my principal conclusions are founded,[2] have still asserted that no difficulty or distress could arise from population, till the productions of the earth could not be further increased. I doubt whether a stronger instance could readily be produced of the total absence of the power of reasoning, than this assertion, after such a concession, affords' (pp. 516–517).

The answer to this apparent inconsistency is obvious, and the fault does not lie with the critics. It is quite possible to grant Malthus his eternal paradox (that is the position of Wallace) without conceding all the intermediate stages. Any population that keeps on growing must ultimately become infinite, but as to the intermediate steps there is room for dispute concerning the relative rates. On his own showing, the American increase of

[1] See for example the illustration of the feast, and the grounds of the rejection of intruders; the notion that the waste of the rich is a possible source of reserve in a scarcity; the lukewarm attitude to increased cultivation; and his defence of his mutton (p. 521).

[2] This shows the importance he attached to the ratios, which later defenders have tended to minimize. Further, the most his opponents granted was the geometrical ratio. The arithmetical ratio was never proved; it was merely enunciated. It is obviously untrue and inconsistent in the short run, but of that more later.

food must have been at least geometrical, or how could the population have subsisted?

He next justifies his denial of the right of the poor to support. No right can exist to what is impossible in practice, a statement with which no one could reasonably quarrel. What he appears to be pleading for is (since everybody cannot be supported) the right to decide who shall starve. And the decision he arrives at is that they must starve whose parents cannot support them. This conclusion he reaches because God has made the passion of self-love beyond comparison stronger than the passion of benevolence. The function of benevolence appears to be to prevent self-love from degenerating into selfishness, between which he makes a decided distinction. Positive precepts (but not apparently legal obligations such as the poor laws) should properly therefore be on the side of the weaker impulse.

Malthus then returns to his plan for the gradual abolition of the poor laws.[1] 'On these occasions the only way I have of judging is to put myself in imagination in the place of the poor man, and consider how I should feel in his situation' (p. 526). The result of this imaginative effort is faintly ridiculous (pp. 526–527).[2] Then follows an astonishing statement.

'I cannot help believing that if the poor in this country were convinced that they had no claim of *right* to support; and yet in scarcities and all cases of urgent distress were liberally relieved, which I think they would be, the bond which unites the rich with the poor would be drawn much closer than at present, and the lower classes of society, as they would have less real reason for irritation, and discontent, would be much less subject to these uneasy sensations' (p. 528).

This is very difficult to understand. How, if the right to support is denied to the poor on the grounds that it is impracticable of fulfilment, will the widespread relief be forthcoming during times of scarcity with such gratifying results? Stripped of sophistry, the real question is: 'Should anyone starve, and if so, who?' It seems that Malthus has replied that someone must starve unless the poor restrict their families by delayed marriage, and lack of earnings is the test he proposes.

[1] For which see *Essay* Book IV, Chapter VII.

[2] For Place's criticism of Malthus's efforts to put himself in the position of the working-class man, see *Place on Population* (Himes's edn.), pp. 154–156.

Having reached this conclusion, Malthus then appears to back a little.[1]

'The power which the society may possess of relieving a certain portion of the poor is a consideration perfectly distinct from the general question; and I am quite sure I have never said that it is not our duty to do all the good that is practicable. But this limited power of assisting individuals cannot possibly establish a general right' (pp. 531–532).[2]

Then comes a proposition capable of mathematical demonstration as sound as anything in Euclid.

'In a country whose resources will not PERMANENTLY (my caps.) admit of an increase of population more rapid than the existing rate, no improvement in the condition of the people which would tend to diminish mortality could *possibly* take place without being accompanied by a smaller proportion of births, supposing of course no particular increase of emigration' (p. 534).

This is very arid logic, if logic. It involves the old confusion between the long and short term possibilities. Excluding the word 'permanently,' the sentence merely states that for an improved standard of living the rate of growth of resources must exceed the rate of natural increase. If, however, the word PERMANENTLY is inserted, as Malthus has done, it is necessary also to insert the word 'permanent' before the word 'improvement'. The sentence then again becomes a mere truism. As it stands it is not true. The way is open for various temporary improvements which were urged by his opponents and which appear to have been anathema to Malthus.

The basis of Malthus's outlook appears to be that unless the poor are stinted of food they will take out any surplus in increased families: i.e., the subsistence theory of wages. And yet, although the whole tenor of his book has been that the poor laws have just that effect, that they multiply claimants by encouraging marriage, he now says 'a closer attention to all their indirect as well as direct effects, may make it a matter of doubt how far they

[1] Hazlitt comments (*Reply to Malthus*, 1807, p. 121): 'It was thought a work of no small labour and ingenuity to make a harmony of the Evangelists. I would recommend it to someone (who thinks himself equal to the task) to make a harmony of Mr. Malthus's different performances.'

[2] He ably defends his own mutton (*Essay*, 3rd edn., p. 521).

really do this. They clearly tend, in their general operation, to discourage sobriety and economy, to encourage idleness and the desertion of children, and to put virtue and vice more on a level than they would otherwise be; but I will not presume to say positively that they tend to encourage population' (p. 547). The reason for this is partly the shortage of houses; also better government and the more respectable state of the people. So 'owing to these causes, combined with the twofold operation of the poor laws, it must be extremely difficult to ascertain, with any degree of precision, what has been their effect on population' (p. 547).[1]

So we end as we began. The Appendix, which was designed to clear away misconceptions, to give Malthusianism in a nutshell, leaves us in doubt as to whether the poor laws do or do not breed paupers. Nevertheless, Appendix or no Appendix, the main body of the book remains unaltered, and the proposal to abolish the poor laws still stands.

MALTHUS AND WHITBREAD

In February 1807 Whitbread introduced a Bill for the improvement of the poor laws, which had served to degrade the poor, to destroy their independence, to hold out hopes which could not be realized, to encourage idleness and vice, and to produce a superfluous population. Nearly one-seventh of the people were in receipt of parochial relief. Poverty was inevitable, but neither Young's plan to limit the total amount of relief given, nor Malthus's to bring about its gradual abolition, was a practical proposition. He, therefore, proposed the establishment of voluntary parochial schools, a national bank for the benefit of labourers, a change in the laws of settlement, and a change in the vestries. He also proposed a system of rewards for labourers who had brought up six or more children without recourse to the parish for relief. Parochial relief granted to the able-bodied was to make their condition less favourable than that of the independent labourer. These proposals were subsequently divided into four Bills, but although two of them were discussed, none of them became law.

[1] Cf. the analysis of Talbot Griffith, *Population Problems of the Age of Malthus*.

As a result of Whitbread's efforts, Malthus (among others) wrote him a letter,[1] and Hazlitt entered the arena.

To banish poverty, wrote Malthus, if not impossible, is beyond the power of legislation; nevertheless its different pressure in different countries gives hope that it can be lightened. The compulsory provision for the poor has produced effects which follow from the law of population, but, though the abolition of the poor laws would be attended by greater advantages than their retention, as a compulsory provision has been so long established, he admits he would be very sorry to see any legislative action taken on the lines he had proposed 'till the higher and middle classes of society were generally convinced of its necessity, and till the poor themselves could be made to understand that they had purchased their right to a provision by law, by too great and extensive a sacrifice of their liberty and happiness' (p. 7). Compulsory provision is almost peculiar to England, and the mischievous consequences supposed to follow its abolition have not been heard of elsewhere.

He defends himself from hardness of heart: 'I have not admitted a single proposition which appears to detract from the present comforts and gratifications of the poor, without very strong grounds for believing that it would be more than compensated to them by the general and permanent improvement of their condition' (pp. 10–11).

'The moral obligation of private, active, and discriminate charity I have endeavoured to enforce in the strongest language of which I was capable' (p. 11). The natural right of the poor to support is only denied because it is impracticable. Attempts to sanction this right will end in disappointment, irritation, and aggravated poverty. The cost is a secondary consideration: if the number could be fixed they should be relieved as a right. But he is still troubled by the fact that the poor laws have not led to the increase his theory suggests.

'In England it appears that the proportion of births and marriages to the whole population is less than in most of the other countries of Europe; and though this circumstance is principally to be accounted for from other causes, yet it affords decisive

[1] *A Letter to Samuel Whitbread, Esq., M.P., on his proposed bill for the amendment of the Poor Laws*, 2nd edn., 1807.

evidence that the poor laws do not encourage early marriages *so much* as might naturally be expected' (p. 16).

This is very disconcerting and might even have involved rewriting several hundred pages of the *Essay on Population*, were it not for the discovery of a specific cause why the injurious effects had not been so seriously felt. There was a shortage of houses.[1]

'Such is the tendency to form early connections, that with the encouragement of a sufficient number of tenements, I have very little doubt that the population might be so pushed, and such a quantity of labour in time thrown into the market, as to render the condition of the independent labourer absolutely hopeless, and to make the common wages of day labour insufficient to support a single child without parish assistance' (p. 18).

Consequently, if poor rates were spread over the whole property of the country, those who employed labour would encourage house building, gaining more by cheap labour than they would lose by dearer rates. The poor laws ought to be restricted so as not to depress wages below the support of the average number of children.

THE REPLY OF HAZLITT

While Malthus was oscillating between the view that the poor laws now did and now did not increase the number of pauper children, and worried at the thought that they might have house-room as well as relief, Hazlitt was provoked to enter the fray. For him too the immediate stimulus was Whitbread's Bill.

Hazlitt wrote three letters to Cobbett's *Weekly Register*. These, together with two further letters and a series of extracts with notes, were afterwards published in book form.[2] He acknowledges that the book is abusive, but holds the attack merited. Malthus attacking the speculative doctrines of Godwin was one thing; Malthus attacking the rights of the poor is quite another.

It was not Malthus's style but his matter that was offensive. The *Essay* contains many loose and incautious statements.[3]

[1] This had been put forward by Townsend in his *Dissertation*, op. cit., p. 429.

[2] *A Reply to the Essay on Population*, 1807.

[3] E.g. 'The infant is, comparatively speaking, of little value to the society, as others will immediately supply its place' (Malthus, 3rd edn., Vol. II, p. 399).

It was especially the attacks on the poor that provoked in Hazlitt a keen spirit of championship. Hazlitt was afraid that Malthus would gain the ear of the legislature and transfer his principles from the pages of his *Essay* to those of the Statute Book.

Commenting on his own work later Hazlitt owns that 'the style is a little exuberant, but of the arguments I see no reason to be ashamed.'[1] And elsewhere: 'I have in a separate work made the following remarks on the above proposal, (The Application of Malthus's Principle to the Poor Laws) which are a little cavalier, not too cavalier;—a little contemptuous, not too contemptuous;—a little gross, but not too gross for the subject.'[2]

The older Hazlitt then was unrepentant, but it would be a mistake to think that because the style is flowery the arguments are contemptible. The book is shot with shrewd logic. His weapon is the rapier, and in places he goads Malthus unmercifully.

Malthus he says, 'is neither generous nor just, to come in aid of the narrow prejudices and hard-heartedness of mankind, with metaphysical distinctions and the cobwebs of philosophy' (pp. 4–5). His reputation may prove fatal to the poor, and his system is a stumbling-block in the way of true political economy.

'The principle itself is neither new, nor does it prove any thing new; least of all does it prove what he meant it to prove' (p. 16). He had been completely anticipated by Wallace who had drawn the same conclusions. The only addition was the geometrical and arithmetical ratios.

At best these can only apply to half the subject. While there are unoccupied and uncultivated lands, the only thing necessary for men to do is to spread themselves. Increased production will be in proportion to increased population. As a general rule it is not true that the increase of population and the increase of subsistence are disproportionate. In a particular and important view of the subject, the extent of population is only limited by the extent of the earth, and the increase in subsistence will be proportionate to the increased surface occupied, and when the earth is full there will be no scope for arithmetical or geometrical progression. Population will be at a standstill.

'Mathematical terms carry with them an imposing air of accuracy and profundity, and ought, therefore, to be applied strictly, and with the greatest caution, or not at all' (p. 37). Till

[1] Hazlitt, *Political Essays*, 1819, p. 424 n. [2] Id., p. 426.

the earth is full, and till it can be proved that the food cannot be doubled by using proper methods, the growth of population is checked neither by the limited extent of the earth nor by its limited fertility, but by other causes, 'not by the original constitution of nature, but by the will of man' (p. 38).

Malthus has confused man's mind by representing population as a growing evil, whereas population is only an evil as it is excessive. In fact, the same degree of restraint will prevent excess whether the population is great or small, whether it has reached its natural limits or been crushed down by arbitrary institutions.

In spite of the check of moral restraint, Malthus still retains the argument against perfectibility. How can the principle of population be an answer to Godwin and others? Are we to believe that 'if reason should ever get this mastery over all our actions, we shall then be governed entirely by our physical appetites and passions, without the least regard to consequences'? (p. 49). This is incomprehensible unless we think that reason has no power over the impulse to propagate.

It is no objection to increasing the means of subsistence by improved cultivation that population will keep up with it. Improved cultivation means that either a greater number of people will have the same degree of comfort, or an equal number of people will have a greater degree of ease and plenty. At no time during the progress of cultivation would distress be greater than it is now when population is held down by artificial causes, by moral and political circumstances.

Malthus's ratios allow for a doubling during the first period. 'It is perfectly immaterial, perfectly irrelevant to the question, *whether we should double our population*, that we cannot forsooth go on doubling it for ever; unless indeed it could be shewn that by thus doubling it once, when we can do it without any inconvenience, we should be irresistibly impelled to go on doubling it afterwards when it would have become exceedingly inconvenient, and in fact till the consequence would be general famine and the most extensive misery' (p. 85).

This is the crux of the Malthusian argument. It is necessary to distinguish between a population's tendency to increase and its power to increase.[1] Power is abstract, and its effects may be

[1] This point was pressed later by Whately and Senior.

represented by a mathematical series. 'The power of population to increase is in fact the same both before and after it has become excessive. But I conceive this is not the case with its *tendency* to increase, unless we mean its *unchecked tendency*, which is saying nothing; for if we speak of its real tendency to increase, this certainly is not always the same, but depends exceedingly on circumstances, that is, is greater or less in proportion as the population is or is not excessive' (pp. 91–92).

Malthus gives two sets of ratios:

Growth of Population	1	2	4	8	16	32	64	128	256
Growth of Food	1	2	3	4	5	6	7	8	9

The suggestion is that you can pass over to the opposite line to see where you are on the scale, but there is no dependence of the two ratios. Two hundred and fifty-six does not depend on the other being at 9, but on being 'so many removes from the root or first number,' i.e. only an abstract tendency (p. 95).[1] Population will only grow as 1, 2, 4, 8, etc. while subsistence does the same. If subsistence can only be made to increase as 1, 2, 3, 4, etc., then population will come down to that rate of increase, 'or supposing it to have generally a certain tendency to excess, it will then increase as $1\frac{1}{4}$, $2\frac{1}{2}$, $3\frac{3}{4}$, 5, etc. The actual, positive, practical tendency in population *to increase* is not therefore always the same, and for that very reason its tendency *to excess* is always the same, neither greater nor less, in consequence of the absolute increase in population' (pp. 92–93).

Motives to resist sexual gratification vary, but there is always a point where restraint causes the excess to cease. That point depends on the 'manners, the habits, and institutions of society' (p. 110).

There is a tendency in population to increase *faster* than subsistence, but not faster and faster. 'It is in fact only a disproportionate superiority in certain motives over others, which subjects the community or certain classes of it to a great degree of

[1] Malthus is aware of this, but, typically, he makes the suggestion (1806 edn., Vol. I, p. 13); the qualification is in Vol. II, p. 110: 'I am sufficiently aware that the redundant millions which I have mentioned could never have existed.' Some indulgence must be accorded the critics when they apparently labour the obvious; they were attacking the impression as much as the book.

want and hardship: and as far as their imprudence and folly will carry them, they will go, but they will not go further' (p. 111).

Hazlitt then lays down the following maxims:

1. While population increases at the tremendous rate described by Malthus it shows that it is wanted, and that if it could increase ten times faster so much the better.

2. When from natural or artificial causes it begins to press upon the means of subsistence, it stops of its own accord. The checks from vice, misery, and moral restraint taken together become stronger as the excess grows. The growth produces its antidote in exact proportion.

3. The same quantity of vice and misery combined with the same degree of moral restraint will always keep population at the same relative point. Therefore less vice and misery together with more moral restraint will produce the same effect. The happiness of a people is to be judged by the prevalence of moral restraint over vice and misery (pp. 115–116).

Thus we should aim at increasing the influence of rational motives, and lessening the operation of vice and misery. Vice and misery may check population, but they do not remedy it. They alone are the evils.

Malthus himself has insisted on these general principles in some part or other of his 'various' work, but in other parts he has contradicted them and himself, and the uniform tenor of his first work leans directly the opposite way. The question is not 'how much Mr. Malthus retains of his old philosophy, as how many of their old feelings his readers retain on the subject, on which he will be able to build as many false conclusions as he pleases' (p. 118).

It is impossible to determine Malthus's real opinions. 'It should not therefore be the object of any one who would set himself to answer Mr. Malthus, so much to say that such and such are the real and settled opinions of that author, as that such opinions are floating in different parts of his writings, that they are floating or fixed in the minds of his readers, and that those opinions are not so correct as they might be' (p. 121).

Malthus is not right in lumping together the need for food and for sexual intercourse as laws of nature. Many persons have abstained from sexual intercourse throughout their lives, and the longer they go without it, the more tractable they find it. Single women who lead pure lives are influenced by moral causes, operating through the institutions of society. The need for sexual intercourse is not at all on a par with the need for food.

According to Malthus the passion between the sexes is necessary and will remain in its present state, but what is this state? It varies with climate, and all other natural and artificial causes. Moreover these causes, especially moral causes, have influenced the prevailing manners of large classes of people and whole ages. He should provide answers to three questions:

(1) How much vice and misery are due to human institutions and human nature, independently of the principle of population?

(2) Whether removing these evils would increase the evils of population and cause more vice and misery than ever?

(3) Whether the tendency to excess is mechanical (inherent) or dependent on the state of society, public opinion and other controllable causes? (p. 151).

Whence, if governments influence morals, and morals population, there is an increased need to remove bad governments, and if the amount of vice in existence may be greater than necessary, its mere existence is no proof of excessive population.[1]

What degree of vice and misery is necessary as a check? Which abuses are necessary? The vague term 'vice and misery' gives us no clue. It applies generally to both good and bad governments, and proves either nothing at all, or a great deal more than Malthus would in all cases wish to prove. The principle goes to the support of all political regulations and evils or it goes to the support of none.[2]

If morals are influenced by religion, then they do not depend upon the state of population. 'If it is true, that the invention of a useful art, which is accident, or the public encouragement of it, which is design, may contribute to the support of a larger population without multiplying its inconveniences, then it is not true that all human happiness or misery can be calculated according to a mechanical ratio' (p. 165).

In Turkey, for instance, human institutions have aggravated and not mitigated the necessary evils of population. Thus the

[1] Malthus tends to assume this.

[2] Thus Malthus defends the luxury of the rich, but is indignant at the use of his principle in favour of the Slave Trade.

state of population is no proof of what it might be. It depends upon government. 'It is a thing *de facto*, not *de jure*' (p. 181).

Malthus uses his principle in his attack against the poor laws. This attack is based on the belief that misery or the fear of misery is an essential check, but wretchedness is not essential as a spur to industry. The American people are not forced to work by the wretchedness of their situation, and 'the way to hinder people from taking *desperate* steps is not to involve them in despair' (p. 277). Poor relief will not be abused: the check to abuse is provided by the precariousness and disgusting nature of the remedy. If the poor are reduced so low as to be indifferent to considerations of this nature, they will not be restrained from following their inclinations by the 'grinding law of necessity, by the abolition of the poor laws, or by the prospect of seeing their children starving at the doors of the rich. . . . The way to obviate those consequences is not by obstinately increasing the pressure, but by lessening it' (p. 287–288).[1]

Malthus proposes 'formally to disclaim the right of the poor to support.' He must give some better reason for thrusting a poor man out of existence than that there is not room for an unlimited number. He has produced 'a complete theory of population, in which it is clearly proved that the poor have no right to live any longer than the rich will let them' (p. 297).[2]

He suggests that any gains to the lowest class must be at the expense of the next highest grade. Even so they can bear it better. 'Is it an argument that because the pressure of a scarcity does not fall directly upon those who can bear it best, viz. the very rich, that it should therefore fall upon those, who can bear it least, viz. on the very poor? Unless Mr. Malthus can contrive to starve some one, he thinks he does nothing' (p. 314).

To say that the rich have nothing to spare, because they have only one stomach each, is to ignore all their hangers-on, who though they do nothing to increase the produce of the ground, devour it none the less eagerly. . . . 'The rich man has not only to supply his own wants, but the wants of those who depend upon

[1] This is the main point at issue between Hazlitt and Malthus. Townsend believed in hunger as a means of driving the poor. Malthus believed that the removal of the claim to support would encourage or enforce industry. Hazlitt joins issue fairly and squarely.

[2] An echo of the celebrated (or should it be notorious) feast illustration.

him, and who do nothing to support either him or themselves' (p. 301).

Malthus devotes much space to proving that, if the wages of the poor were increased from 1*s*. 6*d*. to 5*s*., it would be of no avail.[1] This, says Hazlitt, is nonsense. When I give away money to another I necessarily retrench the quantity of food or other things consumed in my own house, and give him what I have cut off. I give him a title to a larger share of the common produce by diminishing my own share. 'It does not matter to the community whether he or I spend the money: the only difference it makes is between ourselves' (p. 311). If giving the poor more money would not enable them to command a greater portion of food, 'there could be no room for competition, nor for an increase in the price or the demand' (p. 313).

Malthus is obsessed with one idea, that the rich cannot be expected to retrench. The whole burthen of the scarcity ought to fall on those whom he calls 'the least fortunate members of the community.' In fact, the real funds for the maintenance of labour are the produce of labour, and not that portion merely which is left over by the rich. Malthus repeatedly shifts his ground in the course of the argument, but either a rise in wages must be nominal and therefore nugatory, or real and beneficial. Given a quantity of provisions and a fixed quantity of money, and a distribution in favour of the poor: the rich must retrench somewhere. If they retrench on provisions, there is more food for the poor; if on other things, then the poor will have the same food, but can command extra conveniences, 'smart buckles for their shoes, or garters and ribbons for their sweethearts' (pp. 324–325). It would certainly subtract from the luxury of the rich and add to the comforts of the poor.

Malthus talks much about independence, but how can men be independent when poverty and depression make the workhouse a temptation to them? 'The poor live from hand to mouth, because, in general, they have no hopes of living in any other way. . . . If what they earn beyond their immediate necessities goes to the ale-house, it is because . . . they are willing to forget the *work-house*, their old age, and the prospect of their wives and

[1] The extraordinary argument occurs in the 1st edn., Chapter V, and in subsequent editions, Book III, Chapter V. It will be considered more fully later.

children starving, and to drown care in a mug of ale. . . . No human patience can submit to everlasting toil and self-denial. . . . You reduce them almost to the condition of brutes, and then grudge them their coarse enjoyments: you make machines of them, and then expect from them firmness, resolution, the love of independence, the fruits of an erect and manly spirit' (pp. 331–332).

It is not true that the remedy lies solely in their hands, or that the Government is totally without power in this respect.[1] Malthus argues that the waste of the rich has no bearing on the distress of the poor.[2] In fact, viewed in one light, it is an asset, being capable of retrenchment in case of famine![3] Tilling of uncultivated land, it is said, will only help if suddenly cultivated.[4] The effect of uncultivated land is merely the possession of a smaller territory. This is absurd, for it would justify any degree of waste or neglect that can be imagined.

Starving the poor is not the way to deter them from wasteful expenditure, nor are their standards of decency raised by familiarity with unmitigated wretchedness. Restraints to population may ultimately be necessary, but that is no reason why the evil should not be postponed as long as possible. The poor man is not doomed to starve by the laws of nature, and to argue thus is to confound the necessary limits of the earth's produce with the arbitrary and artificial distribution of it arranged by our institutions.

HAZLITT AND THE *EDINBURGH REVIEW*

In August 1810 Hazlitt's *Reply* was reviewed in the *Edinburgh Review*—or rather it was used as a pretext for an article eulogizing the work of Malthus and belittling his opponents. It would hardly be worth attention but for two reasons: first, it clearly illustrates the attitude of the supporters of Malthus towards his critics; secondly, there is at least a strong probability that the article may have been written by Malthus himself, and its authorship suitably disguised by the editor.[5] It repeats the charges of misapprehension and misrepresentation, accuses the critics of

[1] Malthus, *Essay*, 1806 edn., Vol. II, p. 342.
[2] Id., Vol. II, p. 291.
[3] Id., Vol. II, pp. 291–292.
[4] Id., Vol. II, p. 292.
[5] Bonar, *Malthus and His Work*, p. 329 n.

ignorance and of not reading Malthus's work, and undertakes to expound the doctrine to those who are too lazy to read the book in full.

Space forbids the detailed analysis of what is both brief and easily accessible, but the following points are worthy of note. The article disclaims all pretensions that the doctrine is a discovery. The assumption is made, for it is an assumption, that when both food and population are observed to grow together, food is the cause and population the effect. Although the disproportion between food and population is stated, there is no mention of the ratios. Nor is there any hint of the drastic treatment proposed to be meted out to the poor. No measures, it is stated, for the relief of the poor can be effective which do not increase the proportion between the means of subsistence and population. Hence, in order to improve the condition of the lower classes it is necessary to remove despotism, ignorance, and all those causes which promote dependence and weaken exertion, and to strengthen those tending to promote good habits, such as good government, good education, and those which encourage independence and respectability.

'The only change, if change it can be called, which the study of the laws of population can make in our duties, is, that it will lead us to apply, more steadily than we have hitherto done, the great rules of morality to the case of marriage, and the direction of our charity; but the rules themselves, and the foundations on which they rest, of course remain exactly where they were before' (p. 472).

Surely a harmless enough doctrine to have caused such a stir!

Now such an exposition was all very well for those who had no intention of consulting the work itself, and no doubt commended Malthus to such people by presenting the doctrine in an innocent guise and deliberately masking all the obnoxious and repellant features of the *Essay*. It was this aspect which provoked Hazlitt to a reply, not so much to defend his own work, which had not even been attacked, but to unmask 'the vulgar selfishness consolidated into a principle, like marsh water that has become sordid ice.'[1] This reply appeared in Cobbett's *Political Register* for November 24th, 1810.

It was, of course, stupid to assert that Hazlitt had not read

[1] C. M. MacLean, *Born under Saturn*, p. 228.

Malthus's *Essay*. All the evidence is that he had not only read it, but read it very carefully indeed. Hazlitt, therefore, appeals, not like the reviewer to those who were ignorant of the work but to those who had read it and were prepared to form their own opinions.

Hazlitt demonstrates that the defence of Malthus consists in the adoption, point by point, of the criticisms and qualifications made in the *Reply*. The doctrines of the *Essay* are not so much defended as denied; the paradoxes are dwindled into harmless commonplaces, so that there is a coincidence of sentiment between both supporters and opponents of Malthus. The reviewer admits that the *Essay* is not original, that progress depends on diffusing rational modes of action, securing the independence of the working classes, and that the extent of population and its happiness depend very much on political institutions, moral habits, and the state of commercial development, as distinct from the mechanical operation of the ratios. But these were precisely the points insisted on in the *Reply to the Essay*, and hence the reply to the reviewer might well rest there.

But the work of Malthus still stands, and he is by no means the 'man of no mark' that the reviewer makes out. Therefore, Hazlitt concludes by searching the crannies of the *Essay*, and bringing the matter to an issue in a series of eighteen questions which by their very form are incapable of adequate summary.

Nevertheless the main drift is clear. Malthus represents vice and misery as the only checks, except moral restraint which he considers of no effect. The actual state of man in society is a blind struggle between vice, misery, and the principle of population 'as mechanical as the ebbing and flowing of the tide.' Instead of accounting for the differences between countries in terms of their institutions, government, and state of knowledge he does 'expressly and repeatedly declare, that political institutions are but as the dust in the balance compared with the inevitable consequences of the principle of population.'

Malthus should make an effort to determine what proportion the principle of population bears to the other factors which work on the face of society in producing the varying degrees of happiness and misery, instead of repeatedly discouraging every plan of improvement by repeating the senseless objection that after all population will still press as much as ever against the means of subsistence.

The introduction of the principle of moral restraint makes nonsense of his conclusions, yet it remains a dead-letter in the *Essay*, except for the purpose of abusing and keeping in order the poor. The essence of Malthus's approach to the poor laws is 'that by the laws of God and nature, the rich have a right to starve the poor, whenever they cannot maintain themselves.' But this is nothing but the confusion of a trite truism and a wilful contradiction: namely, the truism that the poor must starve if there is not enough food to be found, and the contradiction that the right of the rich to withhold of their surplus is founded on the same necessity. The real funds for the maintenance of labour are the whole produce of labour, and not merely what is left over after luxury and idleness have been satisfied. These two things are fundamentally distinct, and should be kept so in a question of such importance as the right of the rich to starve the poor by system.

The letter ends with the shewd accusation that Malthus has taken the advice of the prudent Friar in Chaucer—

> 'Beware therefore with lordes for to play,
> Singeth Placebo—
> To a poor man should his vices tell,
> But not to a lord, though he should go to hell.'

CHAPTER TWO

POST-WAR CRITICS—GRAY, WEYLAND, GRAHAME, AND ENSOR

THE POST-WAR REVIVAL

DURING the years between the publication of Hazlitt's *Reply* and the end of the war in 1815 the controversy was kept alive in the periodical press of the time, but the early flood was by this time hardly more than a trickle. The first four editions of the *Essay* followed in rapid succession—1798, 1803, 1806, 1807. Ten years elapsed before a fifth was called for. Meanwhile the hold of the Malthusian theory steadily grew. The *Edinburgh Review* had been with Malthus from the beginning; the *Quarterly*, at first openly hostile, was already modifying its tone, the prelude to subsequent conversion. But the lull was only temporary. The end of the war was the signal for the bursting of the dam, and the flood continued till the death of Malthus, and even beyond.

There were good reasons for this. General opinion in a nation engaged in a major war favoured a heavy birth rate,[1] and thus the threat of an increased population had less force. Moreover the landed interests had been faring very well indeed. The harvest of 1807 was scarcely an average one in England; in Scotland it was very poor.[2] This deficiency, combined with the difficulty of obtaining imports, meant that demand was proportioned to supply by means of high prices and the prohibition of distillation from grain.[3] 'The Board of Agriculture average for the year (1808) was 81*s.* 4*d.*, yet the import of wheat was very small amounting to only 85,000 quarters.'[4]

[1] Hammond, *Village Labourer*, p. 174.

[2] Smart, *Annals*, p. 148.

[3] Tooke, *History of Prices*, Vol. I, p. 290.

[4] Smart, op. cit., p. 182.

Then followed four deficient harvests in succession, those of 1809 to 1812. In December 1809 wheat stood at 102*s.* 6*d.*; in June 1810 at 113*s.* 5*d.*[1] The quartern loaf did not fall below 13*d.*; during the harvest it rose to 17*d.*[2] These high prices proved a great stimulus to imports, and in spite of great difficulties and the enormous cost of freight, insurance, and licences an import of 1½ million quarters of wheat and flour and 600,000 quarters of other grain and meal was attained in 1810.[3] The range of price fluctuation during the period was as great as 30*s.*, the October price being below 100*s.* with the loaf at 1*s.* 3*d.*[4]

The harvest of 1811 was defective and that of 1812 scarcely an average; foreign supplies were almost non-existent. On October 26th, 1811, the price of wheat was 101*s.* 6*d.*, in August 1812 the average price in England and Wales was 155*s.*, while finest Danzig wheat fetched as much as 180*s.*[5] Even at these high prices the shortage on the Continent and the restrictions to be overcome made import almost prohibitive. Economy was the only solution, and high prices were the means by which it was brought about. Bread riots made their appearance in many of the towns of the country.[6]

These prices brought great gain to the agricultural classes. Long-sustained high prices gave an illusory suggestion of permanence. Rents were proportionately advanced on the expiration of leases, and in some cases stood at three times the level of 1792.[7] In fact, much of the gain went into the pockets of the landlords.[8] Enclosure bills were numerous.[9] New ground, much of it inferior or worse situated was taken up, but these additional supplies could only be obtained at increasing cost. The tenant gained, but only during the period of his lease; the labourer little, if at all; the gain ultimately reached the property owner.[10]

If the hardship of the labourer was not noticed in public as it was in the dearths of 1795–6 and 1800–1, it must be attributed to the partial adjustment of wages to the new price levels. Dearth

[1] Tooke, op. cit., pp. 294–295.
[2] Smart, op. cit., p. 198.
[3] Tooke, op. cit., p. 296.
[4] Smart, op. cit., p. 225.
[5] Tooke, op. cit., p. 323.
[6] Smart, op. cit., p. 334.
[7] Tooke, op. cit., p. 326.
[8] Cunningham, *Growth of English Industry & Commerce*, p. 727.
[9] Tooke, op. cit., p. 326 (Table).
[10] Cunningham, op. cit., p. 727.

which was unexpected in its intensity in 1795 was by now an institution. Nominal wages had been increased either by actual payments or by parish allowances. Tooke assesses them at approximately double in 1812.[1]

'The average wages of the agricultural labourer, according to Arthur Young's calculations, had been 7*s.* 6*d* a week from 1767 to 1789; 10*s.* from 1799 to 1803; and 12*s.* from 1804 to 1810. In 1811, they were 12*s.* 9*d.*'[2]

The Hammonds put it differently: 'The wolf was at the door, it is true, but he was chained, and the chain was the Speenhamland system. Consequently, though we hear complaints from the labourers, who contended that they were receiving in a patronizing and degrading form what they were entitled to have as their direct wages, the note of rebellion was smothered for the moment.'[3]

Population had grown from 8,675,000 in 1790 to 10,164,256 in 1811. The poor rate which was £1,912,241 in 1783–85 was £4,077,891 in 1803 and £6,656,105 in 1812–13.[4] Increased allowances mitigated distress which would otherwise have been inevitable among the labourers owing to the high prices, but among the factory workers, who had had little or no increase, and who suffered considerable unemployment, hardship was widespread and severe, and led to frequent disturbances.[5]

Nevertheless it was not dearth that created widespread alarm and despondency, but the onset of plenty. The harvest of 1813 was both abundant and excellent in quality. The price of wheat fell rapidly, and the quartern loaf was below a shilling. 'Bread had never been so cheap since May of 1808.'[6] Fortunately the extra yield sufficed to offset the diminished price, but already the first rumbling suggestion of ruin appeared in the *Farmer's Magazine.*[7] The price of corn must be kept up, or the acreage would be curtailed and the country would once again be dependent on foreign supplies.

The harvest of 1814 was rather under average, but was harvested in good condition. Imports of wheat and wheat flour

[1] Tooke, op. cit., p. 329.

[2] Thorold Rogers, *Six Centuries of Work and Wages*, p. 510.

[3] *Village Labourer*, p. 174.

[4] Cunningham, op. cit., p. 935.

[5] Tooke, op. cit., p. 330.

[6] Smart, op. cit., p. 364.

[7] Id., p. 365.

rose to 852,000 quarters, and the price of the loaf kept about 1*s.*, but already the threat of peace was felt.

'It had brought anything but prosperity to agriculture: as one writer put it frankly, "the dark threatening cloud, which has cast a gloom over the British agriculturists, has now, in all its horrors, burst over their heads." To the commercial interests, the end of the war promised not peace but a sword.'[1]

Thus began the battle for a new corn law, a battle in which Malthus took the side of the agriculturists. Others took up the case of the labourer, for the small farmers were not the only sufferers. Nevertheless, the labourer differed from the other victims in that he had not benefited by the prosperity of the days 'when the plough turned a golden furrow.'

'His housing had not been improved; his dependence had not been made less abject or less absolute; his wages had not risen; and in many cases his garden had disappeared. When the storm broke over agriculture his condition became desperate.'[2] The peace brought both unemployment and high prices.

The corn law was passed in 1815, and the importation of foreign corn was prohibited so long as the price of wheat did not rise above 80*s.* Malthus issued two pamphlets on the subject—the first: *Observations on the Effects of the Corn Laws*, published in 1814, professed to balance the arguments for and against the corn laws, and we are told that he did it so successfully that his friends were doubtful which way he inclined.[3] They were not long in doubt, for in 1815 he published a further pamphlet on the *Grounds of an Opinion on the Policy of Restricting the Importation of Foreign Corn.*

The substance of these pamphlets will be considered elsewhere, but one comment from the second is illuminating in view of his persistent advocacy of the abolition of the poor laws. Writing on free trade, he says: 'But I protest most entirely against the doctrine, that we are to pursue our general principles without ever looking to see if they are applicable to the case before us.'[4]

Against this economic background, and with these words of

1 Smart, p. 398—quoting *Farmer's Magazine.*

2 Hammond, *Village Labourer*, p. 176.

3 Bonar, *Malthus and His Work*, p. 223.

4 See p. 16.

Malthus in mind, we return to the renewed volume of criticism which questioned whether the 'general principle' of population were applicable to nineteenth-century England.

SIMON GRAY—*THE HAPPINESS OF STATES*

At the close of the war three book-length replies appeared in quick succession—those of Simon Gray, John Weyland, and James Grahame.

Gray's book, the first of the three, entitled *The Happiness of States*, although it does not specifically attack Malthus by name, puts forward among other matters a criticism of his theory of population. Although written in 1804 it was not published until 1815. A second edition appeared in 1819. Between these two editions, in 1818, Gray published a further volume under the nom-de-plume, George Purves, L L.D., in which his own and Malthus's theories are set in direct opposition.[1]

Gray's approach to the problem is essentially practical and not doctrinaire. It is generous in tone and forms a valuable addition to the literature of the subject. Malthus obviously noticed the arguments,[2] but did not reply to them.

Happiness, says Gray, is the true standard of value, and since existence is better than non-existence, increase of population tends to increase happiness. It consists 'in enjoying health, corporeal and mental, having something to eat and drink, something for shelter from the varieties of the climate, and something to do. But to complete the total, we must add, in being blest with friends and secure from enemies' (p. 5).[3] Most ranks have their own peculiar means and standards of happiness, but all are equal as to their means of obtaining happiness; therefore we should hesitate to make our own notions the general standard, and be cautious how we scatter the terms happiness and misery about.

Perfectibility will not be achieved through the instrumentality of reason, for men are not capable of extensive improvements in points connected with politics, and it is wrong to suppose that progress in knowledge or science means progress in morality.

[1] Purves (Gray) believed quite erroneously that the publication of the three books was evidence that the Populationists were gaining ground.

[2] See A. H. Everett, *New Ideas on Population*, 1822, p. x.

[3] Quotations are taken from the 1819 edn.

Effective government, while it can prevent the grosser forms of crime, cannot promote positive virtue, because heredity is important and is beyond the reach of education. The human mind cannot exist without passions, and much human action therefore tends to be based on passion and prejudice rather than reason. Men who commit wrong know that they are doing so, but they are influenced by physical and social conditions which offer ever more varied temptations; and so, while they think more accurately, they act as inaccurately as ever. Therefore, we should aim at practical not theoretical perfection, for, by seeking to do too much, we may fail to achieve what is in our power. Individual interest should not be sacrificed to the imaginary interest of the state. 'A nation is made up of individuals, and to make the individuals happy is to make the nation happy' (p. 19).

The source of population is sexual desire operating in marriage, and, since polygamy and concubinage are depopulating systems, early monogamatic marriage is the basis of increase. Consequently stimulating causes of population are those which encourage either early marriage or procreation and may be regular or occasional. Warm genial seasons favour conception, which flourishes in the period May–August.[1] Favourable turns in national affairs, the discharge of soldiers, a real rise in income, or even a fashion set by leaders of society may give an impetus to marriage. Improved medical systems render marriages more productive and children more likely to live.

Defecundating causes are regular and powerful and may become so strong as to make population retrogressive. They may be physical, moral, or mixed, and fecundity depends very greatly on circumstances. For a variety of reasons savages are unproductive: irregular employments, their desolate and joyless condition, frequent fastings and voracious eating, lateness of marriage by the males, prostitution before marriage, the length of the suckling period without cohabitation, wars and unhealthy surroundings, all tend in the same direction. In agricultural states, on the other hand, man is very productive, while in commercial and advanced states the rate is again slower owing to the operation of late marriage, immorality, and luxury. Late marriages in particular mean fewer and less robust children.

[1] Cf. the views expressed in *Climate Makes the Man*, by Clarence A. Mills, 1944.

Labouring with the body seems to be favourable to population; labouring with the mind less so.

Population is also checked by positively destroying causes—the principles of disease and death implanted in the human constitution, and these are particularly effective among the young. The causes of death are many, some regular and universal, some occasional and local. Unhealthy seasons and epidemics are powerful but occasional. Mild winters generally mean a lower mortality. Excess of heat is fatal in hot countries, excess of cold in cold countries. Famines, though very destructive in the past, become less serious with the extension of commerce. Moral causes include the operation of luxury and intemperance, war, crime, and illicit sexual intercourse.

The increase of population is the great permanent source of increased wealth; it extends and improves the cultivation of the soil and renders men less dependent on the varieties of climate. It not only enlarges the demand, but also increases the ability to supply that demand. 'It has as strong a natural civilizing as it has a fertilizing influence' (p. 323). Civilization will show itself when population density is one person to thirty acres, will be vigorous when the ratio is one to ten, and universal at one person to four acres. Thereafter the land will be over-civilized (p. 324).[1] The growth of population leads to increased comforts and the divison of labour, but by leading also to luxury it may be accompanied by other evils.

Population has a strong natural tendency to increase because normally the populating are superior to the depopulating causes. This fact is confirmed by history, by the gradual cultivation of the earth, and by the progress of science and discovery. On the whole it would appear that the people of the earth had their origin in a common stock, and have been gradually increasing in numbers ever since. Will this process continue, and is subsistence the limiting factor?

It is probable that the depopulating causes will increase, and

[1] Several times Gray approaches the conception of an optimum and then the controversy carries him away. Cf. for instance Purves, *Principles of Population and Production Investigated*, 1818, p. 254: 'What is the rate of population per square mile, which he (Arthur Young) in his imagination fixes upon as rousing most industry, producing most employment, and, of course, creating most wealth?'

the stimulating causes lose their vigour. The growth of towns, the change of occupations, and the prevalence of luxury support the view that population 'naturally carries in its own increase a preventive against an over-increase' (p. 351). It is possible that an equilibrium point may be reached when the town and country populations are equal. Numbers certainly do not double themselves in equal periods: there is no natural rate of growth. The force of occasional causes is such that, while some territories might double their population in fifteen years, others would not do so in fifteen hundred.

'Population, were it unchecked by the circumstances in which Providence has placed men, would be in its nature infinite, or go on doubling itself for ever. Subsistence is also in its nature infinite. If this were not checked by natural circumstances, it would continue doubling itself for ever in a still more rapid manner. A grain of wheat, if the produce of it, and the produce of this produce, and so on, were sown year after year, would in a few centuries supply wheat for the whole of the present population of the earth. But what do observations of this description tend to? Nothing practical' (p. 357).

The natural increase of population is that arising out of the whole of its circumstances, whatever they happen to be. Because the American increase is rapid it is no more natural than that of any other state, however different. 'Population is essentially connected with territory, climate, diet, education, and other circumstances, and it is affected, consequently, by their permanent or temporary varieties' (p. 358). The United States' increase is due to a large number of favourable causes all happening together, and estimates of rates of doubling are nothing but rough guesses on which nothing can be built. The progress of population is both irregular and uncertain. No fixed ratio can be obtained because there is none. As the world advances and fills, powerful influences will make themselves felt which have hitherto not been noticed in its ill-peopled condition, and for this reason all calculations concerning future population compared with time must be extremely uncertain and inaccurate.

The next question is that of subsistence. A certain quantity of food is necessary for mere existence, but this is very small indeed. The quantity for health and happy existence is greater, but not so great as we imagine. Most people eat too much, and the healthiest men are those who eat little. After considering in detail the various resources of the world it appears that two acres of land would maintain one person. Moreover such a density in one place does not involve overcrowding unless other areas are equally populous, as subsistence can be transferred from one area to the other.

The ratios are certainly not correct. The subsistence drawn from any piece of land cannot exceed a certain amount, which may be reached in a few years or may take centuries according to the vigour or sluggishness of the cultivators. The general amount of subsistence bears a nearly corresponding proportion to the amount of population. Granted that population cannot exist without food, it is not necessary for each district to produce its own: only the total must be enough. In general the amount of subsistence is maintained at a level of 1¼ to 2 years ahead of population, but extra is only evoked in accordance with the laws of supply and demand. 'Food and men must have been at least coeval,' but the moment man began to cultivate the soil, he became the regulator of subsistence. Population is indubitably the author of subsistence, not the reverse. As only one man in six or seven is needed for actual cultivation, the rest are freed for other work, since an over-supply of food is useless unless for export. In fact, overproduction is inimical to increase, because over-eating makes for sterility. Hence the quaint law: 'The increase of population is much in the inverse ratio of the quantity of subsistence used, to the point of a bare sufficiency of mere necessaries' (p. 454).

Supposing, however, that the equilibrium between population and subsistence be disturbed, how is it to be restored? Colonization is clearly one possibility, but the measure of reducing population to subsistence assumes that a country can reduce its population and at the same time find subsistence kept up to the usual amount.[1] The best remedy is to increase subsistence. Importation is possible for a manufacturing country and may be more profitable than self-subsistence, although the latter makes for independence and may be preferable. Britain should aim at supplying her own necessaries.

[1] Gray certainly had the root of the matter in him, in spite of an occasional blunder. This is a piercing criticism of the Malthusian system.

Bounties on exported grain are unnecessary, for, if we are importing, the existence of a market is proved, and, since most foreign nations are exporters, where are overseas markets to be found? The most effectual plan is to apply more labour and capital to agriculture, and to this end the Government should subsidize cultivators to the extent of an average of £6 per acre, not as a flat rate, but in the proportion of two-thirds of the actual cost of waste land brought under cultivation. Manure should also be made available (pp. 478–480).

Britain has been for half a century a corn importer because we prefer the more profitable manufacturing industries. This has drawn men from agriculture into industry, and unless corrected will lead to an increased dependence on other lands. The opportunity is favourable for reversing the process, but there is another view of the subject.

'The friend of mankind and human happiness, the enlightened friend of his own country, for both go together, may take up the matter in a more enlarged point of view. He may consider all the national divisions of mankind, to which his country exports, or from which she imports, as joining to form a larger country of his own. The continent of Europe and America take off our productions, chiefly in the form of manufactured articles, and we take off theirs, chiefly in the form of raw materials, and among others, corn. If they employ our people in the way best suited to us at present, why should not we, in return, employ theirs in the way most suited to them? By means of our importation of corn, the enlightened patriot will see, that we are cultivating the fields of others for ourselves' (p. 486).

THE REPLY OF WEYLAND

The second of the trio of writers now under consideration was John Weyland,[1] who had already published two works[2] bearing on the poor laws.

The present work, *The Principles of Population and Production, as they are affected by the Progress of Society; with a view to Moral and*

[1] Weyland was born in 1774, matriculated from Christ Church, Oxford, in 1792, and was called to the Inner Temple Bar in 1800. He died in 1854.

[2] *A Short Inquiry into the Policy, Humanity, and past Effects of the Poor Laws*, 1807, and *Observations on Mr. Whitbread's Poor Bill and on the Population of England*, also in the same year.

Political Consequences, had apparently been written shortly after the publication of Malthus's second edition, but had not been published until the end of the war made the circumstances of the time propitious. Its most noteworthy feature is the attempt to produce an alternative theory of the growth of population to supplant the geometrical ratio.

Although Weyland holds that Christian morality is the 'very root and principle' of the questions to be discussed, we shall concern ourselves only with the economic aspects of his doctrine. His aim is 'a condition of progressive prosperity and of moral improvement' (p. 6). The natural progress of population varies in its tendencies with every variation in the state of society and seldom tends to excess.

Granting Malthus's premises, his conclusion is undeniable, but he is wrong in his statement of the natural tendency of population to increase. He is wrong in assuming that the quickest tendency to human increase possible in a particular society is natural, and thus theoretically possible, in all. Population has a natural tendency to keep within the powers of the soil in all gradations of society. This tendency cannot be destroyed but may be altered by bad laws and customs which unduly stimulate population or depress agriculture, thus causing undue pressure against subsistence. Population cannot increase beyond the powers of the soil to provide subsistence but, as these are not all called forth, it will in time undoubtedly increase beyond the means actually provided. This incipient pressure against the actual means of subsistence is in fact the root of progress. Far from causing the miseries which afflict men and women, it is the remedy. It is the leading motive to all industry and the primary cause of all advancement in public happiness and prosperity.

He distinguishes four stages of society: 1. Savage and Pastoral; 2. Agricultural; 3. Commercial and Manufacturing; 4. Highly civilized and artificial states of society.

In the early stages it is untrue to say that population increases faster than food can be provided, because land is accessible and capable of tenfold production. It would be truer to say that the wants of the people press against their own ignorance and apathy. Nor is it true that population can only be repressed by vice, misery, or moral restraint, since the most ordinary exertions of a man will produce more than enough to support a family, and when this level of exertion becomes general the community will be carried along to the next stage of development. Unless the necessity of barbarism can be proved, the resources of the soil are adequate.

The step towards agriculture is decisive, and it is rare for a state to slip back into savagery. In newly settled lands population cannot overtake food. The surplus produce can be sold to manufacturing nations. Workmen are scarce, children an asset, and it is easy to become a master. When all the best spots are occupied manufacturing will begin, and the produce formerly exported will be consumed by domestic workmen until finally there is an export of manufactures.[1] The rise in the price of grain will attract capital either to the cultivation of poorer or to the improvement of old lands. As this will be a slower process, it follows that, if the natural progress of population remains the same, population must soon overtake the supply of food; but the natural progress does *not* remain the same.

There is a spontaneous change in the habits of the people, and a diminution in their prolific powers consequent upon their change of occupation and residence. Towns will arise, and there will be two sections of society, townsmen and countrymen, with different habits. Towns reduce robustness, diminish the number of births, and shorten the duration of life. Artificial wants become necessaries and render the support of a family more difficult.

'The abatement in the progress of population is voluntary, natural and unavoidable . . . *the necessary and natural consequence* of the progress of society, and to exclaim against its effects is in fact to exclaim against all advancement of a country beyond the purely agricultural state' (pp. 66–67).

Large towns are the offspring of a full agriculture and should assist the country (p. 73). The co-existence of large towns and a low state of agriculture is a sure sign of decline. Misery may be caused by the folly of governments, but a country which exports food cannot be said to have the whole population pressing on the means of subsistence.

[1] I.e. increasing returns obtained in industry make it possible to devote a greater proportion of resources to raising the standards of both town and country.

In the more advanced stages of society the increased price of produce leads to the diversion of capital from commerce and manufactures to the improvement or extension of agriculture. This is caused by the population pressing against the superfluities of its supply, and this is the only way in which improved agriculture will come about.

'Cultivators will not lay out their capital upon land of an inferior staple, until they find, by an enhanced price of its produce, that there is an increasing demand for it to compensate their additional expenses' (p. 81).

The reponse can only be to a market. Improved methods, consolidation of farms, and improved implements will produce increasing returns, and will free more people for industry, swelling the ranks of the towns and leading to a further retardation in the growth of population. The difficulty of obtaining more food will clearly increase as society advances, but the rate of progress of population will become proportionately slower.

In such an advanced stage of society, one family employed in agriculture will maintain at least three others. Hence three-quarters of the population will be set free for manufactures and non-productive employment. It is a matter of observation that there is a constant stream of people from the country to the town to supply wastage. If a third part of the population lives in towns, it will require to recruit at least one-fifth of its number from the other two-thirds in the country in order to prevent diminution.

It is clear that if population increases indefinitely, in however retarded a ratio, it must eventually reach the end of its resources. The answer to this hypothetical argument is that population will reach the point of NON-REPRODUCTION. The whole increase of the non-sterile portion will be absorbed by the sterile, and this point will be reached whenever more than a third of the population lives in towns of considerable size (p. 109).

If only half the born live to marriageable age, and one-third do not marry, then six children per marriage will be required. According to Dr. Price, the average number of births to a marriage in most European countries is about four in towns and six in the country. The deficit in the towns must be supplied by the country, otherwise the towns would rapidly become extinct. Fortunately, owing to less mortality in the country, two-thirds of the children survive, but if half the people lived in towns there would be a decrease in population. Far from having an inconvenient tendency to press uniformly against the means of subsistence, the rate of population growth becomes gradually very slow, and long before a country reaches its fullest state of cultivation, its population will have ceased to increase; it will have reached its point of NON-REPRODUCTION. This is due to spontaneous physical and moral causes necessarily arising out of the habits and distribution of the people at such an advanced stage (p. 159).

Under a moderately good government, population will automatically restrain itself; under a bad government, where individual selfishness and immorality predominate, the balance will be disturbed, and misery and famine will follow until a better system be adopted. It is not possible to lay all vice at the door of the government, but the foundation of the national economy is laid by the general nature of its operations, and thus far it is answerable to God and to the country.

Far from attempting to check population, the checks should be removed where humanly possible. The poor laws, for example, are a national advantage and not a menace.

'The extent of this advantage is nothing less than the difference of feeling in the whole population arising from the consciousness on the one hand, that they may starve and rot for any care which the state will take concerning them, or, on the other, that no circumstance can preclude them from that reasonable share of assistance, to which all human creatures in distress are entitled, so far as it is possible to afford it' (p. 180).

Malthus thinks that population must *follow* the production of food, but an invariable rule is not possible. In the early stages of society pressure and want are an urge to advance. Population then is the efficient cause of cultivation. Obviously before men can be supported some food must exist, at least sufficient for bare subsistence, but men are not normally on such a small allowance. Hence no general principle can be established.

'If the people, when born and reared, are forcibly prevented from exerting their industry to provide for themselves, and precluded from profiting by the industry of others, their increase cannot of course be permanent. And wherefore? Because the *natural* effect of the demand they create is obviated by tyrannical interference. But if they are permitted and encouraged to exert themselves, the increase both of population and produce then becomes permanent; but the latter is evidently engendered by the former' (pp. 200–201).

Those who argue that improved agriculture must precede a population growth cannot show how a further extension is to be made in a commercial state of society by any other means than by the demand of an increased number of mouths. No government will enforce the cultivation of inferior land until demand renders it profitable. Bounties for export can never permanently answer. Foreign countries will be supplied more cheaply from lands using good soils, and the only permanent source of demand is an increased home population.

It is possible to cause an unwarranted acceleration of population by bad regulations; but not every encouragement is mischievous, provided a corresponding encouragement is given to increased industry. It is also possible to depress the cultivation of the soil below what is natural. With the extension of cultivation, costs increase, and, since production is for profit, a greater inducement is required. Taxation and interest on capital must also be borne, and these will be allowed for in determining whether cultivation is worth while or not. Consequently, as food is raised on inferior land, the cultivator must be preserved from the competition of foreign countries where there is still good land, and must be provided with such a price as will cover a fair rent to the landlord, the tenant's fair expenses and profits, including decent wages for the labourers, provision for the upkeep of equipment, payment for his moral and religious instructors, taxes to the government, and a liberal clear profit as a reward for his industry and exertions.

There is no reason why these aims should not be achieved, but something more is needed than a mere conviction of their political utility.

'This conviction has ever been too weak to overcome the indolent or selfish propensities of mankind. To become effectual, it must be aided by public principle, which can only be founded in moral knowledge and integrity, which, again, can find its source in no other spring but sound and pure religion' (p. 323).

We leave Weyland treating of these moral matters in his third book.

THE REJOINDER OF MALTHUS

Malthus, in the fifth edition of the *Essay*, published in 1817, replied to Weyland in the Appendix. He writes:

'When he enters into the details of his subject, he is compelled entirely to agree with me respecting the checks which practically keep down population to the level of the means of subsistence, and has not in fact given a single reason for the slow progress of population, in the advanced stages of society, that does not clearly and incontrovertibly come under the heads of moral restraint, vice, or misery' (pp. 296–297).[1]

This may be true, but is wide of the mark. All checks to population are resolvable into moral restraint, vice and misery—that is, into diminished births, or deaths: but the premises of Malthus are more extensive than this, although he does not always argue as if they were. In fact, the complete Malthusian scheme involves not only that the checks be due to these three causes, but that the causes themselves are the result of a disproportion between the number of mouths and the food supply. It is this constant shifting of the argument at all stages of the controversy which makes it so difficult to assess.[2]

In Weyland's eyes the checks are the price of civilization.[3] In the eyes of Malthus the checks are the result of a shortage of food. The phenomena are similar, the explanations are quite different.

Malthus was prone to wander off into allegory, and his choice was not always a happy one for the arguments he favoured. For example:

'If in a particular country we observed that all the people had weights of different sizes upon their heads, and that invariably each individual was tall or short in proportion to the smallness or greatness of the pressure upon him; that every person was observed to grow when the weight he carried was either removed or diminished, and that the few among the whole people, who were exempted from this burden, were very decidedly taller than

[1] Quotations are taken from *Additions to the Fourth and Former Editions of an Essay on the Principle of Population, &c.*, 1817.

[2] Malthus used the abuse of his critics as an excuse for not noticing their arguments. If his replies to Weyland and Grahame are any criterion of his powers of controversy, he was very wise to adopt this course.

[3] Hall, of course, took the view that the price was too high.

the rest;[1] would it not be quite justifiable to infer, that the weights which the people carried were the cause of their being in general so short; and that the height of those without weights might fairly be considered as the standard to which it might be expected that the great mass would arrive, if their growth were unrestricted?

'For what is it in fact, which we really observe with regard to the different rates of increase in different countries? Do we not see that, in almost every state to which we can direct our attention, the natural tendency to increase is repressed by the difficulty which the mass of the people find in procuring an ample portion of the necessaries of life, which shews itself more immediately in some or other of the forms of moral restraint, vice and misery? Do we not see that invariably the rates of increase are fast or slow, according as the pressure of these checks is light or heavy; and that in consequence Spain increases at one rate, France at another, England at a third, Ireland at a fourth, parts of Russia at a fifth, parts of Spanish America at a sixth, and the United States of North America at a seventh? Do we not see that, whenever the resources of any country increase, so as to create a great demand for labour and give the lower classes of society a greater command over the necessaries of life, the population of such country, though it might have been stationary or proceeding very slowly, begins immediately to make a start forwards?' (pp. 299–300).

The transition is so easy; the argument flows so readily. But unfortunately the weights are matters of inference and not observation. If we saw the weights and correlated them with the heights, we might deduce the relationship. If we could take a population and allocate to the lack of subsistence its precise effects in moral restraint, vice, and misery, we might deduce a connection. But unfortunately for the case of Malthus the pressure against food supply is not directly visible—are there not unused acres? Rather it is inferred from the existence of slow population growth, the very fact it was intended to prove.[2]

[1] Within a country this would imply a higher birth rate among the rich, who are not short of subsistence, than among the poor who are; and this is contrary to the facts.

[2] From the outset Malthus's supporters took his assumptions for granted and insisted on the critics 'disproving' them (see e.g. Letter from W. F. S. in Cobbett's *Political Register*, May 16th, 1807, col. 881). In a reply on May 30th (col. 981), C. S. says: 'No, Sir, according to the rules of our courts of

There is as awkward a tendency for cause and effect to get mixed up in real life, as there is for premises and conclusions to intermingle in the *Essay* of Malthus, and thus his odd illustration loses its force, or perhaps one should say 'carries no weight!'

Again we read: 'Though he has not advanced a single reason to make it appear probable that a thousand millions would not be doubled in twenty-five years just as easily as a thousand, if moral restraint, vice and misery, were equally removed in both cases . . . ' (p. 305).

Again we are back at our starting-point. Assuming the rate of growth, and assuming the removal of the checks and a constant fecundity, of course Malthus's results follow. The difficulty arises precisely out of the assumptions, which, in spite of the elaborate 'proofs,' remain assumptions.

Of course Weyland has not produced a new theory. His theory of non-reproduction might be deduced from the Second Proposition of the omnivorous *Essay* (3rd edn., p. 29). The question is—whether such an occurrence is the exception or the general rule.

Malthus resorts to the recent events in England. According to Weyland the point of non-reproduction ought to have been reached, whereas in actual fact the population had increased between 1800 and 1811 at a rate such as to double its numbers in fifty-five years.

'This fact appears to me at once a full and complete refutation of the doctrine, that, as society advances, the increased indisposition to marriage and increased mortality in great towns and manufactories always overcome the principle of increase . . .' (*Addns.*, p. 308).

No doubt; but the implications for the doctrines of the *Essay* are no less clear.

law, and I believe of common sense, it is those who lay down positions, or make charges, that are bound to prove the truth of them, and not those who deny or question it.' There is a good deal of substance in this charge. Nowhere, not even in the United States, does Malthus find his theoretical rate of growth. He merely finds different rates in different countries which he explains by (*a*) a constantly operating uniform sexual urge, (*b*) variously checked by moral restraint, vice, and misery. This is one hypothesis; not the only one, or the most likely one, or the most fruitful one. But instead of expecting to prove and justify it, his supporters call upon his critics to disprove it. What began as a hypothesis, soon crystallized into dogma.

'It is quite inconceivable how a man of sense could bewilder himself in such a maze of futile calculations, and come to a conclusion so diametrically opposite to experience' (*Addns.*, p. 309). So Malthus dismisses the argument of Weyland, without apparently a qualm of mental misgiving. Can the author of the *Essay on Population* have forgotten to ask himself: what has become of the checks?

If his *Essay* urged anything, it was the danger of an increase in population. Indeed the attack on the poor laws was regarded as one fundamental way of staving off disaster. And yet what have we? The population of England increasing in arithmetical ratio? No, it has advanced at a rate more rapid than was ever known at any period of its history. The population checked by misery and vice? No, for as Malthus writes on p. 12 of the same volume:

'The returns of the Population Act in 1811 undoubtedly presented extraordinary results. They showed a greatly accelerated rate of progress, and a *greatly improved healthiness of the people*, notwithstanding the increase of the towns and the *increased proportion* of the population engaged in manufacturing employments.'[1]

Here then we have an unusual phenomenon. In spite of the scorn poured on earlier critics this country could sustain an increasing population, growing faster than ever and growing healthier. What has happend to the checks? Can the master have erred? He is so busy criticizing Weyland that he vouchsafes no reply.

DEFENCE OF GRAHAME

The book of the third critic, Grahame, was not nearly so contemptible as either Empson or Bonar would suggest. Empson, in his classification of the opponents of Malthus, says there are some who will not comprehend 'out of sheer stupidity, like Mr. Grahame. . . .'[2]

Bonar's comment reads: 'Grahame's charges were such as owed all their force to the general ignorance of the actual writings of Malthus himself.' In a footnote he adds: 'One of the charges (p. 18: that Malthus recommends the same remedies as Condorcet) is sufficient to stamp the character of the book. . . .'[3]

[1] My italics. [2] *Edinburgh Review*, Jan. 1837.

[3] Bonar, *Malthus and His Work*, p. 376 and note.

Bonar appears to have accepted what Malthus said in his own defence in the Appendix of 1817. It is well, therefore, before proceeding to Grahame's book to remove some of the prejudice, and to dispose of the charge of ignorance, misrepresentation, and stupidity.

Malthus objects to the statement by Grahame:

'Others, of whom Mr. Malthus is the leader, regard the vices and follies of human nature, and their various products, famine, disease and war, as *benevolent remedies* by which nature has enabled human beings to correct the disorders that would arise from that redundance of population which the unrestrained operation of her laws would create.'[1]

The word *benevolent* is offensive and indefensible, but that apart, it should be noted that the statement refers, not particularly to Malthus, but to the 'others of whom he is the leader.' It is perhaps unfair to blame Malthus for the views of his followers, but, once again let it be emphasized, the critics were not attacking an academic doctrine contained in the pages of a book, but a widespread belief which had not kept up with all the changes and modifications, withdrawals and additions which Malthus had seen fit to introduce.

Further on Malthus comments: 'It shews no inconsiderable want of candour to continue attacking and dwelling upon passages, which have ceased to form a part of the work controverted. And this Mr. Grahame has done in more instances than one, although he could hardly fail to know that he was combating expressions and passages which I have seen reason to alter or expunge' (*Addns.*, p. 295).

This is fair comment and clears Malthus himself, though not necessarily the 'others' who have either been led or misled. Nevertheless it is worth pointing out, although the point is dealt with elsewhere, that many of Malthus's alterations amount to no more than dropping a phrase or a premise while still retaining the conclusions. Much of the fog surrounding his doctrines is entirely of his own manufacture. Although the subsequent editions grew in size, they did not grow in clarity.

However, let us apply the criteria of Malthus to his criticisms of Grahame. Malthus appeals (p. 291) to the general tenor of

[1] Grahame, *Inquiry into the Principle of Population*, p. 100, quoted by Malthus in *Additions*, 1817, p. 288.

his work,[1] and also mentions that particular passages are 'so distinct on the subject, as not to admit of being misunderstood but by the most perverse blindness.' He objects to Grahame's harsh interpretation of the words: 'hard as it may appear in individual instances, dependent poverty ought to be held disgraceful,' and again refers to 'the general tone and spirit' of the whole work. It is therefore not unfair that criticism of Grahame should also be applied not only to isolated passages but to the 'general tone and spirit' of his work.

On page 18 Grahame states that Malthus recommends 'immediate recourse to human efforts, to the restraints prescribed by Condorcet,[2] for the correction or mitigation of the evil.' In reply Malthus asserts, and quite correctly, that he has 'never adverted to the check suggested by Condorcet without the most marked disapprobation' (*Addns.*, p. 292).

But he has been too hasty; he has ignored the 'tone and spirit of the work.' Grahame's book shows clearly that he regards the positive check as more desirable than the preventive check, and when he says that Malthus advocates the same check as Condorcet, he only means that Malthus advocates the preventive as distinct from the positive check.

Indeed, a little earlier (p. 15), he quoted Condorcet: 'Men will then know that the duty of propagation is fulfilled by giving, not *existence*, but *happiness*, to a greater number of beings; and that the object of this duty is the general welfare of the human species, of particular societies and families, and not the puerile idea of encumbering the earth with useless and wretched mortals.'

It is only necessary to turn to page 22 in order to clinch the matter: 'The preventive check recommended by Mr. Malthus, is a general extension among the poor of that abstinence from marriage which, at all times, some members of society are induced or compelled to practise.'

[1] This is a favourite expression of defence. Ensor (*Inquiry concerning the Population of Nations*, 1818, p. 130) exclaims: 'Why should an author, and in the fourth edition of his work, appeal from his language, to the reader's gross guess at his meaning, to the bent and spirit of his theory?' The failure of Malthus thoroughly to revise his doctrine in the light of subsequent modifications is either astonishing or significant. Perhaps the structure would not have stood erect!

[2] I.e. birth control.

With which quotation we may leave the question of misrepresentation. Loose expressions abound throughout the controversy, and Malthus is as guilty as any, but enough has been said to remove the stigma applied by Bonar that this particular one stamps the character of the book. Actually, although Grahame's was not one of the best criticisms, it does contain several ideas of real worth. Moreover, according to his own lights, he does present a consistent thesis.

GRAHAME'S THESIS

Increasing population, he writes, is usually regarded as a sign of national felicity, but it is no use enlarging the population without attending to the means of support. The effects of the principle of population have been different in different ages. In primitive states the richest families were the most prolific, in advanced stages they are less so. Yet, powerful though the principle of population is, the earth is still not peopled.

The question is not one of mere animal propagation, but is bound up with the question of marriage, and on the whole monogamy would appear to be more favourable to population than polygamy. A man should support his own family, and, in the early stages of society when children were an asset, this was comparatively easy. With the increased difficulty of maintaining a family, celibacy becomes more attractive; but, if we deprecate marrying without the assurance of a provision for a family, we must not necessarily applaud celibacy undertaken for selfish motives. The sentiments of mankind concur in honouring marriage and disliking celibacy, except for unusual reasons.

Few men enter thoughtlessly into marriage, and the power of supporting a family is nearly coeval with the capacity of begetting it (p. 90). A possible encouragement to discretion would be the prohibition, without consent, of marriage before attaining the age of twenty-one, but to attempt to extirpate a class of society, either partially or wholly, is a wretched way of obviating the difficulty (p. 91).

The limit of caution is bound to vary with the different classes. A poor man has rarely an absolute certainty of being able to support his offspring 'but he must be content to repose some degree of trust in the bounty of Providence, or, more remotely, in the assistance of his neighbours, and to be stimulated to industry by the immediate pressure of necessity.'

'The well-being of society plainly requires that the degree of forethought and caution which every individual should exercise before introducing a family into the commonwealth, should decrease in proportion to the lowness of his class in society—that is, that the caution which begets reluctance to produce a family, should be strongest where there is most ability to rear a family, and should decrease in proportion as this ability becomes narrower' (p. 92).

In the upper levels of society the common excuse for not marrying is that it would involve quitting a certain rank in society. Among the middle classes, the chief consideration is the ability to pass on to children the same advantages and improvements possessed by the parents. The poor have little occasion for these considerations. 'They possess so little, that the odds are ten to one in favour of their transmitting every advantage they have enjoyed.' They weigh the probabilities, but they weigh them in 'coarser scales' (p. 94).

This is a good thing. The marriages of the poor are frequent and fruitful, whereas among the rich where rank counts, marriages, whether common or not, are unproductive. This leads to the principle of a healthy society—'that the lower ranks of society should be, in proportion to their depression, more crowded than the higher ranks; and that the thinness of the ranks should increase even more than in strict proportion to their elevation' (p. 95).

Population ought to be mainly replenished from the lower ranks. The comparative sterility of the rich, by leaving vacancies at the top, stimulates competition down below. Thus there is a constant striving upwards leading to a recruitment of the higher ranks from the lower.

'When the lower ranks are thin, the tide of national greatness is on the ebb' (p. 98). It is a fundamental of society that caution should decrease with depression on the scale. No doubt this principle has its drawbacks by increasing mouths where mouthfuls are fewest, but this apparent disorder is corrected by an opposite principle. The tendency is only mischievous when human institutions are defective.

Nature has provided a remedy—emigration. 'It was long

before legislators found out that a free export of corn is the best security of an ample production of food; and it was still longer before they discovered that a free export of men must be equally advantageous to the growth of population' (pp. 4–5).

Redundance of population must be expected to appear, or the earth would never be replenished. Where Malthus errs is in attributing to this natural principle of increase 'all the *accidental* mischiefs which he has been able to trace to the disproportion that *anyhow* may have existed between the number of mouths in a country, and the quantity of food actually raised in it' (p. 103). The natural principle is only chargeable with those due to 'fair competition between the productive powers of population and the productive capacities of the earth' (p. 103).

Emigration is the natural remedy for excess until the earth is full. Then a different remedy may be necessary. Until that period arrives it is nonsense to talk of multiplying beyond the means of support. Emigration is man's earliest resource; improvement of cultivation comes later. In the early days 'it was easier to follow the beaten track in a new country, than to improve the mode of life and labour in an old one' (p. 105). Hence, early emigrations have greater width than depth.

As emigration extends men are driven to the substitutional expedient of some degree of improved cultivation which delays the necessity for a time, until, when new emigrants do go forth, they take with them improved methods to lands already partially peopled. Thus begins a secondary and richer form of emigration. Malthus replies to this that in any case the phial would soon be exhausted, but confident prophecies of this nature are easy to make when he knows they will not be speedily tested (p. 112).

Emigration has been partially tried with the consequence that not only mankind but also civilization has spread to all the newly settled countries. In its early beginnings it merely added to the numbers of mankind in proportion to the addition made to the inhabited surface. In its later progress it has re-acted beneficially on the previously occupied countries by introducing commercial intercourse, competition, and improvement. What its ultimate effects will be 'we are as little entitled to limit as we are able to foresee' (p. 113).

When Malthus compares the growth of mankind to the growth

of trees in a forest, he overlooks the fact that the forest has no means of enlarging its boundaries or thinning its trees without destroying them. When Townsend compares mankind to the colony of goats on Juan Fernandez, it is a false analogy. 'With the addition of every goat to the flock from the very beginning, the means of subsistence were narrowed; but in a human society, it is only after the numbers have become considerable, that the resources of the country are fully opened and secured to every member...' (pp. 116–117). The goats cannot improve the soil, whereas human beings can. When human beings emigrate, the same numbers that reduce the subsistence bring with them improvements which can increase it. The limit of improvement must be reached before the limit of subsistence can be known. The resources of the earth are capable of an immense extension; fisheries can be improved; fresh products can be introduced on the land. Malthus replies with his geometrical progressions, Jarrold with the shortening of life. The most satisfactory answer is: 'We may fairly leave it to Providence' (p. 120). The earth's coal may be exhausted (probably sooner than the earth will be full) but this causes neither anxiety nor decreased consumption of fuel. 'The difficulty arises from tacitly assuming the eternity of the present system of the world and constitution of human nature' (p. 120).

In addition to the general remedy of emigration there are partial remedies. Infant mortality—the ordeal of infancy—is a necessary check. It is properly severer among the poor than among the rich, because it is 'to every individual, a faithful rehearsal of his probable part in the great drama of after life' (p. 168). Among the poor only the fittest survive. This is why among savage nations few decrepit inhabitants are seen. They perish in infancy. The natural check is confined to infancy: unhealthy employments are an artificial check.

The rich help to maintain the poor in two ways—by luxury and by charity. Luxury appears to be inevitable and its benefits are great. It conveys wealth to the poor and enables an increase in their numbers, at the same time thinning the ranks of the rich through the operation of celibacy. This is a healthy state of affairs. Charity on the other hand is supposed to impair these advantages without offering an equivalent substitute. Nevertheless it makes an important addition in one quarter at the expense of but a slight deduction in another. It often enables the poor to recover from a temporary loss of earning capacity.

It is remarkable that luxury has been defended in books and condemned in the world; charity has been admired in the world and condemned recently in books (p. 206). The establishment of poor laws was caused by the subversion of the monasteries, the break-up of the feudal system, and the general ejection and oppression of tenants, by the extension of pasture and the neglect of tillage. The poor were driven to enormities by despair, and at length came Elizabeth's establishment of poor's-rates. This system has relieved much suffering at the expense of some idleness, but much of the latter is caused not by the system itself but by the law of settlements.

The adversaries of the poor laws are not agreed as to the evils they cause; they seem to have started by assuming that the system is mischievous and have then searched for mischievous consequences. Mr. Malthus, however, is the first English writer to attack the poor laws on the simple principles of the system, without reference to their administration (p. 64).

Individuals should in the first place rely upon their own industry for support, but in an unequal society this should be backed by some reliance upon public protection and assistance, and this needs legislative provision. The virtue of charity is not destroyed when it is enforced by law. The economic system produces inequalities; the laws defend these inequalities and prevent the poor from violating them; hence it is just that 'the sufferings created by the system should be relieved from the overflowings of that prosperity which springs from the same parent' (p. 212).

Originally men produced all their own requirements, but the division of labour has raised new classes divorced from the cultivation of the soil. Employment is the medium whereby they can obtain a share in the products of the land. But the commercial demand for labour may fall short of the demand or permission of nature to increase food. The proprietor may by using machinery raise less but bring it more cheaply to market, may abandon tillage for pasturage, or otherwise make food less accessible to the poor.

'Yet it seems consistent with reason and nature that every man, whether manufacturer or agriculturist, should be entitled to a share of the existing resources of the country in which he lives and is willing to labour. If they who are in possession of the land neither voluntarily raise as much as it can produce, nor suffer him to cultivate any part, nor find it convenient to give him as much for his labour in any other department as will keep him from starving, there seems little hardship or injustice in compelling them to bestow gratuitously a pittance for his support' (p. 214).

A principle of nobility seems necessary for social coherence, but it may prevent property from being developed and improved in the public interest. The advantages to the poor are rarely observed; the advantages to the nobles are sufficiently obvious. Moreover in most countries these artificial institutions have been extended beyond justification. In any case it is in the interests of the rich to remedy evils and vindicate the justice of society by 'sending down the gentle stream of charity some portion of what has been defended from the rude torrent of change' (p. 221). Such contributions should be levied on a legal basis.

There are many objections to the English poor laws, but errors of administration should be distinguished from errors of principle. The corruption of the best things may produce the worst evils. It is true that the burden is unfairly and unequally distributed. Malthus has rightly attacked the attempt to render the wage level stable in terms of corn, which represses the frugality that scarcity demands. 'This is . . . to attempt, by charity, what charity can never effect—to abolish the evils of life, instead of mitigating their severity' (p. 224). But surely the system can be cured instead of being abolished. Malthus has not paid attention to the regard due to a speculative scheme as compared with one actually in existence.

It is said that foundling hospitals encourage vice, but though they may multiply illicit births they do not multiply cases of illicit intercourse: they only prevent abortions. 'What some writers have mistaken for the extension of the evil, is merely the clearer exhibition of it arising from the extension of the remedy' (p. 227). Establishments no doubt multiply claims for relief, but this is no cause for lament. That they multiply cases of evil is difficult to establish. Their main advantage is to secure the application of relief with a fair distribution of the expense. Charity is better than the preventive check. 'Supposing in the end that equal numbers would survive both checks; under the preventive check the deaths might be fewer; under the positive check the survivors will be stronger, and will have a better chance of a happy life' (p. 234).

Malthus's system would injure both rich and poor. The rich would harden their hearts. They would be affected not by present suffering and the benefit which would result from relieving it, but by the fancied evils of the future growth of indigence. They 'will hear with docility that their own imprudent generosity is the cause of public disorder, and somewhat more attention to their own interests the only cure for it . . . and gladly prefer the barren heights of universal philanthropy, to the humbler but more productive region of particular beneficence' (pp. 238–239).

The influence on the poor, however, is of greater importance. That the worth or the happiness of the poor would be promoted by abstinence from marriage is an unusual idea. Marriage is a preventive of vice, and the ties of marriage add worth to character. 'They open their hearts, and render them more benevolent by multiplying the objects of their benevolence. They increase their pride, and, through that, their virtue; they soften the ruggedness of their nature, and form pledges of their industry and tranquillity' (p. 241). A curtailment of affections is not compensated by an increase in animal comforts. The poor, more than the rich, are dependent on the pleasures and endearments of domestic relations, and marriage is better than vice. Vice may not utterly corrupt the rich, but the minds of the poor are always as gross as their vices, and are the forerunners of utter corruption of character.

Necessity is the mother of activity, and necessity derived from an honest source produces an activity which is honestly directed. Consequently the effects of marriage among the poor are the basis upon which the national wealth is erected. Malthus's preventive check would have the most injurious effects. The dissolute would not be restrained by such considerations, and the frugal ought not to be.

Population does not depend upon the existence of food—increased subsistence arises from increased population. In general men do not rear families because they have the means, but having families endeavour to provide for them. It is true that the tendency to redundance has caused some suffering since the beginning of human society. Emigration has meant exile from friends, but it is an evil from which have sprung all the benefits derived from colonization. But not all emigration is caused by lack of subsistence. Malthus underestimates the importance of government and does not always correctly state it. Under a bad government the country overflows without being full; and this redundance he confounds with positive magnitude of population.

THE *ESSAY*—FIFTH EDITION

It was in the next year, 1817, that Malthus published the fifth edition of the *Essay*, now swollen to three volumes. Criticisms of Weyland and Grahame have already been noted. The changes introduced into the body of the work, though considerable, were not basic.

In the preface he writes:

'It would have been easy to have added many further historical illustrations of the first part of the subject; but as I was unable to supply the want I once alluded to, of accounts of sufficient accuracy to ascertain what part of the natural power of increase each particular check destroys, it appeared to me that the conclusion which I had before drawn from very ample evidence of the only kind that could be obtained, would hardly receive much additional force by the accumulation of more, precisely of the same description.'[1]

Referring to the astonishing increase in the population of England and Wales, he denies that it can be permanent (p. 35).[2] Nevertheless the increase is a striking illustration of the principle of population, and a proof that where the resources will permit a rapid increase, and the resources are advantageously distributed, the population will not fail to keep pace with them. Truly, whatever may have been the resources of the British Isles, the resources of the principle of population were enormous. If

[1] The caution with which this is expressed is noteworthy, and might be compared with some of his more positive assertions elsewhere. Note the implications: the natural power of increase is inferred from the supposed absence of checks in America; the ample evidence obtained is the only kind available; no quantitative evidence is obtainable of the extent of the various checks. This clearly indicates the hypothetical nature of the Malthusian scheme, yet the critics are frequently abused for attacking the obvious.

[2] Quotations from *Additions to the Fourth and Former editions*, 1817.

the population increases slowly, it is proof that it is being checked. If it increases rapidly it is proof that it is not being checked. The checks themselves are deduced from the fact that in any event population can only increase in arithmetical ratio which he has just proved untrue. It is small wonder that the critics grew bewildered and impatient, and misrepresented him! In 1798 the principle of population had threatened misery and ruin to a population which did not conform to the arithmetical ratio. In 1817 the rate of increase had grown and healthiness had increased—still in conformity with the same principle.

In spite of the suggestions of friends that he should throw out the attack on systems of equality, he decided to retain it because he had 'some little partiality for that part of the work which led to those inquiries on which the main subject rests' (p. 37). He also desired to leave on record an answer to the systems of equality founded on the principle of population.

Turning his attention to emigration, he remains of the opinion that it cannot be generally effective, but he concedes that 'the subject at the present moment is well worthy the attention of the government, both as a matter of humanity and policy' (p. 85).

Returning to the question of the poor laws, he considers two points to have been established beyond doubt:

'The first is, that the country does not in point of fact fulfil the promise which it makes to the poor in the poor laws (p. 56) . . . And secondly, that with a very great increase of legal parish assessments, aided by the most liberal and praiseworthy contributions of voluntary charity, the country has been wholly unable to find adequate employment for the numerous labourers and artificers who were able as well as willing to work' (pp. 56–57).

The poor laws do not perform their promise, because they cannot. It is not that the efforts have been ill-directed.

'It is practicable to mitigate the violence and relieve the severe pressure of the present distress, so as to carry the sufferers through to better times, though even this can only be done at the expense of some sacrifices, not merely of the rich, but of other classes of the poor. But it is impracticable by any exertions, either individual or national, to restore at once that brisk demand for commodities and labour which has been lost by events, that, however they may have originated, are now beyond the power of control' (p. 60).

The hope of the future lies in a predicted slackening of the rate of population growth.[1] 'But it will be seen probably, when the next returns of the population are made, that the marriages and births have diminished, and the deaths increased in a still greater degree than in 1800 and 1801; and the continuance of this effect to a certain degree for a few years will retard the progress of the population.' This, together with a redistribution of resources and an increase in foreign trade, will restore full employment and good wages (p. 64).

Taxation is not the cause of the distress. 'If the whole of the taxes were removed tomorrow, this stagnation, instead of being at an end, would be considerably aggravated. . . . The effects of taxation are no doubt in many cases pernicious in a very high degree; but it may be laid down as a rule which has few exceptions, that the relief obtained by taking off a tax, is in no respect equal to the injury inflicted in laying it on' (pp. 65–66). There is still a suspicion of tenderness for the wealthy when he refers to 'the very great mistake of supposing that, because the demands of a considerable portion of the community would be increased by the extinction of the debt, these increased demands would not be balanced, and often more than balanced, by the loss of demand from the fundholders and government' (p. 68).

The principal causes of pauperism are the irregular demands for manufacturing labour, and the practice of paying by parish rates what ought to be paid as wages. The remedy proposed remains the gradual abolition of the poor laws.

As might be expected he has something to say on the subject of the corn laws. Bounties on exportation get a cautious and conditional approval.

'The objection then to a bounty on corn, independently of the objections to bounties in general, is, that when imposed

[1] Probably one of the most serious criticisms of the Malthusian theory is the inaccuracy of its predictions. Talbot Griffith, *Population Problems of the Age of Malthus*, gives the appropriate figures.

	1801–11	1811–21
Percentage increase of population .	14·39	16·39
	1806–16	1816–26
Birth rates (per 1,000)	33·84	33·39
Marriage rates	16·50	16·16
Death rates	19·98	20·33

These factors will be considered in detail later.

under the most favourable circumstances it cannot produce permanent cheapness: and if it be imposed under unfavourable circumstances; that is, if an attempt be made to force exportation by an adequate bounty at a time when the country does not fully grow its own consumption; it is obvious not only that the tax necessary for the purpose must be a very heavy one, but that the effect will be absolutely prejudicial to the population, and the surplus growth will be purchased by a sacrifice very far beyond its worth. But notwithstanding the strong objections to bounties on general grounds, and their inapplicability in cases which are not unfrequent, it must be acknowledged that while they are operative; that is, while they produce an exportation which would not otherwise have taken place, they unquestionably encourage an increased growth of corn in the countries in which they are established, or maintain it at a point to which it would not otherwise have attained' (pp. 176–177).

After a lengthy consideration of the pros and cons of restrictions on imports, he seems to incline reluctantly towards them. 'They are essentially unsocial' (p. 211). Free trade is the ideal, but 'a perfect freedom of trade . . . is a vision which it is feared can never be realized. . . . It should always be considered as the great general rule. And when any deviations from it are proposed, those who propose them are bound clearly to make out the exception' (p. 212).

Turning to the effects of increasing national wealth as it affects the condition of the poor, he discerns two disadvantages: first, a diminished power of supporting children; second, the employment of a larger proportion in more unhealthy and more fluctuating forms of employment' (pp. 224–225). The advantages he perceives are: first, the destroying of the pernicious power of the landlords. The workers instead of being hangers-on are turned into merchants, tradesmen, farmers, and independent labourers. Secondly, diminishing returns in agriculture and increasing returns in manufactures will increase the exchange value of corn against other goods (p. 234). The worker will not be able to maintain so large a family, but he will be better lodged and clothed (p. 235). Thirdly, if a taste for luxuries is generated among the labourers in general, those who do wish to maintain a large family will be able to do so at the expense of these conveniences and comforts.

GEORGE ENSOR

In the following year, 1818, George Ensor[1] made his contribution to the stream of replies by publishing: *An Inquiry concerning The Population of Nations: containing A Refutation of Mr. Malthus's 'Essay on Population.'* His style is marred by violent declamation but, that apart, there are not a few arguments worthy of notice.

After opening the book with a survey of the views held on population in both ancient and recent times, he raises his objections to Malthus, which arise from 'his want of science; his infinite contradictions; his inhumanity; his loud abuse of the people; his silence respecting the hard-heartedness of the opulent; his general indemnity for kings and ministers' (p. 79).

Malthus's plan to abolish the poor laws amounts to visiting the sins of the fathers on the children. 'The banquet of nature shrinks into a short allowance ministered by a miser' (p. 80). By what law of nature do some feast and many go short of necessaries in order that others may feast? 'By what view of nature, or God, or man, do some rejoice in all the *delicacies of the season*—that is, all unseasonable things;—and others suffer the privations of grain and roots planted in due time and gathered accordingly' (p. 80). Malthus's view that no one has a right to subsistence unless his labour will purchase it amounts to saying that 'a portion of this man's property is more sacred than that man's life' (p. 81). It is a mistake to think that the rich feed the poor: the poor feed the rich, but the dictum—'If a man will not work neither shall he eat'—is applied only to the poor. It is no more true to say that governments can do nothing for the poor, and that their happiness depends upon themselves, than to say that slavery depends upon the slaves themselves.

Malthus abuses the people. 'Even when they have an opportunity of saving, they seldom exercise it.'[2] And yet 'amidst aggravated taxation and distress, eight hundred thousand labouring Britons are now enrolled in benefit societies' (p. 83). The poor have increased because their wages have lagged behind

[1] Ensor (1769–1843) was born in Dublin of an English father. He graduated from Trinity College in 1790 and devoted his life to political and religious writings.

[2] *Essay*, 1806 edn., Vol. II, p. 174.

prices, and much capital has been destroyed. The real question is, not whether the rich should give or maintain, but whether they should take and impoverish.

Malthus says that population tends to increase beyond the means of subsistence. What is meant by tendency? The disposition of the sexes towards each other is subject to many countervailing tendencies equally powerful. Petty supposed doubling might take place in ten years, but he calculated on much smaller increases and never talked of such an increase continuing. If population has such a strong tendency to increase, why are there uncultivated lands? Or 'how does it happen that the same people grow rich as they grow more populous, and live better as they increase in numbers?' (p. 98).

Malthus's ratios are not always operative. In a new country, where the population doubled in fifteen years, the land cultivated could obviously have been quadrupled or more in the same time. In America the population has increased enormously, and the comforts of life have increased in greater proportion. Man is more likely to be made miserable by misgovernment—taxation, rapacity, waste, and royal splendour—than by overbreeding.

There is urgent misery and poverty in England, but there is no serious pressure of population against subsistence. 'When we talk of population and subsistence, we should consider all the people and all the food. Then, if the sum of one does not exceed the sum of the other, there is no deficiency. If, however, one-fifth of the people take five portions of food, leaving the other four parts of the population short by so much of their proportion, this is not properly a pressure of population against food' (p. 103). Without insisting on rigid equality the English people do not get their fair share of public provisions—'they do not obtain their rights in the article of food. Man has a paramount right to his property; man has also an equal right at least to the produce of his labour, for labour originally determined property' (p. 104). Yet the poor are overtaxed. The evil is not that the rich should be heavily taxed, but that such a burden should fall on the poor, for the rich would only sacrifice some superfluity, whereas the poor have to forgo absolute necessities.

Ensor points to the luxury of the rich and the animals they maintain—horses, dogs, etc. One horse will consume the food of two men. According to Colquhoun, inferior animals in Great

Britain consume eleven million quarters of grain and men eighteen millions. It is not a question of giving this to the poor, but of not taking it from them.[1] 'A lady's pug dog, or a hound, or a pointer is unnoticed; but a child too many obtrudes on *nature's feast*' (p. 108).

Malthus thinks savages fought for food, but what would they gain by fighting? Wars are not undertaken to cure want, but for malice, passion or envy, ambition or fanaticism. Men are not so absurd as to make war for its supposed advantages, but to gratify their passions.

He undervalues mankind. A child is a costly product. The mother is prevented from earning by pregnancy, therefore if the child dies there is so much capital lost. A child saved is so much capital redeemed. How much more serious is the loss of a man! Malthus says: 'The effects of the dreadful plague in London, in 1666, were not perceptible 15 or 20 years afterwards.'[2] The inference is false, for even if the numbers and wealth were restored, progress was retarded; it also leads to extraordinary conclusions. The most deadly diseases cannot stay the growth of population. If you cure one, you render another more fatal. If you abolish one, you pave the way for a new one. Medicine is incapable of lasting achievements, because Nature will task her ingenuity to find new maladies to take the place of old and preserve the balance between men and food. For breed you will beyond the level of subsistence, and die you must in proportion! This is a complete fallacy. Whatever improves health serves society. It saves loss of time and wealth, and is one of the most striking advances of modern times.

This is sordid arithmetic—but thus the new philosophy must be met. Each child represents so much wealth spent on his generation and nurture. If he dies prematurely, this wealth is lost. The loss of an adult is the loss of a machine in full work. Here is a conception concerning an important aspect of population 'in which the best parts of knowledge concur with the charities and affections of mankind' (p. 179).

According to Malthus the peasant is better off as a wage earner. This is not so: he has no locality, no stake in the country, no property. If the parliament had any sympathy

[1] Cf. Hazlitt's views, *Political Essays*, 1819 edn., p. 117.

[2] *Essay*, 1806 edn., Vol. II, p. 57.

with the people it would facilitate enclosures by a general enclosure act, but in that case there would be a substantial loss of legal fees.

The alarm concerning population has no real foundation and represents merely a fluctuation of public opinion. Malthus favours absolute or protracted celibacy, but he forgets that late children are early orphans. Moreover it is not only the poor who are improvident. The rich have children they cannot provide for, but who are thrust into sinecures and waste the produce of many hard-working men. It is a beastly opinion to hold that those who are fed must breed.

The people of Ireland are numerous and poor; therefore it is assumed that they are poor because they are numerous. Malthus says they are degraded; in total want of decent pride; they propagate their species like brutes.[1] His remedy is to make food dearer which would extinguish those who now live on cheaper food. Potatoes and wretchedness are synonymous in Ireland, but the Irish were wretched before a potato was planted. The real trouble is misrule, absenteeism, and exploitation. Ireland exported eight millions of agricultural produce, not in exchange, but to absentees for which there was no return. The Irish peasants are abused for being poor—who makes them so? Their poverty is not their own fault, and the remedies proposed are ridiculous. Feed them on dearer food; on grain instead of potatoes; stimulate exertions; create new wants! The solution is to give them better government—self-government. They are not over-peopled but undergoverned.

A free nation may become too populous, but when the government is bad, the people's misery must be referred in the first instance to that cause. Nations whose government has improved have increased both in population and comforts; no nation which possessed liberty and equal laws has become miserable solely on account of the excess of its people. Bad government, unequal laws, and ill-distributed property are the real evils.

Population is a proof of good laws. The lowest form of labour should be uncontrolled, untaxed, and mobile. The labourer should depend upon his own exertions for his maintenance. Until he is master of his own time, movements, and labour, and excused from all forms of taxation, society will have to provide

[1] Malthus, *Essay*, 1806 edn., Vol. II, pp. 408 and 412.

for distress, because what is taken in taxation must be returned some other way. There should be absolute freedom for anyone to adopt any occupation he pleases.

Malthus identifies all misery with overbreeding, but there are other causes. Changes in fashions or imports cause unemployment and distress. Heavy taxation presses on the working classes. In 1815, when the people were moderately employed, ill-paid, and miserable, the government passed the corn law. It is not a national benefit, but a short-sighted attempt to give the country gentlemen and farmers a monopoly of food production.

The people are poor and growing poorer, not because of what is given, but because of what is taken away. Labour is the source of national wealth but the upper classes squander much of this national wealth in luxury. The House of Commons is a mockery—seats are bought and sold. Jobbery and waste are rife; taxation is enormous. 'At Droitwich salt costs thirty-one pounds the ton, thirty pounds of which are duty' (p. 466). The people are repressed. There are laws against association and meetings. There is a huge standing army which cost nearly seven million in 1817. Is it to be wondered at that the people are poor? Lord Bathurst, in 1815, received of public money as much as the whole of Norwich's poor rates. America, on the other hand, has none of these drawbacks. She has flourished under popular representation.

Some men may propagate improvidently, but improvidence is but one of many causes of misery. The moral check operates perpetually. 'What are all the laws of marriage, but this moral providence authenticated by the supreme authority of nations?' (p. 488). The power to breed is a good and not an evil, strenuous but not self-destructive; it enables society to recover its occasional losses. But there is a power which can neutralize this propensity: it is despotism. 'Man will live and increase where the land is rock, the water ice, under perpetual night. . . . Yet despotism is worse than all these together; and man perishes under misgovernment, though surrounded with a wilderness of enjoyments (p. 492). . . . A rich country is miserable, because it is worth oppressing; and a poor one happy, because it is abandoned to its own management, in despair of extorting any profit amidst its wants' (p. 494).

Populousness is desirable if men are free. Numbers are an

essential precursor to the division of labour. It was the growth of population which turned savages into hunters, hunters to shepherds, and shepherds to cultivators. 'Agriculture became an art, cultivation a science, and many men were born' (p. 498). And these benefits will continue to be felt so long as the government is good.

CHAPTER THREE

COBBETT, GODWIN, AND BOOTH

PARSON MALTHUS

The next great landmark in the controversy was when Godwin broke his long silence and published his second *Reply* in 1820. It has been adversely criticized and has rarely been given the attention due to it. According to Leslie Stephen it was 'the longest answer to the shortest argument in modern times.' Before, therefore, looking at it, we will pause for a moment and regard the shortest answer, that of Cobbett, who replied in one word: 'Parson!'[1]

'I have, during my life, detested many men; but never any one so much as you. . . . No assemblage of words can give an appropriate designation of you; and, therefore, as being the single word which best suits the character of such a man, I call you *Parson*, which amongst other meanings, includes that of Borough-monger Tool' (col. 1019–1020).

Apart from the abuse, which abounds throughout this letter, the reply is noteworthy for its taking up Malthus regarding his so-called 'Law of Nature.'

'You talk of the "*punishment of nature*"; you talk of "the *laws of nature* having doomed him and his family to *starve*," ' writes Cobbett of the proposed withdrawal of poor relief from the destitute.

'When nature causes a country to exist and people to exist in it, she leaves the people, as she does other animals, to live as they can; to follow their own inclinations and propensities; to exert their skill and strength for their own advantage, or rather, at their pleasure. She imposes no shackles other than those which the heart and mind themselves suggest. She gives no man

[1] Cobbett's *Weekly Political Register*, Vol. 34, No. 33, May 8th, 1819.

dominion over another man, except that dominion which grows out of superior cunning or bodily strength. She gives to no man any portion of the earth or of its fruits for his own exclusive enjoyment. And, if any man, in such a state of things, cannot get food sufficient to keep him alive, he must die; and, it may truly enough, then, be said, that "the laws of nature have *doomed* him to be starved" ' (col. 1027–1028).

When, however, the people come to an agreement to associate for their mutual benefit, and to refrain from using their personal advantage for the sake of the advantages which a regulated society can give, it must be understood that this implies that they are entitled to protection from harm and at least to a bare means of subsistence.

Property is the natural outcome of the social compact, but property, especially in land, can never be absolute and unconditional. Men never could have intended to give up the right to live and love, and if the occasion arises when they are neither able to earn a living nor receive sufficient contributions for subsistence from the community, the social compact is at an end. They have a right to act according to the laws of nature, which means that they may take food wherever they find it. The existence of private property makes it understood that the helpless are in case of need to be protected and fed by the proprietors.

'If there be a state of society, which exposes persons to starvation, without any fault on their own part, such society is a monster in legislation; it is worse than a state of nature, and ought to be dissolved. What! . . . A social compact, which does not recognize the right to live!' (col. 1039).

In such a society they would have a right to recur to the law of nature and take whatever houses, lands, and goods they were strong enough to take. The logical outcome of the Malthusian proposal is a state of lawlessness and anarchy.

GODWIN'S SECOND REPLY

However, the arguments of Cobbett are too elusive to be considered in detail at this stage and we must return to 'the longest answer to the shortest argument.'[1] This kind of comment is

[1] The short answer was often given. Why is not the earth full? That is one version. Another: Malthus has written a quarto volume to prove that man cannot live without food.

typical of the general disparagement of the critics and the implied superiority of Malthus. His argument was not short—it was very long indeed. The third edition runs to well over a thousand pages. The first dogmatic statement is short, it is true, but it is followed by hundreds of pages of qualifications and substantiations, often apparently contradictory. Thus, any reply aiming at completeness was bound to be long, if the writer were not to be accused of not having read the *Essay*. To go into lengthy detail is to be accused of verbiage.

There is some substance in the charge against Godwin. His book is verbose. It suffers from grave defects of style. There is much repetition, and much apparent inconsistency; but not all of this is deservedly laid at Godwin's door. The attempt to pin down the Malthusian argument in its entirety is a long and weary process. Godwin spent two years on the task and hardly succeeded. Indeed there is a touch of real pathos in his remark on the last page of the book which embodies this two years' labour: 'I am sensible that what I have written may be regarded in some respects as a book about nothing.' This is a feeling which may well be shared by anyone who has followed the labyrinthine qualifications, the alternate advances and withdrawals, the disappearance of the premises and the retention of conclusions which mark the work of Malthus.

Godwin's concluding sentence—'If I have contributed to place a leading point of political economy on a permanent basis, my labour may not in that respect be found altogether fugitive and nugatory'—expresses a hope which was hardly fulfilled. Nevertheless the work was written in deadly earnest.

'I never was so deep in anything as I am now in Malthus, and it is curious to see how my spirits fluctuate accordingly. . . . On Friday I made an important discovery and I was happy. The weather has since changed, and you know how that affects me. I was nervous and peevish on Saturday to a degree that almost alarmed me. On Sunday I was in heaven. I think I shall make a chapter expressly on the geometrical ratio that will delight my friends and astonish the foe.'[1]

Perhaps the very patchiness of the book itself is due to these ups and downs of Godwin's spirits. If the chapter he mentions did

[1] *William Godwin: His Friends and Contemporaries*, Kegan Paul. Letter to Mrs. Godwin, August 31st, 1819, Vol. II, pp. 259–260.

not have the effect he desired, it is pleasant to think that his conviction was surer than his argument.

'What matters what becomes of this miserable carcase, if I can live for ever in true usefulness? And this must be the case in the present instance: for whatever becomes of my individual book, if I am right the system of Malthus can never rise again, and the world is delivered for ever from this accursed apology in favour of vice and misery, of hard-heartedness and oppression.'[1]

Mackintosh thought, and rightly, that the book was intolerant in tone.[2] There are certainly many errors and inconsistencies and much vain repetition. But it was a sincere book. Godwin hated the things which Malthus stood for, or appeared to him to stand for, and like most of Malthus's opponents he found it impossible to denounce the doctrines without abusing the man.

The book was a failure. It did not end the controversy, which proceeded unabated. Nor did it bring in the funds so sorely needed to save Godwin from insolvency. Malthus thought little of it, and, writing to Francis Place, commented thus: 'Mr. Godwin, in his last work, has proceeded to the discussion of the principles of population with a degree of ignorance of his subject which is really quite inconceivable.'[3]

Publicly he dismissed the book in a note at the end of the 1826 edition:

'Since the last edition of this Work was published, an answer from Mr. Godwin has appeared; but the character of it, both as to matter and manner, is such, that I am quite sure every candid and competent inquirer after truth will agree with me in thinking that it does not require a reply. To return abusive declamation in kind would be as unedifying to the reader as it would be disagreeable to me; and to argue seriously with one who denies the most glaring and best attested facts respecting the progress of America, Ireland, England, and other states, and brings forward Sweden, one of the most barren and worst supplied countries of Europe, as a specimen of what would be the natural increase of population under the greatest abundance of food, would evidently be quite vain with regard to the writer himself, and must be totally uncalled for by any of

[1] Kegan Paul, op. cit., Vol. II, p. 260. [2] Id., p. 275.

[3] *Letters of Ricardo to Malthus* (Bonar, 1887)—Letter from Malthus to Place, February 19th, 1821, note, p. 207.

his readers whose authority could avail in the establishment of truth.'

Bonar treats Godwin very severely, and not entirely fairly, in pointing out some of his inconsistencies.[1] It would be comparatively simple, and equally unjust, to treat Malthus in the same way. It would also be quite unprofitable. Rather let us attempt to extract some of the substance from a book which is extremely difficult to summarize.

The first thing, says Godwin, that occurs to a speculator on population problems is the thinness of man's numbers and the extent of waste and desolate places, but Mr. Malthus thinks otherwise. The danger of over-population, far from being remote, he believes is imminent and immediate. Population will always press against the food supply. This is obviously untrue, for in a civilized state one man can produce more than is needed for his subsistence, otherwise developments in arts and science would be impossible. We should all be cultivators and the only knowledge would be agricultural knowledge (pp. 17–18).

As soon as men associate in nations a small portion of their labour suffices to feed the whole. Hence it happens that, while a minority of the people do the indispensable work of producing subsistence for all, the rest are freed for the development of art, science, literature, and thought, or for the indulgence of refinements of luxury or ostentation. Therefore, if any man starves it is not by a law of nature, but by the law of artificial life whereby some wallow in luxury while others are left to pine in want (p. 20).

If the theory of Malthus is true, why is the earth not peopled? He has found a calculation to show that the population ought to increase at an alarming rate, and then has written three volumes giving vague and indefinable causes why his theory is completely at variance with recorded history. The basis of his argument is the increase in the United States, and he has tried to turn this exception into the rule (p. 25).

His strength lies in his adherence to general statements, but to be more specific: How many children are necessary to maintain a population at its present level? Clearly not less than two per family, and to allow for deaths before maturity, three; most political economists allow four. Hence for doubling a population in twenty-five years an average of eight children per marriage

[1] *Malthus and His Work*, pp. 369–370.

would be required. Why does he not show such a birth rate in the European registers?

Taking the population of England at ten millions of whom five are adults, this population would require ten millions of births for its maintenance during a period of twenty-five years, if allowance were made for infant mortality. To double itself it would require a further ten million births purely for the benefit of the geometrical ratio. Where are the records of these births, and, since for lack of subsistence they must all die, the corresponding deaths? Until Malthus produces these records he cannot prove his rate. If the geometrical ratio is true there must either be a colossal infantile mortality or an enormous operation of the preventive check.[1]

Godwin then proceeds to investigate Malthus's authorities for the American increase and finds them unsatisfactory.[2] The question is 'one of the gravest (if at all grave) which was ever presented to the consideration of mankind.' Malthus should have given his figures. What has a short period increase to do with infinity? Dr. Price calculated that a penny invested at five per cent. compound interest would in less than 1,800 years exceed in value 300,000,000 earths all solid gold, but no one thinks of applying this to the affairs of real life. 'A sound and well regulated mind, that is engaged in other matters than mathematical puzzles and wonders, soon comes to a stand amidst the luxuriances of an infinite series' (p. 137). It would be a good thing if Malthus were to show, by setting down the figures side by side, exactly how the numbers are kept down in terms of births and infantile mortality.

Women are the relevant factor in considering population growth. The rest, men young and old, and children of the male sex (exclusive of those males necessary to give activity to the prolific power of the women) are of no account in this matter (p. 146). It is well established that child-bearing ceases at the age of forty-five. Although there are climatic and racial differences there is an ascertainable time of commencement. Where women begin to bear children earlier, they cease their powers of child-bearing sooner. Consequently a census of human beings is not a

[1] This reasoning is no better and no worse than Malthus's crude statement of the ratios. (*Essay*, 3rd edn., p. 13.)

[2] This point, and many others raised by Godwin, will be dealt with later.

term in a geometrical progression, because only females of child-bearing age are to be considered. Hence, observations of crude rates of population growth, unless taken over a long period, are valueless (p. 147).

Since tables which do not differentiate by sex and age are worthless, the British enumerations of 1801 and 1811 are labour thrown away. The Swedish figures are the only promising ones. These prove that an increase which is reasonably attributed to procreation is sufficient in some situations and under some circumstances to double a population in somewhat more than a hundred years (p. 161). Malthus's summary treatment is not good enough; it is not even 'the semblance of a science.' Patient men will subsequently examine the problem carefully and account for the phenomena, not in one sweeping clause (vice and misery), but on clear and intelligible principles (p. 162).

A study of the Swedish figures leads to the following conclusions:

'First, that the marriageable women in any settled community, or over the whole globe, do not exceed one fifth of the population.

'Secondly, that the number of marriageable women does not increase from generation to generation, or increases in a very inconsiderable degree.

'Thirdly, that the number of children born is pretty accurately in the proportion of one child annually to five marriages.

'Fourthly, that the number of children born annually is nearly in the same proportion to the number of child-bearing women in the state.

'Fifthly, that the number of births to a marriage, taken upon an average, does not exceed the proportion of four to one.

'Sixthly, that the women who live to reach the child-bearing age are found pretty generally to marry; and that, if the bridegrooms are sometimes a little advanced in age, this rarely happens to the brides.

'Seventhly, that early marriages do not greatly tend to increase population. In Persia, where a woman frequently marries at twelve, she is often found to be old and past child-bearing at thirty' (pp. 190–191).

Thus we are assured that the power of increase is subject to strict limitations.

A survey of various British, Danish, and other figures, where there is some age discrimination, bears out the conclusions reached from the Swedish figures, namely that the average number of children falls short of four to a marriage, but this figure may, of course, be confined to Europe.

The next approach is analytical. What is the value of a marriage, or how long does the average marriage last? Some women may die in the first year of marriage, others in the second, third, or fourth, and so on throughout the period of twenty-five years. Moreover, to the mortality of the women we must add the mortality of the husbands. Since comparatively few women marry a second time, the death of the husband is as effective in stopping procreation as that of the wife. After making certain assumptions and calculations, Godwin arrives at the general result that the average marriage lasts sixteen years (p. 209).

In addition there are other considerations. All women do not marry, and of those who do, some marry late. In the case of late marriages, not only is the period of child-bearing diminished, but the chances of the union being broken by death are increased. Sickness prevents child-bearing for longer or shorter periods, and suckling has an important effect. Allowance must be made for sterility in both men and women, for natural abortions and premature births. Some women produce only one or two children during the whole period of marriage, and in general the propensity to produce children diminishes in force towards the end of the procreative period. All these factors, therefore, support the view that four births to a marriage are an ample average allowance (pp. 210–216).

Population is kept down, that is agreed. There is vice and misery, that is also agreed. Population is thinned by war and pestilence; but do these arise from hunger? The proper and ultimate appeal on the subject is to the Bills of Mortality. Is the death rate in Europe greater than it is in the United States? (p. 300). If Malthus had confined his attention to the time when the world was fully peopled, the arguments against him would have been different, but his book would have remained on the shelves.[1] The inference from all history is that population does not require checking, that the happiest countries have been those where mankind has been encouraged. There is an immense

[1] Note once again, the clear distinction drawn between the long-run and short-run positions. Wallace's book did remain on the shelves.

difference between a natural want of subsistence and a lack arising from misgovernment; it is the latter which makes countries a permanent source of desolation (p. 310).

If Malthus had desired to establish his ratio on sound foundations, he should have estimated how many children per marriage were needed for doubling and shown that such a proportion existed in the United States. He should have shown in the other countries how the checks operated, by putting down in columns the numbers born and destroyed each year, so that the difference between the British state of affairs and that in the United States could be clearly seen. In view of the atrocious conclusions he has reached, this negligence is extraordinary. The theory of population rests precariously upon two points: that the birth rate is higher and the death rate lower in the United States than elsewhere. He has made no attempt to establish these two points, nor to fix anything specific concerning them; he has merely cast a supercilious glance at the gross total (p. 321). Not that the figures are very reliable in any case: the only reliable figures are those of Sweden (p. 323).

The Swedish figures show a possible doubling in a hundred years. Why has this not been general? The answer is to be found in occasional causes. Malthus says the increase of population is subject to a uniform, constantly acting check. This is only true in so far as all men must die. In most reductions of population there is much vice and misery. He has compounded these two facts into a theory that population, therefore, must be checked by vice and misery (p. 341).

The question of the American increase is vital to Malthus's principle, but since immigration is possible there is no proof that it is due to procreation. The United States have always attracted emigrants and welcomed them in increasing numbers. Moreover, the American War of Independence in 1775 gave the movement a new and powerful impulse. Multitudes no doubt went there between 1776 and 1789. During the Terror the streets of London were crowded with French emigrants, many of whom doubtless found their way to America. The conquests of Napoleon also helped to swell the numbers. Such evidence as there is supports the view that fruitfulness in the United States is in no way different from what it is in Europe (p. 425). Malthus talks of late marriages in Europe, but since this usually refers to the male, who normally takes a young bride, the effects on fecundity are not what he would suggest. If there is no reason to suspect that the birth rate of the population of the United States is abnormally high, there is every reason to believe that the death rate is at least as high as that in Europe.

Although the figures of the first American census are doubtful, they may be admitted for the sake of argument. The question is not the fact of an increase but its source. Malthus says it is from procreation only, Godwin says it derives from immigration. If Malthus is correct the population should exhibit more children than adults. According to the census of 1810 the free white inhabitants under sixteen years of age numbered 2,933,211; those over sixteen years of age numbered 2,928,882. These are the phenomena of a stationary population so far as it concerns procreation (p. 441).

While the increase of the species is problematical, the most striking fact is the scanty way in which man is scattered over the earth. The productive powers of England are clearly sufficient for the population. The cultivated area is 39,100,000 acres; the commons and waste land amount to 7,816,000 acres. It is estimated that 2¾ acres will produce food for one person. Therefore, on a basis of a population of 10,000,000, and allowing for the subsistence of the horses used in agriculture, there are 6,800,000 acres unaccounted for, and these would feed a further 2,054,380 human beings. This is taking no account of the 7,816,000 acres of waste land. Why then if the quantity of food is insufficient is not more produced? The negative answer is that it is neither want of soil nor want of hands (pp. 458–462).

Here, however, the ambiguity of the term 'means of subsistence' comes to Malthus's aid. It may denote either the possible produce or the actual produce collected, and he always chooses the latter. As long as distribution continues in its present form, population is not kept down by lack of the means of subsistence, but by ignorance or the positive institutions of society. There may be strong arguments for the present distribution of wealth, but 'the saddle should be put on the right horse.' In America a man can get land to cultivate. Here the land is wholly appropriated, but not to the genuine uses of natural man (pp. 463–470). Yet Malthus belittles the influence of human institutions as 'mere feathers on the surface.'

The ratios are the 'shewy and dazzling part' of his theory, but they have nothing to do with the practical part of the proposition that population is at all times pressing against the limits of the means of subsistence.[1] The geometrical ratio of population is bound up with time. For the first term we are safe, since in both geometrical and arithmetical series both population and subsistence are doubled. Therefore, till we see the first step accomplished in England we have no reason to feel alarmed.

There is no end to the improvements in art, and Malthus allows that population may be quintupled in a hundred years, although this is scarcely credible. 'It is this apparently candid spirit of concession, as much at least as any other cause, or all other causes put together, that has given to Mr. Malthus's theory so astonishing a success with his contemporaries.' They said, the writer must be very sure of his ground, who grants to his antagonists more than any of them would venture to ask (p. 489). The food production of Great Britain is adequate if properly distributed. When extensive cultivation fails to produce an increase, more intensive methods will have to be employed. The spade must take the place of the plough. This will retard the reduction in the hours of labour, but there is hope in the introduction of machinery. There are also the resources of the sea, and the possible substitution of vegetable for animal products. There are two steps available: (1) Plough instead of pasture, (2) Spade instead of plough. Since, however, there is no prospect of an immediate deficiency, the argument is merely necessary because Malthus's food concessions are only conditional. 'The more he gives away, literally the more he gains' (p. 499).

The population of Europe, Asia, and Africa may be increasing, but there is no evidence that it is, and our duty is to act on the evidence we have. Looking at the matter from the standpoint of distribution, all are not adequately fed; but the remedy is to change the mechanism of society, to break up more land, and to render enclosed land more productive. If it is ever unwise for a man to marry, it is owing to the partiality and oppressiveness of human institutions (p. 506).

Malthus asserts that the poor laws are an evil 'in comparison of which the national debt, with all its magnitude of terror, is of little moment.' This is gross exaggeration, but it leads him to

[1] Again the immediate view (pp. 474–476).

propose his remedies—the abolition of the poor law and the continuance of low wages (p. 541). And this prohibition of the right of the poor to support extends not only to the idle, but to infants, the aged, the sick, and the unemployed who are willing to work (p. 542). Clearly in many countries they have no legal right to relief, but Malthus has attacked their moral right. He rests on two memorable propositions: that the poor have no right to support, and that the rich may do what they will with their own (p. 549). Children are to be excluded from the operation of the poor laws by fair and distinct notice two years before they are born. They have 'drawn a blank' and therefore they have no right to support, and after the notice, no right to complain. Nevertheless, the fact remains that the poor laws were not something given; they were a substitute for something taken away.

Malthus's remedy amounts to a judicious blend of squandering by the rich and starving by the poor. He says: 'If the diffusion of luxury, by producing the check sooner, tends to diminish the distress, it is surely desirable.'

A man must not marry unless he can maintain a family; but no man can be sure that he will always be able to do this without assistance. What constitutes a fair prospect of being able to support a family? If a man in good health saves a year's wages (at 9*s.* per week) is this a fair prospect? Suppose his marriage produces four children: well. If it produces twelve, he has drawn an overwhelming ticket in life's lottery (p. 576). No labouring peasant has a fair prospect, and Malthus's plan shows an utter disdain for the condition of man upon the earth (p. 579). The labourer may be sick, unemployed, have too many children; he may have a cripple or an idiot; yet he must starve, for he has heard the warning thrice repeated!

DAVID BOOTH—'MATHEMATICAL DISSERTATION'

Included in Godwin's book there is a 'Mathematical Dissertation' by David Booth,[1] who, according to Godwin, had encouraged and inspired the production of the *Reply*. Brief as it

[1] Booth was born in Forfarshire in 1766 and died in 1846. In early life he was a business man, but later he became a schoolmaster. Among his other activities he invented the Brewer's saccharometer. In 1818 he wrote: *Tables of Simple Interest on a New Plan of Arrangement*, and he was also the author of an *Analytical Dictionary of the English Language*, published in 1835.

is, this 'Mathematical Dissertation' contains several points which mark a decided step forward in the progress of the controversy. Instead of being content with gross figures of total population and with crude birth and death rates, Booth insists on the need for taking into account the age distribution.

The important points in connection with the question of growth are the number of propagators, and the number of births each produces. He takes the Swedish figures and, in default of better, standardizes them (p. 268).[1] According to the figures thus adopted, a population of 10,000 can be just replaced by an annual total of 370 births. In such a population there will be

TABLE I.

Ages of living	Average of 9 years, from preceding table	Proportioned to a population of 10,000
Births	88,032	370
Under 5 years	334,899	1,408
5–10	255,965	1,076
10–15	241,521	1,015
15–20	204,297	859
20–25	195,371	821
25–30	187,134	785
30–35	176,309	741
35–40	150,066	631
40–45	132,180	556
45–50	110,505	464
50–55	98,395	414
55–60	84,646	356
60–65	74,643	314
65–70	52,357	220
70–75	40,106	169
75–80	23,230	98
80–85	11,569	49
85–90	4,303	18
above 90	1,566	6
Population	2,379,062	10,000

Table showing the proportions of different age-groups in the Swedish Population from an average of nine years. Taken from Godwin, op. cit., 1820, p. 268.

[1] Table I.

TABLE II.

Years	Born	Under 5	5 to 10	10 to 15	15 to 20	20 to 25	25 to 30	30 to 35	35 to 40	40 to 45	45 to 50	50 to 55	55 to 60	60 to 65	65 to 70	70 to 75	75 to 80	80 to 85	85 to 90	Above 90	All the living
0		1408	1076	1015	859	821	785	741	631	556	464	—	—	—	—	—	—	—	—	—	7892
5	1850	1408	1076	1015	859	821	785	741	631	556	464	—	—	—	—	—	—	—	—	—	8856
10	1850	1408	1076	1015	859	821	785	741	631	556	464	414	—	—	—	—	—	—	—	—	8770
15	1850	1408	1076	1015	459	821	785	741	631	556	464	414	356	—	—	—	—	—	—	—	9126
20	1850	1408	1076	1015	859	821	785	741	631	556	464	414	356	314	—	—	—	—	—	—	9440
25	1850	1408	1076	1015	859	821	785	741	631	556	464	414	356	314	220	—	—	—	—	—	9660
30	1850	1408	1076	1015	859	821	785	741	631	556	464	414	356	314	220	169	—	—	—	—	9829
35	1850	1408	1076	1015	859	821	785	741	631	556	464	414	356	314	220	169	98	—	—	—	9927
40	1850	1408	1076	1015	859	821	785	741	631	556	464	414	356	314	220	169	98	49	—	—	9976
45	1850	1408	1076	1015	859	821	785	741	631	556	464	414	356	314	220	169	98	49	18	—	9994
50	1850	1408	1076	1015	859	821	785	741	631	556	464	414	356	314	220	169	98	49	18	6	10,000
55	1850	1408	1076	1015	859	821	785	741	631	556	464	414	356	314	220	169	98	49	18	6	10,000

Table showing populations ranging from 7,892 to 10,000 each of which, with a given fertility ratio, would produce the same annual number of children. The crude birth rates would, however, be vastly different. Taken from Godwin, op. cit., 1820, p. 272. The above is an exact copy and evidently there were three typographical errors : (1) column 6—the figure 4 should be an 8 ; (2) column headed 45 to 50—the first number 464 should obviously be deleted ; (3) last column—the second total 8856 should read 8356.

2,108 people over 45. If these were cut off by death, there would remain a population of 7,892 of 45 years of age and under, and, though the reproductive capacity of these populations would be precisely the same, the crude birth rates would be entirely different.[1] Moreover the latter population would grow again in the normal course until it reached the figure of ten thousand, when, unless conditions had altered, it would again become stationary. From this illustration he deduces that the effect of increased longevity is to increase the population to a new high level, when numbers again become stable (p. 274).

'In taking a census therefore of an infant colony, we need not wonder that it should double its numbers in a very short period. The emigrants who arrive in small numbers afterwards, are less observed than the primitive founders; and it is extremely probable that many such establishments may double their numbers, apparently from propagation alone, in less than 20 years. The principle however on which this duplication rests, escapes the eye of the common observer. The colony is not a society in the sense which we understand of a nation. It is the first expansion of a set of picked propagators,[2] without parents and without children, which two classes, together with the diseased and ineffective, constitute nearly three-fourths of the population of modern Europe. It is the body of the polypus without its limbs, which its inherent energies are able to renew. Till these are completed, the increase will continue. . . . Mr. Malthus catches the polypus in the middle of its growth;—he measures the length of limbs already attained, and, comparing these with time, he forms a ratio of increase, in which, he asserts, they will expand for ever!' (pp. 277–278.)

Applying this reasoning to the United States: in none is the proportion of persons over forty-five more than 16 to 17 per cent. In newly settled districts it is less than 7 or 8, whereas a quarter is normal.

The extent of immigration can be deduced as follows. It is obvious that everyone who was alive in 1800 and living in America must be over ten years of age in 1810. In 1800 the white

[1] Table II, page 133.

[2] This is illustrated in Table IV, page 139. Although Malthus criticized the use of the Swedish figures, they were the only ones available to illustrate Booth's reasoning.

population was 4,305,971. Death would reduce this number by one-fourth in ten years, leaving probably not more than 3,200,000 still alive. Hence we should expect to find this number in the group aged over ten years at the census of 1810 (p. 281). In fact this group contains 3,845,389, giving a surplus of 645,389 which can only be accounted for by immigration.

The census of 1810 also contains 2,016,704 children under ten years of age. Part of these must also be accounted for by immigration. Moreover the introduction of grown-ups would naturally contribute to this total after arrival. Consequently probably half of the total increase in population can be attributed to immigration. Hence there is no need to assume a power of procreation greater than obtains in Europe (p. 282).

'Assuming the females between 20 and 45 years of age to be the only source from which the continuance of the race can be derived, the series which would denote the varying number of those females, in the order of time, would also denote the law of increase in the censuses of the tribe or nation. All the females now existing between 20 and 45 will be gradually erased from the list, by superannuation or by death, in the space of 25 years. Their place will be filled by others; and if the number of the new mothers be not then double what they now are, we may rest assured that the society does not exhibit a permanent principle of increase, in the ratio and in the time prescribed by Mr. Malthus' (p. 286).

Malthus's geometrical ratio is extremely arbitrary. When he finds that his ratio does not exist in the countries of the world, instead of doubting his hypothesis, he looks round for checks which have retarded its operation. He calls them checks before he has established that the population needs such checks, thus begging the very question at issue.

THE *EDINBURGH REVIEW*

Godwin's book was reviewed in the *Edinburgh Review* dated July 1821. It is described as an 'old-womanish performance,' the result of a fifth edition of the *Essay* acting upon 'an enfeebled judgment.' The first impulse was to ignore the book, but as it had made some impression in London on a certain class of readers, and been referred to in the House of Commons as having refuted Malthus, it was decided to pay some attention to it.

Booth's rule for calculating the volume of immigration is given some credit, but he has misapplied it. He has taken a mortality allowance of a quarter by applying the general mortality figure of 1 :40 and multiplying by ten for the ten-year period, but as the early years are the most mortal this method is unsound when applied to a body of people not being recruited by fresh births. The correct figure is nearer one-seventh, which gives an immigration for the ten years of 165,418, instead of 645,389 as calculated by Booth. After making this adjustment, the American rate of increase works out nicely at a rate of doubling in about 24 years 10 months.

This calculation allows over 16,000 a year for immigration, which is probably above the truth. Further considerations are adduced (p. 367) which would probably bring the figure for the loss during the ten years in question to one-eighth. All the evidence points to an increase such as Malthus uses being free from any essential error.

The reviewer then turns his attention to Booth's comments on the age grouping of the population and explains these phenomena differently and to his own satisfaction, but, as Malthus himself takes up these points subsequently and deals with them himself, we need concern ourselves no further with them here.[1]

The reviewer charitably puts the previous errors down to Godwin's ignorance; but is compelled to note what are glaring misrepresentations, the chief being that Malthus was an advocate for low wages. On the contrary, Mr. Malthus 'has laboured in all his works, even to tiresome repetition, to show the labouring classes how they may raise their wages effectively and permanently, and become more independent of the rich. On this subject, the tendency of his principles, and the tenor of his language, cannot be mistaken by the meanest capacity' (p. 374).[2]

[1] See Malthus's article on *Population* in the *Encyclopædia Britannica* and the subsequent reprint entitled *A Summary View of the Principle of Population*, 1830.

[2] It is true that Malthus frequently refers to his desire, no doubt quite sincere, to see the poor better paid, better fed and clothed, but much of his

Lest we should be in any doubt of the reviewer's own idea on the subject, it is expressly stated: 'The main cause of low wages is the abundance of hands, compared with the work to be done;[1] and that the only mode of raising them effectively and permanently, is to proportion more nearly the supply of labour to the demand for it' (p. 377).

BOOTH'S REPLY

Booth replied,[2] but on his own behalf only and not for Godwin.[3] He complained with justice of the tone of the review, which probably had 60,000 readers, to every one of whom his name was repeatedly held up as that of an author whose extraordinary want of information led him into gross errors, and whose ignorance was unparalleled, while perhaps not one in a hundred of these readers would ever hear of his reply. Nevertheless he addressed the reply to Malthus on the assumption that Malthus had written the review.

He begins by defending his criticism of the ratios which the review dubs 'solemn and absurd trifling.' Booth agrees that he had always thought that the ratios were extremely ridiculous, but had understood that Malthus laid great stress upon their assistance. 'The comparison of Progressions appears at the beginning of

writing leans in the opposite direction. If a poor man refrains from marriage he will have less dependants to support and will, therefore, be better off, but unless the movement is widespread, the level of wages will hardly be affected. If the notion of a wages fund were sound, the poor in general might raise wages, but not any particular poor man. To this extent Malthus was an advocate of high wages. On the other hand, in Book III, Chapter V, he attacks the notion of raising money wages, and he frequently points out the futility of the rich sharing with the poor. While he expresses little faith in the adoption by the poor of moral restraint, and rather more hope of the preventive check, much of his work suggests that to increase wages is merely to invite further propagation. This was the real burden of Malthusianism as understood at the time, and on these grounds Godwin was not far from the mark.

[1] One is tempted to insert here: 'for whom?' The point does not seem to occur to the reviewer.

[2] *A Letter to The Rev. T. R. Malthus, M.A., F.R.S., being An Answer to the Criticism on Mr. Godwin's Work on Population, which was inserted in the LXXth number of the* Edinburgh Review, *etc.* David Booth, London, January 1st, 1823.

[3] '. . . it is not for me, officiously, to become his champion' (Advertisement, p. iv).

every edition of your work, and, whether you have been deceived or deceiving, has had a material effect in the promulgation of your theories' (p. 4).

He corrects the reviewer who imagines that to find the loss of a community in ten years he has merely multiplied the annual mortality by ten.[1] What he has done is to apply the standardized figures for Sweden, as set out in his table,[2] the only reason for choosing Sweden being that only there are the statistics sufficiently detailed (p. 19). The securing of accurate enumerations is extraordinarily difficult, but what can be built on the 'suppositions' and 'conjectures' concerning American mortality relied on by the reviewer?[3]

'In your vocabulary, *to calculate* is not to pore until you are half blind over arithmetical figures, but, by a single figure of rhetoric, to make a bold assertion and trust to the credulity of your readers that you will be believed.[4] . . . You reach, by a single bound, that height of learning, to which ordinary minds can arrive only by patient toil. In these venturous springs, however, it is possible that you may sometimes overleap your mark' (p. 28).

Here then is Booth's comparison of his own derided estimate of the loss of a quarter suffered in ten years by a population, compared with the estimate of one-eighth in the review.

'Should a country, containing 400,000 inhabitants, cease to have any further increase and consequently be allowed to be depopulated by the course of nature, and if in ten years this people should muster only 300,000, I might surely say that they had lost a fourth of their number. This fourth would not be exterminated by an equable annual reduction, for it would vary, from year to year, with the changing value of life.[5] But if,

[1] *Review*, p. 365. Cf. the reviewer's sneers with Booth's explanation.

[2] See Table III, page 139, derived from Table I.

[3] See *Review*, pp. 365–367, and Booth's comment, pp. 25 et seq.

[4] See post, Book III, Chapter V.

[5] Booth's method of splitting the population into age groups and estimating the survivors from the mortality tables was a big contribution to the subject. Ravenstone (see post) appears to have used the same method of calculation and probably Booth's Table to make his reductions. Malthus's method could prove nothing. It is impossible to follow the controversy in detail here, but reference should be made to Booth's contributions and the *Edinburgh Review* mentioned above, and to Malthus's Article in the *Encyclopædia Britannica* or the *Summary View*, 1830. Booth's view that the problem is really insoluble is probably the correct one.

Table III.

Table of a Population of 10,000, *averaged from the Swedish Censuses, exhibiting their gradual Extinction by Death.*

Ages	Living	After 5 yrs.	After 10 yrs.	After 15 yrs.	After 20 yrs.	After 25 yrs.	After 30 yrs.	After 35 yrs.	After 40 yrs.	After 45 yrs.	After 50 yrs.	After 55 yrs.	After 60 yrs.	After 65 yrs.	After 70 yrs.	After 75 yrs.	After 80 yrs.	After 85 yrs.	After 90 yrs.	After 100
Under 5	1408																			
5–10	1076	1076																		
10–15	1015	1015	1015																	
15–20	859	859	859	859																
20–25	821	821	821	821	821															
25–30	785	785	785	785	785	785														
30–35	741	741	741	741	741	741	741													
35–40	631	631	631	631	631	631	631	631												
40–45	556	556	556	556	556	556	556	556	556											
45–50	464	464	464	464	464	464	464	464	464	464										
50–55	414	414	414	414	414	414	414	414	414	414	414									
55–60	356	356	356	356	356	356	356	356	356	356	356	356								
60–65	314	314	314	314	314	314	314	314	314	314	314	314	314							
65–70	220	220	220	220	220	220	220	220	220	220	220	220	220	220						
70–75	169	169	169	169	169	169	169	169	169	169	169	169	169	169	169					
75–80	98	98	98	98	98	98	98	98	98	98	98	98	98	98	98	98				
80–85	49	49	49	49	49	49	49	49	49	49	49	49	49	49	49	49	49			
85–90	18	18	18	18	18	18	18	18	18	18	18	18	18	18	18	18	18	18		
above 90	6	6	6	6	6	6	6	6	6	6	6	6	6	6	6	6	6	6	6	
Amount	10,000	8592	7516	6501	5642	4821	4036	3295	2664	2108	1644	1230	874	560	340	171	73	24	6	0

Table taken from Booth's Letter to Malthus, p. 16, showing the justification for assuming a loss of one-quarter in ten years.

Table IV.

Year of colony	Born	Under 5	5 to 10	10 to 15	15 to 20	20 to 25	25 to 30	30 to 35	35 to 40	40 to 45	45 to 50	50 to 55	55 to 60	60 to 65	65 to 70	70 to 75	75 to 80	80 to 85	85 to 90	Above 90	Number of living
0					859	821	785	741	631	—	—	—	—	—	—	—	—	—	—	—	3837
5	1850	1408			859	821	785	741	631	556	—	—	—	—	—	—	—	—	—	—	5801
10	1850	1408	1076		859	821	785	741	631	556	464	—	—	—	—	—	—	—	—	—	7341
15	1850	1408	1076	1015	859	821	785	741	631	556	464	414	—	—	—	—	—	—	—	—	8770

Table illustrating the enormous contribution immigrants may make to population growth.

Notes. The original immigration of 3,837 consists of the age groups of child-bearing age. To keep this group constant a further immigration of 172 per annum is assumed (i.e. one-fifth of 859). Such a population grows very rapidly indeed, and, although not quite typical of a normal immigration is sufficiently near it to show its effects. (Table from Godwin, op. cit., 1820, p. 276. Full explanation is contained in pp. 274 et seq.)

after the Census is made, the population, instead of being limited like a tontine to the survivors, were increased by an indefinite but a large and continued immigration (from other nations as well as from the cradle), and if I should be told that my now increased society lost annually 1 in 50 of their number, how many of the old and how many of the new inhabitants being left indeterminate, I acknowledge that I should find it a difficult task, even with the assistance of their ages, to separate the deaths. This, however, is the problem which you have attempted to solve, for the purpose of proving that I did not understand the subject' (pp. 29–30).

Booth gives a further striking illustration of his method (p. 31), and displays life tables to show that the expectation of life is less in Philadelphia than in Sweden and Northampton. He admits that the data may not be true, but 'the Company for whom they were formed had no interest in their falsification, for they purchase as well as sell Annuities' (p. 39). He thinks little of Dr. Seybert's book which is anything but official and contains numerous obvious errors (p. 53). Nor does he regard the statistics of registered tonnage as of great importance in view of the use of foreign vessels and indirect routes. Altogether Booth's position commands respect, and his general attitude is that common to so many of Malthus's critics.

'For centuries, at least, there seem to be sufficient room and sustenance upon this globe for all its probable inhabitants; and I see no necessity of legislating for eternity until we are certain that man, in this world, is eternal. While food can be procured by industry, the sole evil to be conquered is its unequal distribution' (p. 63).

Towards the end of the book, Booth gives his reasons for being convinced, though he cannot prove, that Malthus was the writer of the review.[1] The reviewer makes the same mistake as Malthus in imagining that the censuses were taken in 1800 and 1810 in

[1] Ricardo thought so too at first (*Letters of Ricardo to Malthus*, Ed. Bonar, 1887, p. 198): 'I have read a very good critique on Godwin in the *Edinburgh Review*; and I am quite sure that I know the writer. It is very well done and most satisfactorily exposes Godwin's ignorance as well as his disingenuousness.' But in the next letter he writes (p. 206): 'I have mentioned my suspicions respecting the writer of the article on population in the *Edinburgh Review* to several persons. I will not utter them from this time.'

this country.[1] Like Malthus he also quotes, though without specifying it, the fourth edition of Price's *Observations on Reversionary Payments*, although there have been three subsequent editions, all differently arranged, thus making it difficult to follow the references.

There is some truth in the charge of misrepresentation he makes. It is 'rather too mischievous to cite so often from the same antiquated copy, (without even mentioning the edition), when you were writing for the more volatile readers of a modern Review. I grant that to have bought a new copy would have been expensive, but I am told that Mr. Jeffrey pays sixteen guineas a sheet, and your criticism fills fifteen pages' (p. 70). Booth was not alone in regarding Malthus as, in some respects, a 'slippery customer.'

[1] *Edinburgh Review*, p. 376. 'This might have been passed over as a slip of the pen, had I not seen the same error printed in more than twenty different pages of your *Essay on Population*. There is a chapter of ridiculous calculations respecting the population of England, through the whole of which, as well as in other places, you not only persist in the same blunder, but likewise *repeatedly* and *pointedly* assert that Mr. Rickman's "Preliminary Observations on the Censuses" were *printed* and *published*, the one in 1801 and the other in 1811 (that is before the Census in each case was finished), though these are expressly dated 1802 and 1812, and were not published until the close of those years' (pp. 68–69). 'From all this it appears certain, that though there are 80 pages of your *Essay* employed upon the Censuses, you have never seen either of the "Population Abstracts," and must have received the remarks which you published, from some one of your calculating friends' (p. 69). This is perhaps too strong an assertion, although the frequency with which the errors are repeated is rather curious. Moreover, Malthus's misrepresentation of the Table of Süssmilch (see post, pp. 268–271 seems to suggest a similar conclusion, unless one is prepared to accept the view of gross deception. A tentative conclusion would be that some of his statistical work was done for him.

CHAPTER FOUR

RAVENSTONE, PLACE, EVERETT, AND THOMPSON, 1821–1824

RAVENSTONE'S DOUBTS

GODWIN'S *Reply* was published in November 1820. On May 28th, 1821, Piercy Ravenstone wrote the Preface to his extraordinary book entitled: *A Few Doubts as to the correctness of some opinions generally entertained on the Subjects of Population and Political Economy*.

It would be interesting to know who he was, for the name is probably a pseudonym.[1] His argument in many places follows the same lines as that of Godwin and Booth, but the book is incomparably better written, and, as but six months elapsed between the publication of the two books, it hardly seems feasible that the influence was confined to the printed word. Whoever Ravenstone may have been, the conclusion is that he will be found (if ever he is found) within the circle of Godwin during the years 1819–1820.

Nevertheless, if many of the arguments, insofar as the book deals with population, are those of Godwin and Booth, they are presented with a force, a clarity and a persuasiveness of diction

[1] Beer, op. cit., writes: 'Ravenstone was essentially a Tory Democrat, but without any ulterior motives, without any other end to serve than what he considered justice and national welfare. Of an ardent temperament, a religious and cultured mind, his whole being was in revolt against capitalist and Stock Exchange dominion . . . He was indeed Cobbett *édition de luxe*—a Cobbett who could think systematically and consistently, whose knowledge of history was more comprehensive and accurate and less vitiated by prejudice, and whose style was as vigorous as that of the *Political Register*, but of a polish and refinement which only a superior classical education can produce' (pp. 251–252).

which set the book in a class apart. For the masterly criticism of some of Malthus's so-called proofs the reader must, for lack of space, be referred to the work itself.[1] Probably the most striking feature is the insistence on analysing the conditions under which population grows. Throughout the book emphasis is laid on fertility rates as distinct from crude birth rates, and there is an acute application of this fruitful approach to the poor and inadequate statistics then at his disposal. What Godwin and Booth had fumbled to express, Ravenstone brings into clear relief. Whatever may be made of his individual analyses, and many of them are now difficult if not impossible to check, his method was far ahead of his time.

The new doctrine (writes Ravenstone) asserts that, while the powers of the earth to produce subsistence are steadily becoming exhausted, man alone retains his propensity to reproduce at an undiminished rate. Men tend to overrun the world with the rapidity of weeds, thus causing a steady increase of misery, a shrinkage of comforts, and a degradation which must baffle every effort. The ordinary condition of the poor is one of mitigated famine. As there is not enough for all, each man's share in the division must of necessity be reduced. The fertility of the earth is entirely owing to the application of capital. The rich, it has been discovered, feed the poor; those who produce everything would starve but for the assistance of those who produce nothing. Hence the poor are to be checked and the rich encouraged, because their capital is the sole source of wealth (pp. 4–5).

This is not an uncomfortable creed for statesmen, nor would they criticize severely a doctrine which attributes all the wealth of the people to their wisdom, and all the evils to Providence; which augments their rights and diminishes their obligations; which holds their idle expenses to be meritorious, and help given to the poor as mistaken or even mischievous. A system which treats the poor as an encumbrance to society, the product of a mistaken past generosity, which demands no sacrifices in its performance, which bids them worship at the shrine of self-interest, cannot fail to enlist a large measure of support. The circumstances were propitious for the growth of such beliefs; they diverted men's minds from the consequences of their rulers' follies.

[1] Ravenstone, op. cit., pp. 46–106.

It was held that wretchedness was an indispensable spur to industry; poverty the source of all national wealth. The labouring classes were mere engines in the hands of the rich; accessories to the capital from which industry derived all its powers and nourishment. The poor naturally increased beyond the means available for their support. Taxation was no real evil, as it only served to check the increase of the poor, and so anticipate the severer inflictions of nature. 'It was better for man to fall into the hands of his fellow-creatures than into those of God.' . . . 'That part of the produce of a country which was consumed by the labouring classes was so much lost to the nation. Its gain consisted only in the surplus produce, this it was the business of statesmen to augment' (p. 14).

It has not been a question of mere words, but has been translated into action: it has invaded Parliament, pulpit, and even the courts of justice. Nevertheless 'it is a cold and dreary system which represents our fellow-creatures as so many rivals and enemies, which makes us believe that their happiness is incompatible with our own, which builds our wealth on their poverty, and teaches that their numbers cannot consist with our comforts and enjoyments; which would persuade us to look on the world in the light of a besieged town, where the death of our neighbours is hailed with secret satisfaction, since it augments the quantity of provisions likely to fall to our own share' (p. 17).

The consequences of this doctrine for religion and morality are so fraught with peril that it ought to be scrutinized with the greatest care. 'It cannot add much to our veneration for the divine nature, to see that Omnipotence can devise no better plan than misery and extermination, for correcting those defects in our system of society, which might so easily have been obviated by a different constitution of our nature' (p. 17). Those who come to doubt the goodness of God will soon begin to doubt His existence. A cold selfishness will lead to a dreary fatalism.

'It is time to put an end to those cheerless systems, which only look on men as so many beasts of burthen; which class them solely according to their power of production; which assign them no value but the amount of their labour; which consider them in no other relations than as they are workers in brass, or workers in wool, than as they contribute to the wealth of the nation, or augment the comforts of the rich' (pp. 21–22).

With these considerations in mind, therefore, he undertakes his investigation into the real principles of population.

The existence of large families leads us readily to suppose that human fecundity is rarely exercized to the full, but observations on the yield of plants never produce the results which single experiments might lead us to expect. Actually, whether nations are rich or poor, rising or declining, population appears to advance with a uniformity which is independent of the regulations of society.

Everyone will admit that the number of births depends not upon the total population but on the number of productive marriages, yet Mr. Malthus has gone astray through ignoring this obvious truth. By studying population in small insulated spots he has been able to find every variety of anomaly imaginable. But the artificial boundaries of a parish do not sever human relationships.

It has been concluded that population will increase most rapidly where the crude birth rate is greatest. This is not true. A high rate may be due to a shorter average duration of life, and where there is a high death rate, there must necessarily be a high birth rate even to maintain numbers. Nor must it be assumed that an extension of the duration of life is conducive to a growing population: it can only increase the number of old people, and since it adds nothing to the productive classes, it will cease to have any effect at the end of one generation. Consequently crude birth rates are misleading and it is necessary to divide society into productive and unproductive classes. 'We must confine our inquiries entirely to the probable number of marriages in every country, and the fruits they are likely to produce' (p. 33).

The large number of unmarried women among the upper classes is not typical of women in general. Sooner or later nearly all the poor marry. It is the only way to obtain a helpmate, and a poor man hopes that his wife will earn sufficient to keep herself. Statistics bear out this reasoning by showing that nineteen women out of twenty sooner or later become wives (p. 34). The only figures for unproductive marriages are those of Vevay in Switzerland, which give one marriage in twenty as childless. So we arrive at an estimate that of all females born, eleven out of twenty live to marriageable age, and of this number ten become wives and mothers. Thus, half the women born contribute to the continuance of their species. It follows, therefore, that four children to every fruitful marriage are the minimum for the maintenance of a stationary population (p. 35).

Since twenty-one is the average age of marriage and forty-five the end of the prolific period, the maximum period of productivity is twenty-four years. This, however, is clearly too long for an average, since women who begin to breed early, cease early, and the two extremes are rarely found in one woman. A difference of twenty years between the ages of the oldest and youngest child of one family is very rare; it is often as little as five or six. In fact, a period of sixteen years is probably an overestimate of the truth. As a marriage may be ended by the death of either husband or wife we must reduce this period by a calculation of the value of their joint lives, which process reduces the sixteen years to eleven. Two years seems to be the minimum time required for the gestation and suckling of a child, and the Scottish statistics show that in practice the interval between children is rather longer. So we arrive finally at a figure of five and a quarter children as the maximum yield of the average marriage (p. 38).

Under these circumstances a population could double itself from its own resources in seventy-five years. With only four children to a marriage the population would be stationary. With four and a half children, the doubling figure would be 140 years. With five children it would be eighty-six years. A doubling in seventy-five years is the absolute maximum, and has never under any circumstances yet taken place. Malthus's American increase is thus physically impossible: it is equivalent to asserting that each fruitful marriage produces nine children.

If infant mortality could be reduced we could look for a great increase in population, without any alteration in human nature, but there seems to be no ground for such a hope in past experience. The ratio of mortality appears to be the same in all countries, and seems to have all the force of a law of nature. The conquest of one disease appears to be followed by the generation of another through altered habits of life. Man is very adaptable and appears to be able to live in any climate and under almost any kind of diet, but he finds death no less certainly in the tropics or at the polar circle. The death rate appears to be independent of climate, diet, or human institutions (pp. 43–45).

It cannot be taken as axiomatic that what has never happened can never come about, but it is a safe practical rule. The unlimited powers of propagation appear to be checked by the laws of society. We cannot combine the advantages of a state of nature with the benefits of civilization. Since these states cannot co-exist together it is a waste of time speculating as to what would happen if they could. This is the fallacy of Malthus's system. Although mankind has grown in numbers, it has been by small steps, and there is no reason to believe that the rate will become so rapid as to prove inconvenient (p. 50).

A large population is dependent upon the subdivision of labour, which by improving cultivation has increased the output per man and so created a class of people who can devote their energies to improving the conditions and comforts of life. 'Barbarous habits are as impossible in a well-peopled country, as civilization in a desert' (p. 64).

Population has been growing steadily, but the inconvenience has been confined to England, and that in the last thirty years. 'What is peculiar to one country cannot have arisen from causes common to all' (p. 77). In his investigation of various countries Malthus has sought for varieties rather than resemblances, to collect anomalies rather than to establish a general rule, but 'though in some circumstances, the population of different countries may vary, the same law regulates its general progress in every part of the world' (p. 107).

'Every where the inquiry ends in one almost uniform result. In every country, however various its habits, however different its form of government, whether classed by the lovers of classification as a commercial or as an agricultural people; whether its inhabitants be collected in cities, or widely scattered over a wilderness of territory; whether its fields be cheered by the constant presence of the sun, or their powers of production be suspended by the long continuance of a rigorous winter; whether it be habitually an exporter of corn, or whether it derive its sustenance from the fertility of other soils; every where we find the annual marriages bearing nearly the same proportion to the whole number of the people; every where we see the marriages renovating the world by almost exactly the same number of births; every where we perceive the numbers of the people rapidly though insensibly increasing in almost equal proportions;

and, every where we find the means of subsistence rising as it were spontaneously from the earth, to meet the wants of its newly-created inhabitants . . . God . . . hath not bid us to multiply our species only to find food for the grave' (pp. 117–118).

Division of labour results in the means of production outstripping the growth of population. If population really increased faster than subsistence, the state of the savage would be the only state of abundance. But knowledge is power. 'It introduces new modes of cultivation. It converts the barren soil into a garden, and calls forth the hidden powers of nature, which might otherwise have slumbered on for ever useless and unknown' (p. 119).

'This is the true theory of our existence. Population and subsistence are inseparably connected. An increase of numbers is immediately followed by an increase of cultivation. Nothing in nature perishes, it only assumes new forms. What has served for the food of animals is not therefore lost; it becomes the aliment of new vegetation. The destruction of present existences is made the means of giving birth to new beings. Death becomes the support of life . . . (Man) is not taught by nature to look on a son or a brother as one with whom he is to contend for a scanty mouthful of bread. . . . To live in plenty he has only to labour. . . . If in the dread of seeing his children perish with hunger, he fears to become a father: it is not to the will of Providence, but to the abuse of his reason, and the misdirection of his passions he owes his misfortunes' (pp. 119–120).

Human institutions are the real source of our misery, and he who fosters a spirit hopeless to the improvement of man's condition is the enemy both of man and God.

RAVENSTONE—THE AMERICAN INCREASE

European experience serves to convince us that there is one law of population. 'The annual number of marriages will be every where to the whole population in the proportion of from 1 to 116 to 123. The number of children to each fruitful marriage $4\frac{3}{5}$ to $4\frac{4}{5}$. The number of births will, in every year, constitute the twenty-sixth or twenty-seventh part of the people; these appear to be the extreme limits of their oscillation' (p. 121).[1]

[1] This conclusion is based on detailed analysis of the statistics of various European countries (pp. 77–107).

What then of the exceptional American increase? The distinctive factor in this case is immigration. Brazil has the same natural advantages, but until recently, when her shores were opened to immigrants, her increase made no great strides.

The American increase can easily be shown to be the result of immigration, if we compare the two censuses of 1790 and 1810. Clearly all those included in the 1790 census who are still alive in 1810 will be over twenty years of age. The population in 1790, exclusive of slaves, amounted to 3,230,000. According to all the mortality tables these would be reduced by death within twenty years to a total of 1,810,000.[1] If then America had been insulated from the rest of the world, and had derived no supplies from other countries, the total number of its adult inhabitants would have been 1,810,000. Any surplus cannot be natives but must have come from outside.

The census of 1810 returns 2,930,000 inhabitants of twenty years and over. Consequently, of this number, some 1,120,000 persons, or more than a third of the adult population are not natives and must have come to live there from elsewhere within the last twenty years (pp. 130–131). But this does not give the full extent of the immigration. Some of the immigrants will have died during the twenty years. 'If we suppose that each year brought an equal number of emigrants, and that all were of an age least liable to mortality, we shall find the number of deaths in twenty years cannot be fewer than 280,000.' This is an underestimate because all would not be in the prime of life, and the early hardships would tend to increase mortality. Therefore the total number of immigrants cannot have been less than 1,400,000 or 70,000 persons a year. Even this figure does not include those who arrived in childhood and had not reached their twentieth year in 1810, the number of these being unobtainable (pp. 131–132).

Moreover these immigrants will also be responsible for a large share of the infant population. During the period the native adult population averaged 1,625,000, which gives the number of women of child-bearing age as 540,000. Most of the female immigrants would be of child-bearing age; thus there will have been 330,000 women not American born, who have been adding

[1] The rate of mortality is, of course, the vital point. It was here that Malthus later took up the challenge.

to the population, or, if allowance is made for those possibly over-age, say 300,000. From these figures, the children of immigrants would be to the children of natives as five to nine. If it be supposed that all who emigrate are in the prime of life the proportion would be higher still (pp. 132–133).

On the whole it may fairly be assumed that the children born of immigrants were to those of the natives as six to nine. The number of persons under twenty-one in the census of 1810 was 3,125,000. If we allot two-fifths of these to immigrants we have 1,250,000 children which added to the number of adult immigrants gives a grand total of 2,370,000 additions to the population from outside, four-fifths of the total increase. The whole increase from procreation is reduced therefore to 470,000 which gives a rate of doubling of 102 years.[1] This agrees with the Swedish results and the twenty-five year cycle has no more existence in the New World than in the Old (p. 134).

According to the above calculation, the average number of the native population (exclusive of foreigners) between the years 1790 and 1810 was 3,460,000. If births be calculated at 1 to 26, nearly the largest possible rate, they will amount to 133,150 per annum, which in twenty years would add up to 2,663,000 of whom 796,000 will have died, leaving an infant population of 1,867,000 in the second census, or 8,000 fewer than was obtained by the former mode of reckoning (p. 136).

Referring to the census tables, the number of females annually attaining their twentieth year is to the total population as 1 to 110; they will therefore during the above period have been 31,000. But the number of births is to the number of such females as 4·30 to 1, giving an annual total of 133,370, within 4,000 of the number originally found. Subsidiary calculations serve to check these conclusions (pp. 137 et seq.).

The Malthusian theory of a doubling by procreation alone in twenty-five years leads to results inconsistent with all knowledge of emigration (pp. 146–147). 'If the whole number of people,

[1] The reader is referred to the book itself for the full reasoning and calculations. It is impossible to escape the conclusion that Ravenstone must have chosen many of his ratios and reductions with care to achieve such a happy result. Nevertheless, the method is interesting, and the complications introduced into population statistics by constant emigration are exemplified so that rather more than Malthusian care is needed in their interpretation.

who in two hundred years have quitted Europe to settle within her limits, has exceeded 370,000; if the average annual supply of strangers has been more than 1,800—then has her native population not doubled itself in twenty-five years; then is there no evidence that such an increase has ever taken place in any time or in any country' (p. 147).

With the destruction of the geometrical ratio of increase in a period of twenty-five years, the arithmetical ratio also falls to the ground. 'They are twin brothers, conceived in the same hour; one common sympathy connects their existence. One common grave may receive their remains' (p. 155).

Malthus's propositions are very elusive. If any period had been fixed when the ratios were to begin they would have been shown to be absurd. The first step in the two is the same, and there is no reason why each generation should not claim to be the first link. If we project the ratios backward they lead to the most absurd and inconsistent results (p. 157).

If the growth of subsistence is independent of population, why are not the uninhabited lands storehouses of wealth? It would be thought that where there are fewest consumers there should be greatest abundance, but experience contradicts this conclusion. What says the savage? He has no leisure to reply; he is busy 'unkennelling a grub from his fastness in the trunk of a decayed tree. . . . Misery and want are the lords of the wilderness' (p. 170).

The result of our researches is that subsistence depends on human industry; it increases most rapidly where labour is directed with the greatest skill and exerted with the most perseverance. If nature had produced for all his needs, man would have been but a beast of the field; whereas from man's necessities have sprung all inventions and improvements. The basis of property is industry; it owes its existence to the division of labour which cannot exist without an abundant population. When the labour of one half of society suffices for the subsistence of the whole, the other half will be freed for pursuits 'whose excellence is not the less because their utility is not immediately obvious.' It is to the increase of population that all the comforts of life owe their full development (p. 174).

The real cause of advance is not diffusion of knowledge but increase of numbers. By promoting the division of labour it released from toil those who could devote themselves to the extension of the boundaries of knowledge. The most populous nations are those which live most at ease and have most comforts. 'The very offal from the tables of the rich in a populous country would be more than sufficient to maintain, in unusual luxury, a whole nation of savages' (p. 177).

Statistics seem to prove that there is a return from land strictly proportional to the amount of labour bestowed upon it (p. 181). In any case, large numbers are essential for the introduction of machinery; without large numbers the labour involved in the construction of the instruments would be greater than any possible saving: far from being an economy they would be a waste of labour (p. 184).

Why should we imagine that the world is at the end of its tether? That nature can no longer advance and that her powers are effete? 'The means of subsistence will increase with the improvements in cultivation. Science will come in aid of industry. Chemistry, exhausting all the secrets of nature, will teach new modes of decomposing and organizing matter. New means of production will be discovered. The elements, rendered subservient to the authority of man, will put forth all their powers for his benefit; and the spirits that dwell therein, yielding to the spell of knowledge, shall glory to work his will' (p. 188).

Limits to population there must be, but they are only the limits of space. Of the limits of subsistence we know nothing till we have calculated the limits of future improvements in knowledge.

FRANCIS PLACE—THE ADVOCACY OF BIRTH CONTROL

In the following year, 1822, Francis Place[1] published his notable book, *Illustrations and Proofs of the Principle of Population*,[2] notable because of its open advocacy of birth control. James Mill had hinted at this solution in his article *Colony* published in

[1] Place was born in 1771, and had an unfortunate childhood, his father being a drunkard and an inveterate gambler. He was rescued by an early marriage from what might have proved moral degradation, and finally worked his way from apprentice to master tailor, and became well known for his political views and efforts at reform. The influence of his personal experience on the writing of this book is very marked.

[2] Quotations are taken from the reproduction by Norman E. Himes (George Allen and Unwin, 1930).

1818. There are also a couple of guarded passages in his *Elements of Political Economy*. Place's book contains more than a hint: it amounts to a recommendation.

The book was a reply to Godwin, apparently provoked by Place's misapprehension of the importance of Godwin's book which had been 'extolled in Parliament, quoted from with praise in various publications; and represented both by the public press, and by many intelligent persons, as a satisfactory refutation of the principle of population' (p. viii). He flattered Godwin in thinking that the work had had such an effect, but he set to work to expose Godwin's inconsistencies in no uncertain fashion, refuting statements made in the *Reply* in 1820 by others contained in that of 1801. This interesting, amusing, though at times rather laboured and not quite fair treatment need not detain us.

Godwin's *Reply*, says Place, is a 'plausible attempt—utterly destitute of proof' (p. ix). The population of the United States has repeatedly doubled itself from procreation in periods of less than twenty years. In England the population has for several ages been increasing as fast as the means of subsistence would allow, and that rate of increase has been very much accelerated during the last seventy years (p. x).

Place is particularly severe on Godwin and Booth in regard to their interpretation of both the Swedish and American statistics. Godwin's two main fallacies being (1) that in order to double the population eight children per marriage are needed, and (2) that the Swedish figures are applicable to the United States (p. xii).

The most striking feature of the book, however, and the one which above all gives it the title to an important place in the history of the controversy, is the advocacy of contraception. Admitting almost completely the Malthusian analysis, he rejects the Malthusian remedies, and carries the theory consistently and fearlessly to its logical conclusion.

Legislation, particularly piecemeal legislation, is vain. Only drastic legislative change combined with instruction of the people is adequate to the purpose in hand. Place expects censure, and expresses his willingness to face it. 'He is fully persuaded of the usefulness of his suggestions, and will not be much affected either by censure, or by the words in which it may be conveyed' (pp. xii–xiii). He admits Malthus's premises, but does not approve of the whole of his expedients; neither would Malthus himself if he had not been in too big a hurry for results, and too often disposed to favour the prejudices of the rich (p. 8).

'No effectual check to the progress of population, at all beneficial to the people, can be expected, but by means of increased knowledge; to teach which to the great body of them must be a work of some time, requiring in the teachers great urbanity, great diligence, great patience, and great clearness of statement; and yet, if it were set about in the right spirit, there is no knowing how short the time might be before a visible alteration for the better would become apparent' (p. 9).

Godwin emphasized the importance of government and social institutions; Malthus, on the other hand, is frequently desirous of keeping the facts of bad government out of sight. 'There are passages in his book in which its desolations are noticed, but they are finally declared to be of little moment' (p. 127). Consequently, although such was not Malthus's intention, the effect of many passages in his book has been to encourage hard-heartedness and oppression, and increase illwill between the different classes.

'The condition of the mass of the people will be wretched in any country, no matter what its population, so long as it is wretchedly governed, and one of three things must happen: 1st, Government must be reformed, and made to impede human happiness as little as possible. Or, 2d, it must conform itself to the increase of knowledge among the people; or, 3d, It must subdue them, and rule them as slaves' (p. 129).

Malthus's object was to increase happiness, but his methods can only impede it. His sincerity is unquestioned, 'but the belief in his sincerity is at the same time a belief of his extreme ignorance of human nature, in some very important particulars' (p. 137). He denies the right of the unemployed poor to eat, but grants it to the unemployed rich. He attempts to satisfy the starving man with statements about abstract rights. The poor have a legal right to assistance which he proposes to destroy. The abstract right of the rich (but not the poor) to live without working, designated as the 'Law of Nature, which is the Law of God,' has no meaning.

'No such *right* as Mr. Malthus speaks of, was ever instituted by nature. *Nature* never ordained that one man should labour for another man, *nature* made no such relation among men: *nature* left *every thing* in common, and the appropriation of any of her gifts, however acquired, can only be maintained and secured by compact; and it is by compacts and conventions among men, that *right* has any existence in the sense Mr. Malthus uses the word.

'A man in possession of the good things of this life has a *right*, *a right created by law*, to keep what he has from others, if he choose so to do; but take away this *legal right*, as Mr. Malthus has done, and substitute his "*law of nature*," and the whole is at once resolved into a question of brute force, and the one has as much *right* to take as the other to withhold; and in a case of possession on the one side, and starvation on the other, to kill the possessor, to obtain the means of subsistence, if by other means he cannot obtain it' (p. 138).

This denial of right to the poor has been wholly mischievous, and has impeded due recognition of the principle of population by the people. The other proposition for the gradual abolition of the poor laws is equally mischievous. Since few labourers have a prospect of being able to maintain a family, scarcely any of them can marry without committing an immoral act. Malthus seems to have overlooked this aspect of the situation (p. 140). 'As for the rates eating up the produce of the land . . . they eat up but a small portion, which under a better state of things would not [sic] be paid as wages' (p. 143).[1]

The real objection to the poor laws is that they degrade both those who administer them and, even more, the labouring poor; and insofar as they increase population, they do it in the worst possible manner. Malthus's scheme would reduce the poor rates, but it would cause greater evils. It would degrade the poor, while decreasing their numbers but little, for few marry owing to the encouragement these laws give. On the other hand, parents deprived of Parish relief would undercut wages and in a very short time their condition would become 'ignorant, stupid, and brutish' (p. 145). Actually Malthus's idea of starving the

[1] Himes's comment is: 'Evidently the *not* is an error, and should have been omitted.' (Typographical errors.) Not evidently or necessarily. The inclusion of 'not' gives a different meaning which probably Place intended to convey: that is the present writer's view.

poor, and Godwin's suggestion of infanticide, both start at the wrong end. The real remedy is preventive.

When Malthus says the poor man 'is to be told that *his* King and country do not want more subjects, that *he* is not fulfilling a duty to society by marrying, that he is *acting directly contrary to the will of God, and his repeated admonitions*,'[1] his language is absurd. The poor are not so ignorant as to talk of king and country in that way (p. 154). They have their grievances—their exclusion from the franchise, the laws of settlement, the payment of wages out of poor rates, heavy taxes, restraints on emigration, trade restrictions, impressment, the combination laws, and the corn laws: of all these things they complain and not unreasonably. But Malthus hardly ever alludes to these causes except in general terms. Instead the poor man is denounced for being idle and improvident (pp. 152–153).

'Idle he is not, improvident he generally is, to some extent, and it can hardly be otherwise. He must spend an odd sixpence or a shilling now and then, although he had certainly better save it. But as to his idleness—all the work is done that is desired to be done; and there he stands, ready and willing to be engaged to do the hardest, the most disgusting, and the most destructive kind of work' (p. 154).

Such men as Malthus cannot form correct notions of the working people. They can know little of the shifts, privations, and efforts made against terrific odds to keep up a decent appearance. The dissolute poor are obvious; the virtues of the rest are hidden (p. 155).

'How then, I ask, can these be taught by those who are ignorant of their habits, and do not understand their real situation, who confound them with those whom they themselves despise, who suppose them infinitely less intelligent, less honest, less disposed to be virtuous, and less willing to be instructed than they really are; who attribute to them the most puerile notions, address them in the language of children, or goad them like slaves, who accuse them of making complaints they do not make, and pay no attention to those they do make?' (p. 156).

Malthus is on sound ground when he observes that 'it does not seem entirely visionary to suppose, that if the true and permanent cause of poverty were clearly explained, and forcibly

[1] Abridgment of pp. 342–343 of the *Essay*, 1806 edn., Vol. II.

brought home to each man's bosom, it would have some, and perhaps not an inconsiderable influence on his conduct: at least the experiment has never yet been fairly tried. . . . We must explain to them the true nature of their situation, and show them that the withholding of the supplies of labour is the only possible way of really raising its price; and that they themselves being the possessors of this commodity have alone the power to do this.'[1] But he looks to the prudential restraint from marriage to achieve this result. Godwin, too, in his first *Reply*, looks for the operation of the preventive check in an improved state of society.

If the poor were taught without cant or the appearance of self-interest, in clear language without figure and metaphor, that the overstocking of the labour market was the cause of low wages, that indiscreet marriages frequently led to poverty, misery, crime, and disgrace; that even a small degree of surplus labour deteriorated the condition of every labourer; and if on the other hand they were clearly shown that by abstaining from marriage for a few years the supply of labour might be reduced to the level of the demand, and their chances of respectable maintenance be greatly improved, a great change for the better could be expected.

'If, above all, it were once clearly understood, that it was not disreputable for married persons to avail themselves of such precautionary means as would, without being injurious to health, or destructive of female delicacy, prevent conception, a sufficient check might at once be given to the increase of population beyond the means of subsistence; vice and misery, to a prodigious extent, might be removed from society, and the object of Mr. Malthus, Mr. Godwin, and of every philanthropic person, be promoted, by the increase of comfort, of intelligence, and of moral conduct, in the mass of the population.

'The course recommended will, I am fully persuaded, at some period be pursued by the people, even if left to themselves. The intellectual progress they have for several years past been making, the desire for information of all kinds, which is abroad in the world, and particularly in this country, cannot fail to lead them to the discovery of the true causes of their poverty and degradation, not the least of which they will find to be in overstocking the market with labour, by too rapidly producing

[1] See *Essay*, Book IV, Ch. III.

children, and for which they will not fail to find and to apply remedies' (pp. 165–166).

In spite of their professions, the rich have persistently opposed the improvement of the poor. They have prevented the mobility of labour by the law of settlement. The landowners, magistrates, and principal farmers have formed what amounts to a conspiracy, and have reduced allowances to the level of animals. At the same time efforts at combination among the workers to improve their conditions have been called a crime 'worse than felony, and as bad as murder' (p. 168).

The whole practice of government has been to depress wages, and to reduce the workers to an abject state of dependence. In legislation three things are needed to improve the conditions of the working people:

1. Repeal of the combination laws.
2. Repeal of the laws restraining emigration.
3. Repeal of all restrictive laws on trade, commerce, and manufactures, and particularly the corn laws.

Unless the rich agree to this, they should cease from complaining of the conduct of the poor and the pressure of the poor's rate (pp. 171–172).

Malthus seems to shrink from discussing the prevention of conception because he fears to encounter the prejudices of others,[1] yet on his own showing no general improvement in the condition of the poor is possible without an increase in the preventive check.

'It is time, however, that those who really understand the cause of a redundant, unhappy, miserable, and considerably vicious population, and the means of preventing the redundancy, should clearly, freely, openly, and fearlessly point out the means. It is "childish" to shrink from proposing or developing any means, however repugnant they may at first appear to be; our only care should be, that we do not in removing one evil introduce another of greater magnitude. He is a visionary who expects to remove vice altogether, and he is a driveller who, because he cannot accomplish what is impossible to be accomplished, sets

[1] There is probably some substance in this view, but there is a more fundamental objection apparent in the *Essay*. If the poor could control the size of their families by voluntary measures a great stimulus to activity would be removed. Malthus desired the stimulus, the prospect of marriage, without too many children, the fruits of the marriage.

himself down and refrains from doing the good which is in his power' (pp. 173–174).

If all could marry young without the fear of breeding more children than they desired to have, wages would rise to a comfortable subsistence for all, and all might marry. Marriage would be the happiest state, and open prostitution would cease. The poor's rates would be at a minimum and might be remodelled or confined to the aged and helpless. There is no cause for despair; but reason for hope, that moral restraint will increase and the reasonable adoption of birth control will so regulate the supply of population that an adequate subsistence can be provided for all.

AN AMERICAN CRITIC—A. H. EVERETT

The next critic of note was A. H. Everett, who published in 1823 (with a second edition in 1826) a book: *New Ideas on Population with Remarks on the Theories of Malthus and Godwin.* If the ideas were not so new as he claimed, the book is well written, and like most of the post-Godwinian writing free from abuse and vituperation.[1]

He is as good as his word when, unlike most of the other critics, he says, 'I have principally aimed at brevity.' He was apparently introduced by Sir James Mackintosh to Malthus, of whom he writes: 'I have rarely met with a finer specimen of the true philosophic temper, graced and set off by the urbanity of a finished gentleman, than is seen in his person' (p. viii).

The basis of Everett's case[2] is that, as population grows, civilization, science, and the division of labour increase productive power more than in proportion to the demand. An increase in population increases both the supply of labour and the demand for its products, yet Malthus has either not perceived this, or not kept it clearly before him. 'He appears throughout his work to consider the increase of population, simply in its effect upon the consumption of the means of subsistence, without regarding its

[1] Sadler (1830) is a notable exception.

[2] Malthus drew Everett's attention to the similarity between his ideas and those of Gray, whose book Everett had not then read. In the second edition Everett comments: 'Mr. Gray is, I think, rather wanting in precision, and too much inclined to coin new words.' Nevertheless his work is a valuable addition to the literature of Political Economy (p. xxii).

operation upon their supply' (p. 21). He treats every individual as a consumer, but not as a producer, yet the real question is one of proportion.

'Does an increase of population produce an increased supply of the products of labor in proportion to the demand, and consequently a greater abundance of the necessaries and comforts of life; or does it, on the contrary, produce an increased demand for the products of labor in proportion to the supply, and consequently a comparative distress and scarcity' (p. 22).

This is the real question which Malthus settles by a mathematical formula. Everett inclines to the former view; Malthus to the latter.

If the labour of a man and his product are fixed quantities, an increase of population will not alter the proportion of subsistence to numbers. But these quantities are not fixed. Although labour varies with the dispositions and motives of men, this fact can be neglected for the present purpose, leaving two circumstances which determine its productiveness: the natural advantages under which it is applied, and the skill employed in its application. The advantages of nature may be considered uniform, since increased population cannot alter climate, soil, etc. The only important variable, therefore, is the skill with which the labour is applied. Does an increase in population produce a favourable or an unfavourable effect on this skill?

The answer is obvious. Increased population is followed immediately by the division of labour, which leads to rapid progress in inventions, improvement in methods, and development in all branches of arts and science. In order to substantiate Malthus's theory it is necessary to assume that labour becomes less efficient in proportion to the skill with which it is applied.

Man is intended for society, and only in society does he find his true level. The instinct of nature and the dictates of reason both lead to the establishment of social institutions. In a savage state, like that of North American Indians, scanty population is inevitable owing to the immense labour of gaining even a mere subsistence. But if through some accidental cause the population were doubled, they would hunt in larger companies and employ better implements and stratagems. Life would be easier and would probably lead to the adoption of agriculture as a livelihood.

Agriculture is the natural employment of man, and its adoption is soon followed by the development of manufactures and commerce. This arises out of the abundance of the produce, the superfluous portion of which is changed into new and more agreeable forms.

'While a part of the community is exclusively employed in obtaining by the cultivation of the soil, the natural products required for the use of the whole, another portion would in like manner be exclusively employed in giving new forms to the superfluous portion of these products: and these two divisions of society would exchange with each other the fruits of their respective labours.' This gives rise to commerce. 'These three occupations therefore, each of which supposes and requires the existence of the others, and of which agriculture is the principal, form together the natural employments of the human race' (p. 34).

An increase in population enables such a society to extend its power in any chosen direction. New uses will be found for the surplus products, additional tracts will be cultivated, and new fields opened in manufactures and commerce. Increased division of labour will lead to even more remarkable improvements in methods and productivity. In the U.S.A. the growth of population stimulated agriculture; in England it stimulated manufactures and commerce. In both cases growth in numbers has been the source of wealth and abundance.

The degree of abundance will depend on the political and physical situation of the country. Where there are large uncultivated tracts, an increase involves no danger; but mere extension of cultivation does not alter the proportion of the means of subsistence to population.

'It is only when the population begins to increase upon a territory already appropriated, that it produces the effect of augmenting the supply of provisions in proportion to the demand' (p. 39).

In this case skill increases, and as productivity depends almost wholly on skill and science, it is obvious that the same increase of population will be more productive in the latter than in the former case. On a limited territory increased population introduces a new element—increased skill.

The growth of manufactures and commerce, the sending out

of emigrants and colonists mainly devoted to agricultural pursuits, these have led to reciprocal trade.

'A dense and increasing population on a limited territory, instead of bringing with it any danger of scarcity, is not only an immediate cause of greater abundance to the nation where it exists, but a principle of prosperity and civilization to every part of the world' (p. 42).

It is obvious that an unlimited number of people cannot live on a limited territory, and Malthus's conclusions are a fair deduction from his premises, but these are erroneous. Political boundaries are quite arbitrary. 'It is not true that the human race possesses a rapid and indefinite power of increase, under the checks to which the progress of population is subject, and it is not true that the inhabitants of a given tract of territory must necessarily subsist upon the direct products of the soil they occupy' (p. 46).

Malthus's estimate of increase in America is too low if all the checks were removed, but too high for a real rate of increase. To assume the highest known increase as a standard is like assuming the wisest man as the standard of intelligence. It is unsafe to draw a general conclusion from a single instance.

'The proper course would be to inquire, first, what is the natural power of increase in the human species? Secondly, what are the checks, ordinary and extraordinary, that oppose the development of this power? and, lastly, what is the real rate of increase which we observe to occur in fact under the operation of these checks?' (p. 54).

Malthus has not attempted to calculate this real rate of increase, and all his checks resolve themselves into want of the means of subsistence. But if the power of increase is checked by an accidental want of subsistence arising from moral and physical evil, before it is checked by a necessary want arising from the exhaustion of the earth's resources, then, in order to ascertain the real rate of increase for the purpose of comparing it with the possible resources of the soil, it is necessary to examine the effects of this prior and accidental check. Consequently we should observe all known cases and find a mean rate of growth.

If the quantity of provisions which a country can produce is fixed, there must be some cause to fix it, and Malthus's theory offers no guide. If the supply of food is not regulated by numbers, but numbers by food, no imaginable cause regulating food remains except the influence of soil and climate, but this cause is quite insufficient, since on similar soils at the same time, and on the same soil at different times, we find the most various quantities of the means of subsistence. Compare for instance the Indians of North America with the rest of the nation. If population is determined by the supply of food, by what cause is that supply determined, and why under similar circumstances do the colonists expand and flourish while the Indians perish of actual want?

Both Malthus and Godwin admit that there is a check to population. Only in their remote origin do their theories differ. For Malthus it is a law of nature; for Godwin vicious political institutions. But vicious political institutions are only one form of evil. There is physical evil wholly independent of human agency; there is private vice; there are vicious political institutions, and there is barbarism.

'Population and depopulation are the forms in which good and evil, virtue and vice, happiness and misery, exercise their operation upon man; and wherever we find the effect, we are sure to find it attended by the corresponding cause, population by virtue and happiness, and depopulation by misery and vice' (p. 74).

The rapid growth in the United States is due to the natural power of increase operating under the most favourable circumstances. Checks to growth will be epidemics, natural evils, physical hardship, and war with savages. Checks from vicious institutions and private vice will be less considerable than in other countries, and agricultural pursuits are favourable to morals and health.

Society has a right to regulate marriage, but to give a monopoly to the rich is neither just nor safe. An age could be calculated for rich and poor alike, or lots might be drawn. If such methods seem absurd, it is because the suppositions leading to them are false and groundless. It is the order of nature for men to marry young, and any system against early marriage is contrary to the law of nature and therefore false.

With regard to provision for the poor, so far as this concerns the aged, infirm or destitute, it is unaccompanied by ill-effects. Foundling hospitals may encourage vice in the parents, but it is the child who is the object of their attentions. Generally speaking, it is one of the least agreeable consequences of Malthus's system that it leads to a low estimate of the value of life, though this is not his intention.

Wages are the products of labour, hence it is natural for them to rise, but each member of society does not receive the fruits of his own labour.

'It may be taken therefore as a general rule, that the population and productiveness of labor being given, the rate of wages will depend upon the circumstances, political and economical, which regulate the distribution of the fruits of the labor of the community among its members' (p. 116).

The extent of the population is determined almost exclusively by the degree of civilization, and its increase is checked at every stage by particular forms of moral and physical evil, which may be diminished but cannot be wholly removed and will always prevent the earth from being over-populated.

A CO-OPERATIVE VIEW—WILLIAM THOMPSON

Yet another noteworthy addition to the controversy appeared in the following year from the pen of William Thompson.[1] The work, which is well known, was entitled: *An Inquiry into the Principles of the Distribution of Wealth most conducive to Human Happiness; applied to the newly proposed system of Voluntary Equality of Wealth.* The contribution to the subject of population is incidental and comes near the end of the book, but the ideas expressed are none the less of considerable importance.

Taking the book as a whole, one is bound to agree with Sir Alexander Gray's assessment: 'Thompson has great merits; but he torpedoes himself by his unconquerable dreariness and prolixity.'[2] The section on the principle of population, being incidental to his main theme, suffers somewhat less in this respect than many other parts of the book.

According to Thompson, the Malthusian view is based both on a mis-statement of fact and a misunderstanding of the human mind and of social combinations. It is true that human beings

[1] For further information about Thompson, see: Beer, *History of British Socialism*; Gray, *The Socialist Tradition—Moses to Lenin*; Stark, *The Ideal Foundations of Economic Thought.*

[2] Gray: *The Socialist Tradition—Moses to Lenin*, p. 269.

are physically capable of so increasing in numbers that they outstrip the possible food supply, but this is also true of sheep and silkworms. And since men control the breeding of such animals so as to keep them within the limits of their food supply, why should they not, on the same principles of prudence, control the growth of their own numbers? This is a sufficient answer to the general question.

But the matter does not rest there, for Malthus has produced particulars by which he intends to establish that man is devoid of prudence in regard to his own reproduction, and that he is constantly breeding himself into a state of poverty (p. 536).

Even if this were proved of the past it would not mean that the evils were irremediable, and that prudence could not be acquired. To adopt the view that, if an evil exists and if no immediate means are known whereby it may be avoided, therefore it must remain for ever, is one which would stop all inquiry in any field. The discovery of a defect is the first step towards its removal.

The defect alleged is the tendency of man to increase beyond the food supplies available, and this defect arises from want of prudence due to the ignorance of mankind. Hence, if prudence can be imparted, the situation is not without hope. Such prudence has prevailed among the rich, and involves 'habits of self-controul restraining immediate inclination for the sake of greater preponderant good' (p. 537). And if one portion of society can acquire such habits of prudence, there is clearly no law of nature which makes it impossible for others.

The solution therefore to the alleged problem is the spread of knowledge, and this is opposed by the rich as being incompatible with their institutions, which are based on large numbers of ignorant poor. 'This, the diffusion of knowledge and self-controul amongst the individuals of all communities, the only important part of the population question, has been altogether kept out of view by its supporters' (p. 538).[1]

Actually the real facts of history are the reverse of those stated. Every advance in civilization tends to engender habits of

[1] This charge cannot fairly be made against Malthus, although it might well apply to many of his supporters. It may be, however, that Thompson has in mind birth control, which he favours. In which case, Malthus too is chargeable.

prudence, and instead of producing a greater proportion of population to food, the uniform tendency is to lessen this proportion. 'A greater *absolute* population always follows increased industry and comforts; but as certainly a smaller *relative* population, a smaller population in proportion to the increased comforts and necessaries of life' (pp. 538–539).

Increased comforts have always produced in any community permanently enjoying them increased prudence, and, although there is an absolute increase in numbers, such increased comforts prevent, in fact pre-suppose that there does not exist, a relative increase of numbers to food. And, since all these effects on population have been achieved without conscious instruction, but merely by the community finding itself in new circumstances, furnishing new motives for action, what effects can be expected under a more positive approach?

History confirms this view. In Ireland there are no comforts and conveniences, and yet amongst the most destitute there are no prudential habits. In the North of Ireland, where comforts and industry prevail, so also do habits of prudence in regard to marriage.

'Once in the habit of enjoying certain comforts of food, clothing, dwelling, furniture and other conveniences, they form a part of our scheme of life, they are associated with our very notions of existence. Any change that will increase them, we hail with pleasure; but reject any arrangement that would abridge them. . . . When to this is added, the force of public opinion, bestowing its unmerited sympathy on those who possess most, without regard to use or merit, can we wonder that the possession of increased comforts engenders habits of foresight and caution as to the risk of decreasing them by marriage, or in any other way? It is no enlarged view of benevolence that is here wanting, no prospect of the misery that may await children brought up without means of support. Nothing more is wanting than a selfish love of immediate comforts' (p. 540).

The Irish increase of population has been accompanied by misery; the increase in the United States by comparative happiness. 'In Ireland, deprived by insecurity of comforts, the increase has been *both absolute and relative*; absolute as compared with the preceding numbers, relative as compared with means of support. In America, on the contrary . . . the increase has been absolute merely, not relative' (p. 541). Wherever there is comfort, there the prudential check is in operation to preserve it. Wherever people are destitute and enslaved, 'the habit of yielding to motives immediately stimulant, chiefly those of force, render them incapable of calculation and quite indifferent as to the effects of breeding beyond these means' (p. 542).

This is borne out by comparing England and Ireland, where the ratio of increase during the preceding fifty years was fifty per cent. higher in the latter than in the former. It is true that wretchedness is widespread in England, but this is due to causes which not the most prudent could provide against or even foresee. Political power, excessive demands of capital, fraudulent and devastating changes in the currency, national debt, capricious changes in taxation. It is beyond the worker's ability to provide against such things, and 'these were the events, and not the pretended folly of overbreeding under increased comforts, that have been bringing down the English people to the situation of paupers, and that must keep all mankind in a state of want, vice, and misery, as long as they are permitted to exist' (p. 544). There is no truth of economy or morals more certain than that increased comforts engender prudence, and arrest rather than encourage an increase of population faster than the food supply.

Thompson then applies his reasoning to a co-operative community, which was the purpose for which he had raised the discussion. In such a state, the abundance of comforts would produce the same unwillingness to part with them, and such unwillingness would be better informed. True the inconveniences of a family would not press so heavily upon individuals, 'but a regard for the common welfare and common loss of comforts in which their own would be included, would soon become at least as powerful a curb, in such minds as those of the co-operators, as the simple individual motive produces in the minds of competitors' (p. 546).

Moreover there is birth control. 'Many married persons in such communities, under such circumstances, would doubtless study the means of enjoying in the highest degree, every pleasure of personal attachment, and even increasing those pleasures, without the necessity of a continual increase of births—an object, simple, reconcilable with the utmost delicacy, and demanding nothing but a mental effort from the party whom a new birth would most inconvenience' (p. 547).

Having then pointed out that there would be physical checks in a stationary population due to the shortage of accommodation, which might lead to something like marriage rotas, he again returns to the topic of birth control.

'There is a way, before alluded to, by which early marriages and universal healthiness, may co-exist with a stationary population. Sexual, intellectual, and moral pleasures would be much increased thereby to the married parties. A mental effort on the side of refinement, not of grossness, is all the price necessary to be paid, and by only one party, for early marriages and mutual endearments, where the circumstances of society permit no increase of population. If this expedient of *gentle exercise* be not adopted, the risk of the evil—at whatever it may be estimated—of illicit intercourse, must be incurred. . . . Were it possible that the pleasures of casual intercourse could be enjoyed without any risk to population, or any consequential evil to either of the parties, the morality of utility and benevolence, would look on such connexions with more than an indulgent eye' (pp. 549–550).

The Malthusian alternative is useless. Why should parents be punished by diminished comforts for having large families? It cannot prevent premature marriages, as parents will only calculate on having the average number of children. The sheer burden of having a constant succession of children is inconvenience enough to restrict the desire to moderate proportions without adding comparative poverty in the midst of general prosperity. If there is room for the increased numbers, why should those suffer whom chance (i.e. high fecundity) has made most instrumental in bringing this increase about? 'The parents, particularly the mother, should be assisted and relieved under such circumstances; their means should be increased, not diminished' (p. 553).

We leave Thompson passing to a discussion of the ethics of marriage, and pleading for an improved status for women. Sexual enjoyment, he laments, has become degraded into a matter of trade; and animal pleasure is all that is left to the male. Marriage is 'shorn of all its enchanting capabilities of sympathetic and intellectual association, which can only be enjoyed in the perfectly free intercourse of equals' (p. 556). The differing treatment of men and women as to adultery, the scandalous exclusion of women from property, and from civil and political rights, should be ended, as it would be in a co-operative society; and this would strengthen motives of prudence and restraint.

'Where women are brought up and treated like rational beings, and enjoy in all respects equal advantages with men, they will not, like ripe fruit or bales of cloth, be fought for; their opinion will be of some trifling weight in the disposal of their persons and happiness for life' (p. 558).

CHAPTER FIVE

MALTHUS: A SUMMARY VIEW

RESTATEMENT IN 1824

THE year 1824 is noteworthy for the fact that Malthus's article on 'Population' was published in the Supplement to the *Encyclopædia Britannica.*[1] This article gave Malthus an opportunity to restate his principles in the light of subsequent knowledge and the criticisms they had received. Freed from much of the lumber of the *Essay*, and re-arranged in a more logical form, they reveal a far more cautious Malthus. True, most of the old ingredients are there, but the qualifications are substantial. Many of the criticisms had found their mark; even the arguments of Booth command a little attention. Therefore, as the most mature statement of his views, it is worth considerable notice.[2]

Although, he admits, the potential rate of increase of foodstuffs such as wheat or sheep is very great, the actual rate of increase is slow, owing to the impossibility of man making the necessary preparation and improvement of the soil.

Man is not exempt from natural law, but he is distinguished from other animals by his power of increasing the means of subsistence. This power is obviously limited by the scarcity of land, the natural barrenness of much of it, and the decreasing fertility of land already under cultivation.

The great check to the increase of plants and animals is lack

[1] Bonar thinks it was probably written late in 1821 or in 1822 (*Malthus and His Work*, p. 79).

[2] The Article was reprinted with minor alterations under the title: *A Summary View of the Principle of Population*, in 1830. As being more accessible, quotations are taken from this reprint.

of room and nourishment, and where there is plenty of room and nourishment their increase is very great.

'On the same principle, we should expect to find the greatest actual increase of population in those situations where, from the abundance of good land, and the manner in which its produce is distributed,[1] the largest quantity of the necessaries of life is actually awarded to the mass of the society' (p. 6).

THE AMERICAN INCREASE

The one distinguishing feature relating to the growth of numbers in the United States appears to be the abundance of good land and a great demand for labour. The increase is not due to immigration. In fact, all accounts tend to show that the maximum amount of immigration is under ten thousand per annum. Booth's method, though useful and unobjectionable, is difficult to apply because the means are deficient. The annual mortality in the United States is not known, and even if it were known, the amount which would be lost in ten years by a population depends upon the rate at which it is growing. Milne provides a table based on the same law of mortality as operated in Sweden from 1801 to 1805.

'We see from this table, that, under the same law of mortality, the difference of loss sustained in ten years, by a people not increased by fresh births, would, in the three cases supposed of a stationary population, a population doubling in fifty years, and a population doubling in twenty-five years, be as 1 in 5·3692, 1 in 6·6786, and 1 in 7·9396; and that when thc population is doubling itself in twenty-five years, the loss would be little more than one-eighth' (p. 11).

The censuses form a *prima facie* evidence that the population of the United States has been doubling itself in periods of twenty-five years. This assumption is warranted until better evidence is produced on the other side. Applying Booth's rule, and deducting one-eighth for the loss during each ten-year period, the volume of immigration works out at 71,653 for the period 1800 to 1810, and 106,608 for the period 1810 to 1820. Hence 10,000 persons per annum appears to be an ample allowance for immigration (p.12).

[1] This modification now gets some of the attention it deserves.

Supporting evidence is given by another calculation made by Milne, the author of a book on *Annuities and Assurances.* Using the Swedish mortality figures, he calculates the age distribution of a hypothetical population which had been increasing in geometrical progression for more than a hundred years so as to double every twenty-five years. The result of these calculations (Table, p. 16) shows that the hypothetical population has a distribution by age groups very similar to the distribution actually found in the various American censuses.

There is an element of circularity about the conclusions.

(1) Since the censuses agree with the hypothesis, they are probably correct!

(2) The law of mortality assumed in the hypothesis cannot be much different from what obtains in the United States.

(3) Since the actual structure of the population differs very little from what it should have been by hypothesis, it cannot have been seriously disturbed by immigration (p. 16).

Even this rate of growth must be short of what is possible under the most favourable circumstances. The best proof of mankind's capacity to increase at a certain rate is the fact that it has done so. If an isolated instance were unsupported by other evidence, it might be due to error or accident, but this is far from being the case. The rate of increase in other countries, even under the substantial checks there operating, shows what might happen if the checks were removed. For instance, in England the period of doubling is approximately forty-eight years, in spite of the many who are engaged in unhealthy occupations and the lateness of a great proportion of the marriages. If these checks were removed, a doubling every twenty-five years would be quite feasible.

'It may be safely asserted, therefore, that population, when unchecked, increases in a geometrical progression of such a nature as to double itself every twenty-five years' (p. 25). This does not mean that it does this exactly in each period. Practically it would be sometimes slower and sometimes faster.

It must be owned that he has limped rather to this position, and there is an element of tenacity in the way he clings, rather unnecessarily, to the original period of twenty-five years, which is not fundamental to the main conclusions of the theory. But his defence of the arithmetical ratio is lameness itself.

THE GROWTH OF FOOD SUPPLIE

The question of the ratio of the increase of food i
but it is quite obvious that an increase of food in a
must proceed on a different principle. Obviously
land is in plentiful supply, the geometrical increas
outstrip that of man. But then all the serviceable lands would soon be taken up, and man would be driven either to the use of poorer land, or to the very gradual improvement of lands already taken up. In these circumstances there would be a greater resemblance to a decreasing geometrical ratio than an increasing one. The amount of increase of each successive ten years would probably be less than that of the preceding ten.

'Practically, however, great uncertainty must take place. An unfavourable distribution of produce, by prematurely diminishing the demand for labour, might retard the increase of food at an early period, in the same manner as if cultivation and population had been further advanced; while improvements in agriculture, accompanied by a greater demand for labour and produce, might for some time occasion a rapid increase of food and population at a later period, in the same manner as if cultivation and population had been at an earlier stage of their progress. These variations, however, obviously arise from causes which do not impeach the general *tendency* of a continued increase of produce in a limited territory to diminish the *power* of its increase in future.

'Under this certainty with regard to the general *tendency*, and uncertainty in reference to particular periods, it must be allowable, if it throws light on the subject, to make a supposition respecting the increase of food in a limited territory, which, without pretending to accuracy, is clearly more favourable to the power of the soil to produce the means of subsistence for an increasing population, than any experience which we have of its qualities will warrant' (p. 27).[1]

[1] Godwin rarely equalled this! What are these earlier and later periods? Presumably periods of the geometrical increase; but since no one knows exactly where we are in this respect, it is begging the whole question. Apparently at any time food can grow as fast or as slow as it likes; at least no prediction is possible. But this does not affect the 'general tendency' which on his own showing only arises when there is no more 'moderate land' or when diminishing returns have begun to operate. There is no reply

Hence we arrive at the arithmetical ratio which exceeds the most sanguine human expectations.

It is unquestionably true that many parts of the earth are thinly peopled and could produce food for a few periods at such a rate as would keep pace with an unrestricted increase of population, but to put this capacity into action is most difficult. The local people are unable to do it; immigration will involve war and extermination, and when combined with all the hardships involved will only be undertaken when home conditions are well-nigh intolerable. Even if it does occur, the new lands will soon be full and the position restored as before.

Consequently, whatever temporary or partial relief may be obtainable by emigration, considering the subject generally, 'the supposition of a future capacity in the soil to increase the necessaries of life every twenty-five years by a quantity equal to that which is at present produced, must be decidedly beyond the truth' (p. 30).

DISCUSSION OF THE CHECKS

There must be a powerful check at work restricting what would otherwise be the normal rate of growth. If the soil were evenly distributed the check would be obvious. No single farm could sustain a group increasing at the rate observed in the United States. But what is true of a single farm is true of the whole earth.

Improved methods and inventions will have some beneficial effect, but they are more potent in increasing conveniences and luxuries than in increasing food supplies; and though improved methods may lead to the cultivation of inferior lands, they can never supersede for any length of time the operation of the positive and preventive checks. If the workers cannot earn enough to maintain the largest families, there must be either delayed marriage, or else the diseases arising from malnutrition will be introduced and mortality will be increased.

here to Hazlitt's criticism. Malthus has to admit that his theory sheds no light whatever on anything that may happen in the short-run. In the long-run a growing population must be checked, if only by lack of standing room. In the short-run we have to look elsewhere than to Malthus for guidance. Yet, since we are not sure of anything, we might as well have a ratio, and the arithmetical ratio proved very serviceable in the past.

'According to all past experience, and the best observations which can be made on the motives which operate upon the human mind, there can be no well-founded hope of obtaining a large produce from the soil, but under a system of private property. It seems perfectly visionary to suppose that any stimulus short of that which is excited in man by the desire of providing for himself and family, and of bettering his condition in life, should operate on the mass of society with sufficient force and constancy to overcome the natural indolence of mankind' (p. 35).

All past attempts at communism have either been insignificant or have failed completely, nor does education seem to offer much hope for the future. Only a system of private property has any chance of providing for the large and increasing populations in the many countries at present.

But though the laws of private property are the grand stimulus to production, they nevertheless make the actual produce of the earth fall short of its ultimate capacity, because under such a system there can be no adequate motive for the extension of cultivation unless it can both pay a wage and leave a profit on the capital employed. This excludes from cultivation much land which might therefore bear crops, and such land under a system of common property might be cultivated so long as it would yield a single quarter. The price of such measures would be great distress and complete degradation.

'And, if a system of private property secures mankind from such evils, which it certainly does, in a great degree, by securing to a portion of the society the leisure necessary for the progress of the arts and sciences, it must be allowed that such a check to the increase of cultivation confers on society a most signal benefit' (p. 37).

Yet the price may be too high; the check may go too far, and this is particularly likely to happen when the original divisions of the land are very unequal. The only effective demand comes from the owners of property, but what they actually demand may not be the things most conducive to the progress of national wealth. There may be a premature check to cultivation, and a premature check to profits. But this is of little real consequence.

'It makes little difference in the actual rate of the increase of population, or the necessary existence of checks to it, whether that state of demand and supply which occasions an insufficiency of wages to the whole of the labouring classes, be produced prematurely by a bad structure of society, and an unfavourable distribution of wealth, or necessarily by the comparative exhaustion of the soil. The labourer feels the difficulty nearly in the same degree, and it must have nearly the same results, from whatever cause it arises' (p. 38).[1]

Whatever the cause of the labourer's poverty, it may safely be said that population is checked by the difficulty of procuring the means of subsistence. And since good wages are a rare occurrence, this pressure is not to be regarded as remote but, with few exceptions, is constantly acting.

It is true that in no country have the institutions been such as to call forth the full powers of the soil. This creates the delusion that a man can always produce from the soil more than sufficient to support himself and his family.

'In the actual state of things, this power has perhaps always been possessed. But for it we are indebted wholly to the ignorance and bad government of our ancestors' (p. 39). If this had not been so, population would have grown so rapidly that the pressure instead of being premature would have been occasioned entirely by the necessary state of the soil. If man had only directed his efforts from the first in an enlightened manner, our plight would have been even worse, and the condition of the working classes deteriorated (pp. 40–41).

Consequently the check arises from the laws of nature and not from the institutions of man. Nevertheless a great responsibility still rests on man. The population could be greatly increased if the institutions of society and moral habits of the people were more favourable to the increase of capital. Moreover, though man has little control over the amount of the checks, or their degree of severity, he has a great and extensive influence on their character and mode of operation. Progress lies, not in superseding the checks, but in modifying their operation and directing them.

In most of the more advanced countries of Europe the principal check is the prudential restraint on marriage, but the

[1] This is the dreary fatalism attacked by Ravenstone.

registers show vast differences. The source of increased population is the excess of births over deaths. The excess of births is due to three causes: the prolificness of marriages, the proportion of those born who live to marry, and the earliness of these marriages compared with the expectation of life. To achieve the full power of increase all these circumstances must be favourable, and they probably never have been. Even in the United States, although the first two operate powerfully, the distance between the average age of marriage and the average age of death is not so favourable as it might be. On the assumption of the same natural prolificness in the women of most countries, the smallness of the proportion of births will indicate with tolerable correctness the extent of the preventive check.

The absence of the preventive check is characterized by an increase in mortality or a shortening of the expectation of life. It is not a law of nature that half the human race should die before the age of puberty. This only occurs in certain situations where 'the constant admonitions which these laws give to mankind are obstinately neglected.'

The growth of population in accordance with the geometrical ratio is not inconsistent with a reasonable rate of mortality. Although the power of growth is immense, it may be restrained by a comparatively moderate force. The laws of nature, which make food necessary for the existence of man, prevent the existence of an increase which cannot be supported, and thus 'either discourage the production of such an excess, or destroy it in the bud, in such a way as to make it scarcely perceptible to a careless observer' (p. 68).

It is not useless to lay stress on tendencies which do not for any length of time make themselves felt by producing their natural effects. The rate of increase of mankind under the fewest known obstacles is a tendency which cannot safely be lost sight of.

THE POOR LAWS AND PRIVATE PROPERTY

The tendency of mankind to increase beyond the possibility of an adequate supply of food on a limited territory disposes of the natural right of the poor to full support. The question arises as to the necessity of the laws of private property. To assert the right of the strongest is to surrender the right of man to claim to be a rational being.[1] The laws of nature dictate the cultivation of the earth as a means of increasing supplies. Similarly, the laws of nature seem to have told man that any kind of rule is preferable to anarchy. 'The consequence of this universal and deeply seated feeling, inevitably produced by the laws of nature, as applied to reasonable beings, is, that the almost certain consequence of anarchy is despotism' (p. 72).

The right of property is positive law, but the law is so fundamental that, if it cannot be called natural law, it must be considered the most natural and necessary of the positive laws. Its obvious tendency is to promote good; its absence to degrade men to the condition of brutes. It follows that it may be modified with a view to the more complete attainment of the public good. But the concession of a right of full support to all who may be born is quite incompatible with the continuance of the right of property.

The extent to which relief can be given without defeating the law of property is a practical question which can only be determined by experience. It depends on the feelings and habits of the working classes. If the receipt of relief is held to be so discreditable that great efforts are made to avoid it, then it will be possible to give relief without increasing the number of paupers. But if the numbers of the poor are so numerous that the discredit of receiving relief is disregarded, the partial good done by the relief will be more than counterbalanced by the general deterioration of the mass of the poor. At all events, whatever steps are contemplated with respect to poor relief, the tendency of the labouring classes to increase faster than the means of their support is one which must be constantly borne in mind.

So runs the revised version. Moderate in language, reasonable in tone, lacking the picturesque and often misleading metaphors of the *Essay*, paying due attention to the criticisms with which it has been riddled, maintaining the same general viewpoint but with less dogmatism and a clearer grasp of limitations. Yet withall, it is still dominated by the ratios. Unlike many of his apologists, Malthus was aware of the strength of his ratios in captivating the reason of his readers. The first *Essay* created a stir; it made

[1] Curiously enough the adoption of some eugenic criterion never appears to enter his head.

his reputation. The older Malthus can afford to write in a more restrained tone, and admit more of the weaknesses in his 'impregnable fortress.'[1] But a book like the *Summary* would have been shelved if it had appeared in 1798. Nevertheless it is a pity he could not have shaken off to a greater extent the dominance of the ratios. He approaches the threshold of a great contribution, but dogma prevents his opening the door.

[1] Preface to second and subsequent editions.

CHAPTER SIX

NASSAU WILLIAM SENIOR

TWO LECTURES ON POPULATION

THE earlier critics of Malthus were a mixed bunch: doctors, writers, tory philanthropists, and social reformers. In 1828, however, we observe the entry of an opponent who can claim to be a genuine political economist—Nassau William Senior. The substance of his criticism was contained in two lectures delivered before the University of Oxford in 1828, supplemented by a correspondence with Malthus in March and April of 1829. There was some amplification and refinement in his *Outline of the Science of Political Economy*, 1836, but the earlier lectures and correspondence, published in 1831, form the real landmark.

Senior remarks that his first outline of the laws of population was: 'That the population of a given district is limited only by moral or physical evil, or by deficiency in the means of obtaining those articles of wealth; or, in other words, those necessaries, decencies, and luxuries, which the habits of the individuals of each class of the inhabitants of that district lead them to require' (p. 2).

Subsequent reflection suggests the substitution of the words 'apprehension of a deficiency' for the word 'deficiency,' because 'it is not the existence of a deficiency, but the *fear* of its existence which is the principal check to population, so far as necessaries are concerned, and the sole check as respects decencies and luxuries' (p. 2).

Necessaries are those things essential to health and strength; *decencies* are needed to maintain social rank; *luxuries* comprise all those things outside these two categories. None of these terms is fixed and invariable; they depend upon the place, the time, and the rank of the person in question. The class of necessaries fluctuates least, being dependent upon climatic and physical requirements; conveniences and luxuries are constantly varying.

All plants and animals are capable of increase in geometrical ratio, and observation suggests that the period of doubling of the human race in temperate climates may be twenty-five years. This would lead to phenomenal growth unless there were some checks; these checks are classed by Malthus as positive and preventive.

The positive check is physical evil and comprises all causes tending to cause premature death. Some of these causes are natural and some moral, but all result in physical evil; and the final and irresistible check is death from hardship or starvation, which is in fact almost the only check amongst animals or the lower groups of man. In civilized societies famine is replaced by substitute checks which produce the same effects by imperceptible degrees.

Since each doubling of the population provides the means of a further doubling, while each doubling in food production (owing to the operation of the law of diminishing returns) makes a further doubling more difficult, the process must end somewhere, and if all the moral and physical checks were removed, the ultimate result would be universal famine. But this state of affairs never has existed, and never will exist. A society wise enough to abolish moral and physical evil will not lack either the wisdom to foresee such a catastrophe or the prudence to avert it: the preventive check would be in full operation (p. 14).[1]

Famine is the outcome of dependence on that type of subsistence which is most abundant. It results from the lack of variety of wants; and mere seasonal variations in the staple crops must produce want or even calamity. In civilized societies, where there are many varieties of produce, temporary scarcities are met by the reduction of luxury, by recourse to cheaper foods, and by importation from other countries (p. 17).

The rate of increase of a population depends upon two factors—the death rate and the birth rate. Neither taken alone is sufficient basis for a forecast. Nevertheless the death rate is a less deceitful

[1] References taken from *Two Lectures on Population delivered before the University of Oxford in Easter Term,* 1828. N. W. Senior, 1831.

test of prosperity than the birth rate, and 'the extraordinary duration of life in England, exceeding, as it does, the average of any other equally extensive district, is a convincing proof of the general excellence of our climate, our institutions, and our habits' (p. 22).

Of the preventive checks, the chief is abstinence from marriage. This is 'almost uniformly founded on the apprehension of a deficiency of necessaries, decencies, or luxuries, or, in other words, on prudence' (p. 25). Englishmen seldom fear want; they have the fence of the poor laws. They do, however, fear loss of rank; they desire their children to enjoy the same advantages which they themselves have enjoyed, and it is this fear of losing the decencies of life (or in many cases the prospect of acquiring them by abstinence) which is the greatest check to early marriage. Men delay marriage from fear of sinking or in the hope of rising: often they delay too long and lose the opportunity.

From this standpoint, therefore, luxury is not detrimental to society. If each individual confined his attention to the acquisition of necessities alone, the result would be intense misery. If the whole population devoted itself to agriculture, England might feed 100,000,000 people, but it would have no reserves. A succession of bad harvests would mean the rigours of famine, whereas, when a nation indulges in the production of luxuries, bad seasons are counteracted by such measures as the diversion of grain used for brewing or animal fodder to human consumption, or the importation from abroad of necessaries, of corn instead of wine (p. 33).

A high standard of living is the only protection against recurrent hardship, consequently it is only as nations advance in wealth that the positive check is likely to be replaced by the preventive check. As wealth increases, the luxuries of one generation become the decencies of the next.

'Not only a taste for additional comfort and convenience, but a feeling of degradation in their absence becomes more and more widely diffused. The increase, in many respects, of the productive powers of labour, must enable increased comforts to be enjoyed by increased numbers, and as it is the more beneficial, so it appears to me to be the more natural course of events, that increased comfort should not only accompany, but rather precede, increase of numbers' (p. 35).

These are not the received opinions, which are that population has a tendency to struggle past the means of subsistence, and is held back principally by vice and misery. Population may have the power (considered abstractedly) but under wise institutions that is not its *tendency*: the tendency is just the reverse.

Malthus, M'Culloch, and Mill all assert that population has a natural tendency to outrun the means of subsistence, production, or capital. The real issue is the question of subsistence, and its rate of growth relative to that of population. If the present state of the world, compared with earlier ages, be one of relative poverty, their reasoning is unanswerable, but if its means of subsistence have increased more than proportionately to the inhabitants, their reasoning is false. Savage tribes present a picture of habitual poverty and occasional famine: 'a scanty population, but still scantier means of subsistence.' It is admitted that the masses of the people even in modern societies are poor and miserable, but so they always have been. The question is—are they as poor and miserable as they were?

'If a single country can be found in which there is now less poverty than is universal in a savage state, it must be true, that under the circumstances in which that country has been placed, the means of subsistence have a greater tendency[1] to increase than the population' (p. 48). 'If it be conceded, that there exists in the human race a natural tendency to rise from barbarism to civilization, and that the means of subsistence are proportionately more abundant in a civilized than in a savage state,

[1] In the *Outline of the Science of Political Economy*, 1836, Senior quotes Whately's interesting comments on the ambiguity of the word 'tendency' (p. 47).

'By a "tendency" towards a certain result is sometimes meant, the existence of a cause which operating unimpeded, would produce that result. . . . But sometimes, again, "a tendency towards a certain result" is understood to mean "the existence of such a state of things that that result may be expected to take place."' Population has a tendency of the first kind, but not of the second, to outstrip subsistence . . . 'and (as may be proved by comparing a more barbarous with a more civilized period in the history of any country) in the progress of Society, subsistence has a tendency to increase at a greater rate than population. In this country, for instance, much as our population has increased within the last five centuries, it yet bears a far less ratio to subsistence (though still a much greater than could be wished) than it did five hundred years ago.' Whately, *Introductory Lectures on Political Economy, Lec. IX.*

and neither of these propositions can be denied, it must follow that there is a natural tendency in subsistence to increase in a greater ratio than population' (p. 49).

Therefore those causes which tend to elevate a people, tend to make numbers increase more slowly than subsistence; those which tend to degrade, make for over-population. A population increasing more rapidly than its food supplies is usually a symptom of misgovernment, and this growth is only one of the results.

A LETTER TO MALTHUS

On March 15th, 1829 Senior opened a correspondence with Malthus in order to elucidate certain aspects of their respective beliefs and attempt to bring about a reconciliation. In effect he was inviting the older man to change his mind.

He states that he has been misled into a misunderstanding of Malthus's views, principally by the conduct of the writers who have followed Malthus and have assumed that he believed the desire for marriage to be a stronger force than the desire to better one's condition.[1] In view of the importance of the subject, he endeavours to state what he believes to be Malthus's real views.

'In an old country, under wise institutions, in the absence, in short, of disturbing causes, though population is likely to increase, subsistence is likely to increase still faster. In short, that the condition of a people so circumstanced is more likely to be improved than to be deteriorated. If I am right in this view,[2] the only difference between us is one of nomenclature. You would still say, that in the absence of disturbing causes, population has a *tendency* to increase faster than food, because the comparative increase of the former is a mere compliance with our natural wishes, the comparative increase of the latter is all effort and self-denial. I should still say, that, in the absence of disturbing causes, food has a tendency to increase faster than population,

[1] It is not possible to agree with Bonar's view (*Malthus and His Work*, pp. 3–4) that Senior had been really misled. The correspondence shows clearly that he was politely trying to restate what was sound in the doctrine, in an attempt to get Malthus to endorse the restatement. In spite of Senior's best efforts the gulf was not bridged, and the so-called agreement was a 'fiction.'

[2] Malthus refuses to accept this restatement. There was no real misunderstanding, but a difference of opinion.

because, in fact, it has generally done so, and because I consider the desire of bettering our condition as natural a wish as the desire of marriage' (p. 58).[1]

In his reply, March 23rd, 1829, Malthus takes up the challenge on the word 'tendency.'

'The meaning which I intended to convey by the expression to which you object was, that population was always ready, and inclined, to increase faster than food, if the checks which repressed it were removed; and that though these checks might be such, as to prevent population from advancing upon subsistence, or even to keep it at a greater distance behind; yet, that whether population were *actually* increasing faster than food, or food faster than population, it was true that, except in new colonies, favourably circumstanced, population was always pressing against food, and was always ready to start off at a faster rate than that at which the food was actually increasing' (p. 61).

To such lengths do the ratios commit him! Whether the condition of man be improving or getting worse, we are still compelled to say that it is tending to get worse. This Malthus still regards as being the most natural use of the term.

With regard to Senior's reasons for adopting the opposite view, namely that population has generally increased slower than the food supplies, he challenges the generality of this statement. As to the second reason, that the desire for bettering our condition is as natural as the desire for marriage, this is feeble, because 'the most intense desire of bettering our condition, can do nothing towards making food permanently[2] increase, at the rate at which population is always ready to increase' (p. 63). In any case, the mere desire of the labouring classes to improve their condition can do nothing to increase food supplies, since they do not accumulate farming capital or bring about improvements. They are passive as to food production and active in providing consumers. There is a much less tendency to restraint than to marriage, and although it may differ at different periods,

[1] Cf. Hazlitt, *Reply*, 1807, p. 111: 'a disproportionate superiority in certain motives over others.' Senior has drawn largely on earlier critics, but such matter as he uses he has arranged in more telling form.

[2] Once again, when hard pressed by a short-run argument, he slips in the word 'permanently' and all is well. His mind is dominated by the geometrical ratio, upon which he relies whenever the argument runs against him.

and prevail more in civilized than in uncivilized countries, and although we may hope that restraint will improve as knowledge advances, 'yet as far as we can judge from history, there never has been a period of any considerable length, when premature mortality and vice, specifically arising from the pressure of population against food, has not prevailed to a considerable extent; nor, admitting the possibility, or even the probability of these evils being diminished, is there any rational prospect of a near approach to their entire removal' (pp. 64–65).

This is sheer evasion of the point at issue. The question is—not whether there is pressure, that is admitted, but—Is it getting less? If it is then, using the word 'tendency' to signify what is likely to happen, Senior is quite justified in saying that food tends to increase faster than population.

After pointing out that increases in population are fitful and depend on the rate at which food happens to be increasing at the moment, Malthus asserts that the hope for the future lies not in exertions to increase food, but in moral restraint (p. 71). Consequently, Senior's mode of stating the issue is harmful, as directing attention to the wrong aspect of the situation.

'The main part of the question with me, relates to the cause of the continued poverty and misery of the labouring classes of society in all old states. This surely cannot be attributed to the tendency of food to increase faster than population. It may be to the tendency of population to increase faster than food' (p. 72).

But this ignores completely the real question, whether this poverty and misery is greater or less than it was formerly.

FURTHER CORRESPONDENCE

Senior replied promptly on March 26th. The difference between them is greater than he had imagined. He had not intended to convey the impression that he believed that upward progress had been a uniform upward movement, but taking any country at periods of two or three hundred years distance, the ratio of food to population showed in most cases a definite improvement. Progress was rather like that of the snail in the puzzle which climbed up four feet and then fell back three. Nevertheless, if there had not been progress we should still have been ill-fed savages.

'I fully admit, that in all old countries, perhaps in all countries whatever, population is always pressing against food; and that the pressure not only prevents the increase which would take place, if it could be removed, but occasions premature mortality. But as society advances in what appears to me to be our *natural* course, for it is the course for which nature has fitted us, this pressure generally, though not universally diminishes. The proportion of those who now die in England from want, is probably less than it was two hundred years ago; it certainly is less than it was six hundred years ago. I still think myself, therefore, justified in saying, that there is a tendency in the pressure to diminish' (p. 76).

It may be true that, strictly speaking, man has no natural tendency to produce food or to better his condition, but to consume food and to have his condition bettered, but he is a rational animal relating means to ends, and he pursues ends requiring the existence of forethought as well as those dictated by passion. In this sense people desire to increase their subsistence (for that is the meaning of a tendency of subsistence to increase) more strongly than they desire to increase their numbers.

The most important question, however, is the effect of the two modes of expression on the reader's mind. While mischievous conclusions might be drawn from the statement that the increase of food can outstrip the increase of population, 'inferences as false and as dangerous may be drawn, and in fact have been drawn, from the proposition that population has a tendency to increase faster than food' (p. 78). This is taken by many readers to be a proposition without qualification. They believe that the expansive power of population is a source of unmitigated evil, incapable of being subdued. 'They consider man not as he is, but as he would be if he had neither forethought nor amibition; neither the wish to rise, nor the fear to sink, in society' (p. 79). The spread of these views, often sincerely held, leads to despondency, and furnishes an easy escape from the effort and expense of reform. What is the use of emigration or the abolition of the corn laws, population would immediately grow and we should be as ill off as before?

'Undoubtedly these opinions are not fair inferences from your work; they are, indeed, directly opposed to the spirit of the greater part of it; but I think they must be considered as having been occasioned by a misconception of your reasonings.[1] They are prevalent now: before the appearance of your writings, they were never hinted at. I trust, however, that, unsupported as they are by your authority, they will gradually wear away; and I anticipate from their disappearance not merely the extinguishment of an error, but the removal of an obstacle to the diffusion of political knowledge' (pp. 81–82).

On March 31st Malthus replied. He is evidently tired of the correspondence, but he defends his adherents. They may have been a little incautious in their statements but they are essentially correct. Any improvements in food supply will soon be swallowed up by increased numbers. The only real hope is in an increase of the moral checks which do not *necessarily* follow increased facility of obtaining food.

This does not mean that we should not improve cultivation. An increased population is worth while if there is no increase of vice and misery. The period during which the pressure is lightened, though not long, is advantageous. Nevertheless attention should be directed not to this temporary improvement, but to the only permanent source of gain, namely moral improvement.

On April 9th Senior decided to close down the correspondence with a pretence of agreement. The source of improvement is an increased proportion of food to population. This can be brought about by promoting production or by preventing a corresponding multiplication of consumers.

The old doctrine was that numbers were good in themselves, irrespective of the food supply. Malthus's doctrine effected a complete revulsion in opinion. But the revulsion has gone too far. Because additional numbers *may* bring poverty, it has been assumed that they *will*. Because increased subsistence *may* be followed and wiped out by increased numbers, it has been assumed that this *will* happen. The different points of view are thus easily explained, by the state of opinion at the time of writing. Malthus found the principle of population disregarded,

[1] The tone of the whole correspondence is that of a polite invitation to disown the reactionary tendencies which were deduced from his writings. Malthus did not disown them. They were fair deductions and he knew it, and so did Senior. The correspondence at least showed both men, as well as their readers, where they stood.

and rightly stressed the need for some control of numbers. Senior found the principle 'the stalking-horse of negligence and injustice, the favourite objection to every project for rendering the resources of the country more productive' (p. 89).

Attention should be directed both to increasing production and preventing population from advancing proportionately. The former is the province of the higher orders; the latter depends mainly on the lower, and is on the whole the more efficient. But in the present state of public opinion, and commercial and fiscal policy, more good is to be done by insisting on the former. 'The economist who neglects either, considers only a portion of his subject' (p. 90).

The Malthusian influence had begun to wane.

CHAPTER SEVEN

MICHAEL THOMAS SADLER

ATTACK ON THE RATIOS

IN 1830 Sadler produced his *Law of Population.* It is contained in two large volumes, the promised third never having been written. It is a striking work containing an elaborate statistical investigation, much violent denunciation, and a scathing criticism of the doctrines of Malthus. It also enunciates Sadler's Law.

'It is the purpose of the new school to treat and regard men as animated machines, and indeed to supplant them by inanimate ones were it possible; to pronounce them as worthless or otherwise, just as it may please the capitalists' (p. 10).

But men are equally producers and consumers, and under proper regulations equally necessary to each other. The growth of mankind in Europe has been accompanied by more than a corresponding increase in the means of subsistence; where numbers have diminished, conditions have deteriorated, not as the Malthusian theory asserts, improved.

It is a singular fact that apprehensions concerning the growth of population have always been strongest when inhabitants have been, comparatively speaking, fewest. 'The aboriginal American, with less than a square mile of the foodful earth to his individual share, exclaims, we are told, "It is time for our young men to go to war, or we shall starve"' (Vol. I, p. 41). The South Sea Islander adds cannibalism to infanticide, and Townsend, to whom the merit of discovering the theory really belongs, imbibed it in one of the worst countries—Spain.

The geometrical increase is an unsubstantiated hypothesis. Such an increase would fling nature into chaos; it is what an ant might have deduced of the growth of a tree if it had observed its progress in the early stages. Human increase does not proceed in geometrical ratio, but is regulated by an entirely different principle. As for the arithmetical ratio, it has no basis at all.

There is still plenty of room; animals are more prolific than men, and their natural increase, if unchecked, is greater than man's. True the immense fertility of nature is only an abstract idea, but so is that of man. They should both be treated on the same footing, either practically or theoretically. Actually the regulation of the means of sustentation depends on the number, intelligence, and industry of the human species, and the necessity and demand for such means. As society advances, the division of labour and enlarging knowledge produce an improvement in conditions.

The ratios, if they do develop a law of nature, ought to be applicable throughout time, but they obviously do not hold at the commencement of society. The relationship between numbers and food may be disturbed, but such fluctuations are more severely felt in earlier than in later periods of society, and privation is least felt in the most populous times. Combined effort produces results far in excess of individual and disconnected efforts, and past experience suggests that we might within two centuries sustain thrice our present numbers.

Malthus's notion of diminishing returns is based on 'the presumed incurable sterility of the soil now uncultured' (Vol. I, p. 94). This is a fallacy. Fertility is largely a product of industry, and infertile land, by calling forth greater efforts, is often made to produce more not less. The produce of the earth grows in proportion as man multiplies. Apart from the action of manure, fertility depends more on exposure and pulverization than on all other circumstances combined. Talk of diminishing returns should be set against the cries of overproduction of the late 'teens. Life is of all things the most important, and the provision is abundant because human increase will cease before the increase of subsistence.

There is a connection between population and food, but which, as a general rule, precedes? Man must work to live, and human wants are a spur to human exertions. A child's first food is prepared by nature, and before it makes any serious demands on external produce, two harvests have passed on an average—

ample time to arrange for an increase of subsistence. Obstacles to the acquisition of food encourage ingenuity and resourcefulness; horticulture is added to agriculture, and recourse is had to more intensive methods.

The foundation of the social system is necessity. On commercial and manufacturing principles, no more food will be produced than is wanted, but when wanted it will be forthcoming. The most densely peopled nations are the most prosperous, the thinly peopled are miserable, and as their numbers decrease their wretchedness is augmented.

DISCUSSION OF THE CHECKS

It is true that checks to population exist, but they are not called into being by lack of food, and they aggravate the situation instead of remedying it. War is not a struggle for room and food, it is the outcome of ambition, jealousy, hatred, revenge, rapacity, tyranny, covetousness, and the like. It diminishes the natural plenty man would otherwise have enjoyed. If there have been struggles for food, it is to obtain by violence what nature would have provided more abundantly to peaceful industry. The same extent of ground, which now supplies a million men, would not sustain a hundred thousand lazy warriors.

Infanticide is not resorted to as a remedy for excessive population, and far from being best calculated to balance the human species with its food, it is best calculated to keep it in savage barbarism and wretchedness. Where infanticide has prevailed, it has been among the wealthy rather than among the suffering poor. Dearth and famine are peculiar to scanty populations, and, like the other checks, are usually misplaced. Where room is abundant they are active, where men are plentiful they operate languidly.

The checks have decreased in intensity as mankind has advanced. Wars have become less fatal and less frequent. The influence of Christianity has changed the character of war, purged it of much of its barbarity, and abated its carnage. The use of gunpowder has made it a business of tactics rather than slaughter. Epidemics are less frequent and less fatal; many old scourges have disappeared. Vaccination has extirpated smallpox, and, although according to the Malthusian theory there should have been a corresponding increase in mortality from some other cause, actually mortality has declined. However, the theory still has a loophole—agriculture has made a sudden start![1]

As for the preventive check—all-important as it is, it was an afterthought. Malthus says he doubts its importance if not its existence. The distinction drawn between moral restraint and the prudential check is purely academic. Physically speaking, mankind may remain chaste without marriage; morally speaking, it is impossible, and it is idle to assert otherwise, as Malthus himself admits. The check is adduced to remove a slur on the goodness of the deity. 'But how these imputations, which he seems conscious the theory naturally generates, and which it most certainly does, whether it be acknowledged or not, should be removed, by allowing ourselves to hope what we do not believe, appears inexplicable' (Vol. I, pp. 318–319).

Purity is consistent with celibacy if the motive is strong, but interfering with marriage would produce the most mischievous results. It would produce universal profligacy and the corruption of manners To say that the check only delays marriage is to say nothing, for, if the youthful period can be passed in celibacy, no apprehension need generally be entertained about the remainder of a man's life. The preventive check is necessarily connected with vice. It is unnatural, unlawful, and wicked, and against true morality, which knows nothing of the balancing of vices.[2]

The happiness of poverty is based on a few simple enjoyments found almost exclusively in the domestic scene. The preventive check, if applied at all, ought to be applied to those who have other resources, yet those who lay no restraints on themselves, who would impose on the youthful poor a check which is irreconcilable with happiness or morality propose for the higher ranks no check, except to rectify the precedency of old maids and young wives.[3]

Malthus would exclude the poor from nature's feast, but elsewhere he apologizes for the dogs. As for the proposed poor law reform: What is meant by marrying with a fair prospect? Not one marriage in ten could make out a fair prospect under all

[1] Cf. Malthus, 1806 edn., Vol. II, p. 367.
[2] Cf. Malthus, 1806 edn., Vol. II, p. 351.
[3] *Essay*, 1803 edn., pp. 551–552. See *post*, p. 317n.

circumstances to the satisfaction of an anti-populationist. And even if a man had a fair prospect, he will fare no better if he falls on hard times. Private benevolence, under the pupilage of such a system, would be worse than useless.

'A system which only prescribes to the rich that they should reform their drawing-room etiquette, but which demands, as it regards the poor, the surrender of their natural, moral, and legal right to sustentation in their distresses, is, in the highest degree, partial and unjust' (Vol. I, p. 357).

It takes no account of the condition of the poor, for whom celibacy is a disaster. A man would have to retire to his hut after work to prepare his own meal; if smitten with disease there would be none to nurse him. His wife is his solace, assistant, companion, nurse, even his servant. The system is also impolitic. A female who delays marriage will have lost her bloom, and may have outlived her affection. It would disturb the natural order of successive generations and their ages. There would be older parents, immature offspring, a real danger of more orphans, who under the new system would be deprived of the right of support.

Moreover, the theory of the preventive check is applied in a most inconsistent manner. When the doctrine is to be upheld, the English people are held to be responsive to it. When the poor laws are to be attacked, they are held to be regardless of it. Actually the people do marry, and they marry early.

THE AMERICAN INCREASE

Turning to the American increase in Book II, he submits it to an extensive statistical examination. The figures do not show the required geometrical increase. America has become the colony of all Europe and there are few American writers who can reckon two pure American descents, yet they pronounce the increase independent of immigration.

The American censuses show a majority of males, whereas from a very early age females outnumber males. This discrepancy is not due to a less favourable mortality among females in the United States, but is due to immigration. The majority of emigrants are young men in the prime of life, some are married couples, some young children, and a few single women.

THE AMERICAN INCREASE

The total population in 1775 was 1,700,000. The number over forty-five in the census of 1820 was 957,853. Could that number possibly have survived from the numbers of 1775? Using Milne's table, the survivors would have been 466,656. The difference 491,197 gives the number of immigrants of forty-five and upwards in 1820. Furthermore the preponderance of young people in the census is also evidence of emigration. Milne asserts that the figures agree with a geometrical increase; they also accord with the fact that immigrants are usually young people and therefore the proportion of the old would tend to be smaller.

Examination of the Bills of Mortality shows an abnormally high mortality amongst men in the prime of life which can only be explained if this group is swollen by recruits from foreign sources (Vol. I, p. 548).

Malthus only begins to admit the volume of immigration when it is supposed to be no longer of any consequence, and he underestimates the importance of immigrants as a source of increase. As a class they increase much more quickly than an equal number of individuals taken from a normal population. It is a mistake to assume that if the immigrants are males they add less to the population than the other sex. It is true that the basis of increase is the number of child-bearing women, but since this number in a normal population is greater than the number of men, an increase of males of marriageable age will have a disproportionate effect in increasing the population. Dr. Price calculated that the prolific part of the community might be taken at a quarter of the whole. Consequently married immigrants have twice, and unmarried males four times the normal effect in augmenting numbers. It is fantastic to assume that the effects of immigration can be neglected. Of 10,000 immigrants no calculation will produce less than 5,000 in the marriageable class. The annual marriages, therefore, in the United States, which are about 20,000, will be reinforced by a quarter. It is not the increase of population in the United States that is denied: it is the source that is in question.

THE LAW OF POPULATION

Finally, in Book IV, we come to Sadler's effort to establish his own *Law of Population*. Not that his failure to do this will impair the earlier criticism of the Malthusian doctrine (Vol. II, p. 308).

It is a striking fact that man is one of the most sterile beings in creation, and slight as the increase of mankind is under the most favourable circumstances, it is subject to strict regulation. Causes, apparently unconnected, produce remarkably consistent statistical results.

Marriage is quite distinct from affection and love: it is an institution not of religion but of nature. It ensures the rearing of the young, and without it the sexual propensity would contribute little to the propagation of the species. Inequality of the sexes would be fatal to its preservation, and nature does preserve this equality in a wonderful way.

There is a near, but not an actual, equality of the sexes at birth, but this slight inequality strengthens rather than weakens the argument. In England, from 1800 to 1820, the proportion of births was twenty-five males to twenty-four females, but this does not doom certain males to celibacy. In every stage of existence the death rate of males is greater than that of females, and at about the age of puberty the sexes are balanced. Thereafter the females become a majority, but here again the surplus females are not doomed to spinsterhood. The male has a longer period of fruitfulness and, when marriages are dissolved by the death of either party, more males than females contract a second marriage. Thus does Providence govern the proportion of the sexes by certain and beneficial, if mysterious laws. Moreover, even the proportion of the sexes born is influenced by the difference in the ages between persons who marry, so that the sex of the older parents predominates among the children, thus helping to preserve the equality of sexes at the normal age of marriage. This he endeavours to prove from various statistics, including a Table of the Peerage (Vol. II, p. 341).

There is little need to fear too rapid multiplication. The period of prolificness is barely half the duration of life in a female. Suckling further curtails the period when pregnancy is likely, and although earlier commencement of child-bearing would speed up the generations, the length of term of the female is proportionately abbreviated.

Sadler then enunciates his law of population. THE PROLIFICNESS OF HUMAN BEINGS, OTHERWISE SIMILARLY CIRCUMSTANCED, VARIES INVERSELY AS THEIR NUMBERS. Prolificness will be greatest where numbers on an equal space are fewest, and smallest where such numbers are largest. It is necessary to modify this law with reference to the quality of space occupied, and to consider space with reference to the means of subsistence. Both this theory and Malthus's have an equal tendency to people the world when the ranks are thin, but under Sadler's Law there is no tendency to promote excess which would cause suffering.

In support of this principle he adduces a large volume of statistics, tabulated to show all its ramifications. He studies the comparative prolificness of marriages, in different countries, similarly placed except in regard to population; in different districts of the same country; in towns; in the same countries and districts at different dates; and in places where population has diminished. He draws analogies from the vegetable kingdom, and from animals.

Sadler's book provoked two essays by Macaulay in the *Edinburgh Review*. The first appeared in July, 1830, and led to a refutation by Sadler, published by Murray in the same year.[1] The rejoinder by Macaulay was equally prompt and appeared in the *Edinburgh Review* of January 1831.[2] Space forbids our following this interlude of derision. It is interesting enough in its way, though Sadler is as verbose as ever, but it would carry us too far from our present survey.

[1] *A Refutation of an Article in the 'Edinburgh Review' (No. CII), etc.*, Michael Thomas Sadler, M.P.

[2] Reference might also be made to *Observations on the Law of Population being an Attempt to Trace its Effects from the Conflicting Theories of Malthus and Sadler*, by the Author of 'Reflections on the Present State of British India.' London, 1832.

CHAPTER EIGHT

THOMAS ROWE EDMONDS AND W. F. LLOYD

THE VIEWS OF EDMONDS

Two more works remain for consideration before we draw our chronological survey of the critics to a close. The first, *An Enquiry into the Principles of Population Exhibiting a System of Regulations for the Poor; designed immediately to lessen, and finally to remove, the evils which have hitherto pressed upon The Labouring Classes of Society*, though published anonymously, is generally attributed to Thomas Rowe Edmonds. As a criticism it is not outstanding, although the practical proposals put forward are very comprehensive.

Progress in social science (he writes) is slow and precarious, and there is a dangerous tendency to frame premature generalizations. The correct procedure is to accumulate facts, formulate tentative hypotheses as a stimulus to further research, and only subsequently to establish general laws. Time will elucidate many apparently insoluble problems.

Abundant food is the result of knowledge, security of property, industry, and good government; while scarcity, poverty, and misery are due to the absence of these causes, As civilization advances, the tendency for food to increase faster than population becomes conspicuous. Food has no tendency to produce its own market, and, like any other commodity, will not be produced in excess of the demand. If it were more durable we should see gluts of food, as we do of other products.

It is admitted that the present population is redundant, and this is due to the growth of capital and the division of labour. Inequalities have become steadily more marked, all the land is appropriated, and the social system has developed on the lines of two distinct classes—master and servant. A labourer is thus completely dependent on his ability to find an employer. It follows, therefore, that prosperity depends upon the number of the middle class—the potential employers; and since this class is generally more prudent concerning the size of its families than is that of the labourers, there has developed a relative shortage in the numbers of the middle class. The trouble is lack of entrepreneurs, not lack of capital.

It is no good taking a parochial view for, where there is world competition, corn will follow the highest prices, and, owing to this increase in competition, less labour is now devoted to corn production than formerly. 'It is not only in England but in all other parts that the produce of the soil has been increased by diminished labour, in consequence of improvements in cultivation. . . . The result has been to reduce the price of corn in its real, as well as in its money price, throughout the world, and this probably will continue to operate for the next century' (pp. 46–47).

The idea of a fixed wages fund is a fallacy: the fund rises or falls according to circumstances. Production could be increased with the same equipment, given greater energy and extended credit. The distress of the labourers is due, partly to the introduction of machinery, partly to great fluctuations in wages, but principally to the relative disproportion between employers and employed. This can only be met by teaching the labourers the same habits of restraint in marriage as obtain among the middle classes, by enabling them 'to shape out work for themselves,' or by promoting the best workers to the status of master producers.

Malthus's theory of a population doubling in twenty-five years has overwhelmed his readers by suggesting that nothing can cope with the flood of people, and that danger is imminent. Its application to England has unduly restricted our ideas as to the possible expansion of food supplies. If the doubling takes as long as eighty years, and if we regard the whole world as being open to cultivation, the overtaking of subsistence by population recedes into the future. It is true that this reasoning only postpones the evil; it does not attack the main principle, but it abates the immediate alarm, and allows the taking of a cooler view of the situation (p. 59).

There appear to be no bounds to the advance of science. Already we have the rotation of crops and the transformations of chemistry, therefore why should we assume that the field of man's operations is limited? Since by decomposition renovation succeeds decay,[1] we are not justified in saying that the materials for vegetable organization cannot keep pace with the materials for animal creation. The decay of the animal world nourishes plants, and 'the operation of this harmonious action and reaction is inexhaustible' (p. 63). There may possibly in the future be more than one crop a year from the same land. If this sounds fantastic it is in fact no more so than Malthus's idea of an earth fully cultivated by normal methods. Meanwhile the Malthusian law can still be held under discussion during the period that it is inoperative.

Thinly peopled regions are held down by positive checks, but with the advance of civilization these evils diminish. The preventive check, peculiar to man alone of all animals, arises from reason, which is his distinguishing feature. 'Didactic admonitions' are likely to have little effect amongst the lower classes. They feel marriage to be virtuous, and will not regard its consequences as an evil in the way Malthus suggests. Thus, the only way to restrict their numbers is to make them imitate the middle classes, whose actions are dictated as much by selfish as by moral motives. 'A strong propensity and governing motive of conduct can only be controlled by opposing to it another still stronger' (p. 78). Subsistence does not enter into the calculations of the upper classes: the motive is either the desire for comforts or the fear of their loss. Among the workers, clerks marry late because they say they cannot afford it, although many workers who earn less marry early. The reason is that clerks must keep up appearances; they are restrained by the habits and customs of society. The lower birth rate in towns generally, arises from the same cause—namely a higher standard of living. Hence, paradoxical though it may sound, the real cure for a redundant population is to improve the standards of the working classes (p. 86).

The rate of increase of population is no criterion of improvement. The real tests are increased longevity and the reduction of child mortality. In England the death rate has steadily decreased. 'From 1700 to 1780 it has varied from one death in

[1] Cf. Ravenstone, op. cit., p. 119.

thirty-one to one death in forty-two. In 1790 it was one in forty-five, and according to the statement prefixed by Mr. Rickman to the last population returns, the average of 1796 to 1800 was forty-eight, 1806 to 1810, fifty-one; 1816 to 1820 fifty-seven, 1826 to 1830 it had declined to fifty-four' (p. 89). The aims of statesmen ought therefore to be: reduction of infant mortality, increased expectation of life, physical development of the people, and extension of moral progress.

There are three classes of poor people: those unable to work; those able to work but defective in character; those unwillingly unemployed. There is general agreement that the first should be supported, and the second have no moral right to support. The third class present the problem.

'So long as a man is willing and ready to offer his services, and to say, I am desirous to work, and to perform to the utmost of my ability, the other branches of the community are called upon to support him. He offers in exchange the only thing he can give, his labour; and the state, having established artificial regulations for the purpose of supporting the gradations of rank, should grant in exchange a fair equivalent for that labour, not probably equal to what it would produce if left to its own accord in an ordinary state of commerce, but certainly sufficient for existence' (pp. 104–105).

The funds for this purpose should be raised by taxation, which is fairer to contributors and leads to more efficient administration.

The English poor laws as they exist give rise to several evils. They do not inculcate restraint, they encourage improvidence, they do not discriminate between industrious and depraved, or between married and single. Consequently charity is soured by discord, and marred by sullenness, envy, and malice. Suggestions for improvement are that a jury of workmen be appointed to investigate claims for relief; that schools be established for the young, infirmaries for the old, and workhouses for the idle. The use of district journals and other publications would result in an informed public opinion. Means should be provided to enable workers to employ themselves in non-competitive industries, since it is useless to attempt to compete by hand-labour with the products made by superior methods. In particular, steps should be taken to make it easier for operatives to become master manufacturers and so widen the field of employment.

In order to strengthen the self-respect of the workers, education should be widely diffused; every parish should have a school and a library, and mechanics institutions and public parks should be opened. District courts should undertake the exclusive insurance of the lives of labourers in order to promote thrift as well as to provide protection. The drink menace should be countered by the provision of alternative luxuries.

These measures would be sufficient to deal with the general problem, but there remains the particular problem of the present redundancy, and immediate steps should be taken to deal with this so as to give the general proposals a chance to take effect. Such projects would include the sending abroad of suitable persons in the prime of life (though not so as to cause an unbalanced population), the cultivation of waste lands, the encouragement of cultivation in Ireland, which could supply our corn deficiencies, the development of fisheries, and the formation of corps for various public purposes. By such a combination of long- and short-term schemes there should emerge a steady improvement in the standard of life of the people.

TWO LECTURES BY LLOYD

In the next year, 1833, the Rev. W. F. Lloyd, M.A., Professor of Political Economy in the University of Oxford, published his *Two Lectures on the Checks to Population*, which had been delivered the year before. His work is sound and important.

Earlier unpublished lectures had dealt with the rates of growth of population and subsistence, and he is concerned to examine how equilibrium is to be maintained. Clearly the increase of food cannot keep pace with the theoretical increase of population, but this is not the important point. What is important is the difference between the theoretical and the actual rate of increase, and the mode by which the check is brought about.

There are two checks—the preventive and positive; but poverty and hard living, as well as being responsible for some of the positive check, may act in a preventive way by reducing fecundity. Nor do the checks enumerated by Malthus all arise from want of food, but many may equally well exist in places where food can be had in plenty. So long as man possesses reason, motives leading to prudential restraint present themselves in all forms of society. Common diseases and epidemics, wars, and plagues, are included among the positive checks, but wars are not universally the result of scarcity, though they may be connected with it. Consequently a sounder analysis of the effects of the checks provides three possible rates of increase:

(1) A theoretical rate supposing the absence not only of a shortage of food, but also of all other causes tending either to diminish human fecundity or to case premature death. This might double the population in ten years.

(2) Another theoretical rate supposing only the absence of a shortage of food, and not of the other causes. This is not an imaginary case, but one of which occasional examples may be found, and it probably leads to a doubling in thirty-five years.

(3) An actual rate such as occurs in every country under its existing circumstances. This leads, in England, to a doubling in forty-nine or fifty years.

Of these rates, the first is nearly invariable, the second is less stable, and 'though . . . not accurately geometrical, it yet preserves those main features of a geometrical progression, which are essential with regard to practical considerations, viz., that the increase of one period furnishes the power of a greater increase in the next, and this without any limit' (p. 13). The third rate is most variable of all.

Malthus's checks comprise the whole of the difference between the first and the third rates, and not that part merely which depends on the scarcity of subsistence. The two classes of checks —those produced by scarcity and those due to other causes— add up to a constant. Therefore in unhealthy countries there is little need, while in healthy countries there is great need, for moral restraint. As wars become less destructive and medicine improves, so a wider field is opened for checks arising from scarcity of subsistence, 'and it has become a matter of importance, instead of encouraging marriage, rather to discourage it, and by restraining the number of the births, to prevent the sickness and misery, arising from a want of food, which would be otherwise inevitable' (p. 16).

Systems of equality are highly unfavourable to the preventive check. 'Prudence is a selfish virtue; and where the consequences are to fall on the public, the prudent man determines his conduct, by the comparison, of the present pleasure with his share of the future ill, and the present sacrifice with his share of the future benefit' (p. 20).

The obligation of prudence is a collective one, and each man can clearly foresee the results of his actions. Yet the advantage to himself is so great compared with his share of the communal loss, that he acts against his better judgment. Marriage is a present good; the difficulties lie in the future; therefore under a system of communal provision all may marry early, and all are reduced to want and distress.

'Each therefore, will feel ill effects, corresponding precisely, in character and quantity, with the consequences of his own conduct. Yet they will not be the identical effects flowing from that conduct; but, being a portion of the accumulated effects resulting from the whole conduct of the society in general, would, therefore, still be felt, though the conduct of the individual should be changed. Thus it is that the universal distress fails to suggest to individuals any motive for moral restraint' (p. 22).

Consequently over-population is not in itself sufficient evidence that the fault lies in the people themselves; the fault may rest, not upon the people as individuals, but on the structure of the society in which they live.

The bearing of this on the condition of the working classes appears to have escaped observation. If there is a population of 10,000,000, and a man produces a child, he adds one mouth to be fed, thus reducing the potential share of each person from 1/10,000,000 to 1/10,000,001—which is negligible. All suffer from the act of one and this is no encouragement to moral restraint. It is enough that all people feel that they have an equal chance of gaining employment, even though some may be unemployed. No one has any particular reason to think that he will be unlucky, and, since he is exposed to competition from all round, no man fears the competition of his own children. Prudent individuals do not alone reap the benefits of prudence, nor do the imprudent alone feel the evil consequences.

The result is that it is idle to expect labourers to abstain from marriage, for the simple reason that every personal prompting is in favour of it, and there is no adequate individual benefit flowing from abstinence. The natural age of marriage for labourers coincides with the time when their income is greatest and their vigour is at its height, when they can best bear the privations or increase their exertions. To expect prudence to arise by the spontaneous and collective will of the working classes is to expect an impossible unanimity.

The fact that unemployment exists means that the wages of those employed are higher than they should be, thus giving a false stimulus to marriage (p. 40). Life must be conducted with some risks, and the most that a mariner can do is to choose a prudent time of departure. 'A labourer obtaining good employment, with a prospect of its continuance during ten or twelve years, may marry upon that prospect without violating the rules of prudence' (p. 43). Suppose he should save instead of marrying, the benefit he would derive from it depends on such saving being partial. If all attempted to save, they would counteract each other's expectations of advantage. The notion of punishment too is ill-founded, for the efficacy of punishment depends upon its certainty.

'In the case of the preventive check, not only is the punishment uncertain, but, what is equally pernicious, there is the like uncertainty as to the character of the offence. Marriage cannot be put even in analogy with crime, except *sub modo*. It cannot, like crime, be simply and without exception reprobated' (p. 45).

It is important to distinguish between the motives and the disposition to prudence. *Motives* are external conditions which operate on the reason and furnish grounds for prudence. *Disposition* is something internal to the mind itself, depending on strength of reason, self-command, and response to prudential considerations. Both are important in determining the strength of the check. The motives depend principally upon the constitution and structure of society, and on the degree of pressure entailed by dependency. The disposition depends on the reasoning powers of individuals as improved by education and experience.

The remedy is to lengthen the period of dependency of the young on their parents by deferring earning power till the age of ten, and thereafter increasing it with age. In this way all the pressure of the scarcity would fall on the young who would be increasingly dependent upon the counsel and the assistance of the old. Young children would be a heavy financial burden, but the older people would have ample means to enjoy a comfortable existence with their children so long as the latter remained at home. To leave home and marry would have immediate consequences, and would involve the consulting of parents, who are older and therefore more prudent. This is the type of check which operates among the well-to-do, and might well be extended.

Actually among the poor it is only the arrival of children which causes extra expense. The parents would have had to be maintained separately in any case, and the extension of manufactures, by providing employment for women and young children, relieves the head of the family from liability for their maintenance, so that practically the only motive to prudence is the cost of a little furniture and the difficulty of finding a house. Meanwhile the progress of medicine and hygiene, and the extended duration of infant life, make the need for moral restraint more urgent than ever.

THE DEATH OF MALTHUS

In the following year Malthus died, and so we leave the controversy at this point; not that it was ended. Alison, Doubleday, Thornton, Henry George, and a host of others were to follow. Indeed the controversy flares up and dies down from time to time according to the fluctuating economic fortunes of society. But the passing of Malthus enables us to pause, to gather up some of the threads, and to assess the state of the doctrine as he bequeathed it.

BOOK THREE

CRITICAL ANALYSIS

CHAPTER ONE

THE GROWTH OF POPULATION

THE GEOMETRICAL RATIO

THE idea of a population doubling in geometrical ratio, fortunate as it was for Malthus in popularizing his theory and in capturing the minds of his readers, was nevertheless disastrous in its effects on the development of the controversy. It was long before the discussion could rid itself of this incubus.

This notion immediately shifts the argument from the actual causes of the growth of population to the properties of a geometrical series. Malthus did not originate this form of stating the problem. Petty sought out doubling periods, but he was wise enough not to project them indefinitely and with mathematical precision into the future. Hale, Wallace and many others also concentrated on the rate at which a population would double itself. Malthus, however, by laying down the series: 1, 2, 4, 8 . . . immediately imported into the question of population a paradox similar to that of Zeno.[1]

David Booth protested: 'Time therefore, the most metaphysical of all metaphysical beings, is an ingredient mixed up with the consideration of the abstract numbers of the progression.'[2] Godwin drew the parallel with Price's calculation of the produce of a penny invested at compound interest, and

[1] 'If the tortoise has the start of Achilles, Achilles can never come up with the tortoise; for, while Achilles traverses the distance from his starting-point to the starting-point of the tortoise, the tortoise advances a certain distance, and while Achilles traverses this distance, the tortoise makes a further advance, and so on *ad infinitum*. Consequently, Achilles may run *ad infinitum* without overtaking the tortoise.' *Encyclopaedia Britannica*, 11th edn., Vol. 28, p. 970, col. 2.

[2] Godwin, op. cit., 1820, p. 245.

there are many such puzzles which have been regarded with amusement but never taken seriously.[1] It was the genius of Malthus to import this concept of compound interest into the sphere of population problems, and to sustain it so cleverly as to command in his day almost universal assent.

Once Zeno's method of stating the problem is accepted, it becomes difficult to explain how Achilles can catch the tortoise; but since he is known to be capable of such a feat, the problem is relegated to the study and left for the philosopher, while ordinary life proceeds as though the philosophical problems of time and motion were non-existent. But in the realms of speculation on population problems little was known and much was feared, and the geometrical ratio, once bound up with the growth of population, proved as difficult to attack as Zeno's paradox, and lacked the certain refutation of practical experience. The main strength of Malthus lay in his form of statement, and those who deny that he set much store by the ratios would do well to ponder the status of the theory without them. Before, therefore, any satisfactory progress can be made in the discussion of the issues, it is essential to ascertain precisely what is involved in the apparently infinite succession of doublings.

No one has ever denied that if population were to double itself successively in any finite period of time, it would in due course exceed any given finite number. But that is not the point at issue. The critics of Malthus looked at the matter in a different light. Assuming that the population at any moment is a given quantity, and that it has a tendency to grow, at some future time it will no doubt reach a figure double what it is at the outset. At this point reasoning should halt. There is no particular virtue in the point taken as the origin: it is quite an arbitrary point of time. Every one is well aware that to human consciousness the succession of instants of time appears infinite. What Malthus does by his statement of his theory is to make men's minds reel in an attempt to reach infinity by counting.

At the earliest moment of the controversy it lost its bearings, and, instead of being concerned with the laws of population growth, it degenerated into a wrangle over the properties of an infinite geometrical series, and for this Malthus must take the prime responsibility. Several of the critics, notably Gray, tried

[1] Godwin, op. cit., p. 136.

strenuously to extricate the discussion from the quicksands of infinity, but in vain. It was impossible to grapple with the eternal succession of ones and twos. Ravenstone prefaced his attempt to do so by saying:

'The success of the new system may, indeed, be ascribed not a little to the dexterity with which Mr. Malthus has confined himself to general assertions, and the studied watchfulness he has displayed, in always contriving to keep clear of details.'[1]

Godwin came sadly, and not altogether erroneously to the conclusion that he might have been writing a 'book about nothing.'[2]

But these writers had little alternative. The ratios dominated the situation, and an attempt had to be made to counter them. The existence of Noah made matters a little simpler by providing a starting-point for the calculations, and the critics were easily able to show the inconsistency of the ratios at various periods of history. How a believer in evolution can cope with the matter is as unnecessary as it is impossible to determine. Nevertheless some effort must be made to clear the ground.

THE BASIC ASSUMPTIONS

Malthus assumes two postulata, which form the basis of his whole theory:

(1) Population cannot live without food. (This, so stated, is a mere truism.)

(2) The passion between the sexes is necessary, and will remain nearly in its present state.

It is this second postulate which is the basis, and the only possible basis, for the building of the geometrical series, and Malthus makes no attempt to justify it. It is treated as a self-evident truth, as obvious as that man cannot live without food. It is linked, quite unnecessarily from the point of view of logical soundness, though with great advantage from the point of view of practical advocacy, with a comparatively rapid rate of doubling—namely once in every twenty-five years; that is approximately once in every generation.

[1] I.e. where we are in the geometrical progression. Ravenstone, op. cit., p. 161.

[2] Godwin, op. cit., p. 626.

The critics have been scorned for attempting to show that the period of doubling might be longer or shorter than Malthus had stated. This, it is said, is of no importance, and, if the period were longer it would only delay the inevitable. This scorn is to some extent misplaced. Malthus must have realized the truth of this contention, but he clung with unnecessary zeal to the twenty-five-year period.[1] The rapidity of the doubling period had given the matter a sense of urgency which, considering the state of knowledge on the subject, meant that quick decisions might have to be taken on very speculative grounds. To allay this sense of urgency, if only by extending the doubling period to fifty years, would allow time for calmer consideration of all the possibilities.[2]

But there is a more fundamental criticism which the more enlightened opponents were trying to bring to bear—namely that the periods of doubling varied with circumstances; that the pressure towards increased population was by no means the uniform force represented by Malthus. This, if it could be sustained, would make a very serious breach in the doctrine, and would destroy the foundation of the geometrical ratio, which can only rest upon the absolute invariable operation of the sex instinct. The theory might support a few minor variations, or clearly defined cycles, but ultimately it demands a universal sex pressure, producing, or tending to produce, progeny with machine-like regularity.

Malthus made little or no attempt to justify this postulate. It has a certain air of plausibility when viewed apart from its consequences, though these alone make it suspect. Malthus treated it as axiomatic. The instinct to reproduce 'appears to exist in as much force at present as it did two thousand, or four thousand years ago. . . . Assuming my postulata for granted. . . .'[3] On such slender foundations was the great edifice erected. The passion does not appear to produce uniform results at present, but this is, of course, attributed to the checks. The doubling rate is deduced from one nation, the United States, and all the other countries of the world are explained away as exceptions. The basis for this view, and it is a legitimate view if the postulate is correct, is that there is a uniformly operating

[1] Malthus, *Summary View*, 1830, q.v.

[2] Rowe Edmonds, op. cit., 1832, p. 58.

[3] *Essay*, 1798 edn., p. 13.

sexual force ever and overwhelmingly tending to increase population. He assumes that this force was equally in operation four thousand years ago, without vouchsafing any guide as to his source of information on this point, and he stands or falls by this basic assumption.

The sexual impulse to procreation is so irresistible that it must come under the influence of checks. He does not treat of all human motives as equally at work to produce various rates of increase (as Gray suggests) but of one overpowering and almost disastrous urge towards population, which only the most vigilant and constant efforts, and the most drastic remedies, can prevent from producing universal famine, misery, and despair.

That is the meaning of the Malthusian tendency of population to increase. Sexual forces are sufficient to produce a doubling every twenty-five years, and to go on doing it. The only obstacle resides in the checks: ultimately lack of food; proximately vice, misery however arising, or restraint, moral or immoral.

THE TENDENCY TO INCREASE

Hazlitt admitted the abstract tendency, but asserted that to talk of an unchecked tendency was a wrong use of terms.[1] Whately and Senior[2] showed that *tendency* had two possible meanings:

(*a*) What would happen if one force operated in isolation.

(*b*) What is likely to happen given the existing array of forces at work.[3]

[1] *Reply to Malthus*, pp. 91–92.

[2] Quoted, ante, p. 183 n.

[3] Note the following, *New Monthly Magazine*, Vol. I, 1821, p. 204. 'In what respect, then, can it be said by Mr. Malthus, that population has a "tendency" to increase beyond subsistence? Can he mean, that because there is an abstract *capacity* in man (if such a thing can be conceived) to increase faster than subsistence, that, therefore, there is a *tendency* in men so to increase? If Thomas is *capable* of running faster than James, does it follow that he has a *tendency* to leave James behind? Or does Mr. Malthus only mean, when he speaks of man's *tendency* to increase beyond subsistence, that such *would* be the rate of his increase, if he were governed exclusively by the "principle of population"? This might, perhaps, be true; but it would be a gross abuse of language, and must produce an utter confusion in all our ideas, to call it a tendency on *that* account. . . . It would justify us in saying, that a man had a tendency to be whatever he would become, if directed in his conduct by *any one* propensity in his nature, to the exclusion of the rest; but is that a tendency? Has the earth a tendency to fly from or

Malthus's tendency is the first, but, even as an abstract tendency, it has certain defects. The only unchecked population is in Paradise where men never die.[1] Lloyd analysed clearly the difficulties arising from this approach to the question.[2] Malthus's tendency was mainly an empirical generalization drawn from what must be admitted to be very inadequate data. It was very rash to assume that the rate of growth of an infant colony of a few million souls, whose age composition was a matter of speculation, the extent of immigration to which, though substantial, was difficult to determine, and whose death and birth rates were mere matters of conjecture, could be taken as a basic biological tendency of universal operation.

A much more careful examination of the potentialities of population growth was clearly called for, and many more factors needed to be taken into consideration. If one is to concern oneself with abstract tendencies, there is a sense, and a strict sense, in which it may be said that every female has a tendency to conception once in every four weeks between menarche and menopause: that is she tends to reproduce every time she ovulates. Celibacy apart, there are obvious interruptions, of which the chief is the period of pregnancy, which would reduce the number of births possible to one a year, but clearly if we are looking for maximum tendencies, the most obvious is that every woman tends to produce one child per annum, but for the operation of obvious and powerful checks.[3]

into the sun, because it would do either, if released from its centrifugal or centripetal direction? In truth and in good logic, the earth has *neither* of these tendencies: its tendency is to move in the orbit it actually pursues, in obedience to the combined forces, that actually impel it. And so it is with man: his tendency is not to deviate into every eccentricity, to which he would be driven by *each* appetite or principle of his nature, taken *singly* and unconnected by the others, but to move in the line, in which he is impelled by the *combined* influence of all the various principles and feelings that form his character. The principle of population, as estimated by Mr. Malthus, is one of these principles, and accordingly it exercises its proper influence upon his conduct; but this is only *that* degree of his influence which is compatible with the influence, which is as surely exercised upon him by the *other properties* of his nature.'

[1] Purves, *Principles of Population and Production Investigated*, 1818, p. 57.

[2] Lloyd, *Two Lectures on the Checks to Population*, 1833.

[3] This ignores the number of children possible at one birth. As these words are written the press reports that an American woman gave birth to twins in three successive years.

Neither Malthus nor his followers, nor anyone else for that matter, would seriously suggest such a standard. There are obvious biological and social checks to the attainment of such a result. But the illustration serves to show that Malthus's tendency is not a tendency at all in a strict sense. It is merely an inference drawn from a statistical aggregate, showing what is possible in certain conditions for short periods in a small community very specially circumstanced. Such a growth is the outcome of many tendencies, only imperfectly grasped and certainly not statistically measured. To give such a rate of growth the force of a universal law of nature, to use it as the foundation for such widely applied generalizations and such ruthlessly applied remedies, can only be justified as an act of faith, and not as the exercise of reason.

Many of the critics analysed in a rudimentary way the conditions determining fertility and fecundity. For Hazlitt the passion between the sexes was 'as various in itself and its effects as climate and all other causes, natural and artificial, can make it.'[1] Jarrold suggested many influences which might profoundly modify the fertility of human beings.[2] Gray made a serious attempt in the light of available knowledge to assess the strength of certain stimulating and defecundating causes.[3] Malthus, however, appears to have regarded the production of children as more or less automatic once marriage had been undertaken. There were individual differences, true; but the statistical result was inevitable, universal and eternal in the absence of economic or similar checks. The only way to keep want and misery at bay was to restrict the number of the people and the period of marriage. Otherwise, everywhere and at all times, the same appalling redundancy would make itself felt, with its necessary consequences—vice and misery.

[1] Hazlitt, op. cit., p. 129.

[2] Jarrold, op. cit., pp. 275 et seq. Cf. Jarrold: 'Contrary to what might have been expected, hereditary diseases are great promoters of population' (p. 303) and 'An unsound constitution, in a civilized country, most commonly proves prolific' (p. 305) with Malthus (on the Swiss increase): 'The fact may be accounted for without resorting to so strange a supposition, as that the fruitfulness of women should vary inversely as their health' (1806 edn., Vol. I, p. 400).

[3] Gray, *Happiness of States*, pp. 300 et seq.

It is probably true that, other things being equal,[1] a reduction in the period of marriage would produce corresponding statistical reductions in the number of children, although what the proportion would be is a matter of doubt. Evidence is naturally difficult to obtain, but Pearl has tabulated a mass of information which shows how varied the purely biological factors affecting fertility are.[2] Sexual desire varies very greatly in different people, and is modified by educational and social influences. Innate reproductive capacity seems to show enormous variations, and alters with the advance from menarche to menopause. The span of reproductive life also varies considerably from woman to woman. Both spermatozoa and ova have short lives, so that, although a woman ovulates once in four weeks, and a single ejaculation of human spermatozoa would suffice for the whole repopulation of America, the average number of births per marriage remains extremely small. The marvel is not the fertility, but the sterility of the human organism.

Pearl's figures, though the sample is small and open to criticism, suggest that the frequency of coitus varies considerably with age and with social class and occupation. The frequency is less with advancing age, and is relatively higher among farmers than among merchants and bankers, and still less among professional men. From a small sample of married couples he obtains the astonishing result that only one copulation out of 254 that might have been effective was actually productive, even though no attempt at contraception had been made.

Without laying too much stress on the relative importance of these several factors, about which the information is naturally sketchy, incomplete and to some extent inconclusive, it can hardly be said that, with all these variables, the notion that the passion between the sexes has remained constant for long periods and in all countries is a truism which can be dismissed in a single paragraph.

Then there is a real distinction, which Malthus does not always maintain, between sexual passion and reproductivity. The operation of the sexual instinct is highly conventionalized,

[1] The qualification is important. The use of contraceptives and the decision to have (say) two children only would produce families of two in so many cases as to render the age of marriage a minor factor.

[2] Pearl, R., *Natural History of Population*, 1939.

and Hazlitt was prepared to rest the whole of his case on the fact that single women frequently dominate the instinct, insofar as it has any connection with population, during the whole of their lives.[1] Social and religious environment profoundly influence such things as age of marriage, education, occupation, physical health, and the diversity of interests which compete with the sexual instinct for gratification. It is possible that there is a correlation between a high standard of living and a low sexual activity and also between a low standard of living and a high rate of sexual activity.[2]

Moreover, if Pearl's conclusions are ultimately established it would appear that the density of population greatly influences the physical mechanisms of human reproduction.[3]

Those critics who attacked the geometrical ratio felt constrained to offer alternative theories of population growth. In fact the Malthusian period was essentially one of premature generalization.[4] Gray thought that the rate of population growth would slow down or stop altogether.[5] Weyland thought that the progress of population varied with the different stages of society, but would ultimately reach the point of non-reproduction.[6] Sadler deduced the law that the prolificness of human beings, otherwise similar circumstanced, varies inversely as their numbers.[7] These theories were naïve in conception and proof, but were probably nearer the truth than the sweeping ratio proclaimed by Malthus.

One last point deserves mention before we pass from the biological to the statistical side of the question. Malthus assumes that fertility persists through time, i.e., that if two thousand people become four thousand in twenty-five years, they can

[1] Hazlitt, op. cit., pp. 126–127.

[2] Gray, *Happiness of States*, p. 358. 'Population is essentially connected with territory, climate, diet, education, and other circumstances, and it is affected, consequently, by their permanent or temporary varieties.' See also his footnote advising married people without offspring to live on bread and water (p. 448). Cf. Pearl, *Biology of Population Growth*, 1926, pp. 164–166.

[3] Pearl, *Biology of Population Growth.*

[4] Rowe Edmonds, op. cit., pp. 1–3.

[5] Gray, op. cit., p. 625.

[6] Weyland, op. cit.

[7] Sadler, op. cit., Vol. II, p. 352.

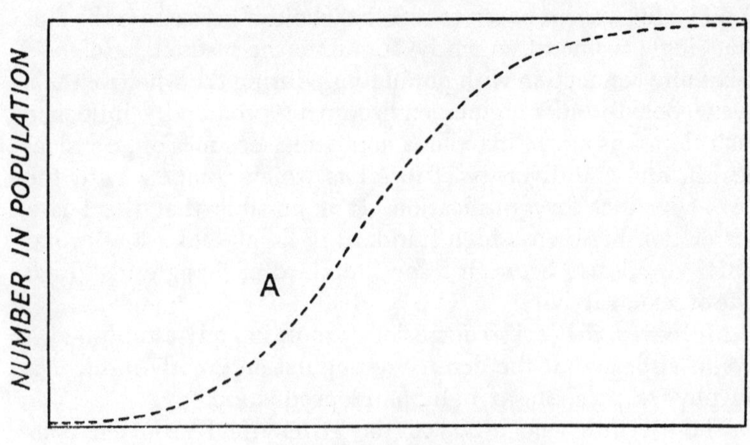

Diagram 1. A typical logistic curve.

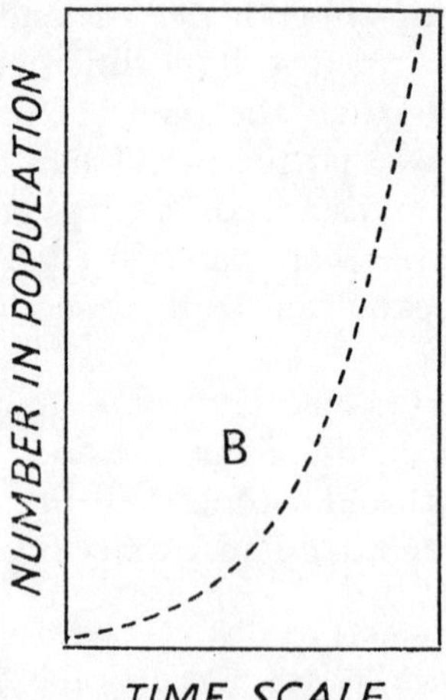

Diagram 2. Showing growth in geometrical ratio. (Not to same scale.)

Note. The logistic curve is typical of the growth in weight of a rat or a pumpkin, of the growth in size of a population of yeast cells or of fruit flies (*Drosophila melanogaster*), and also, if Pearl's hypothesis is correct, of the growth of a human population too. The Malthusian rate of growth, depicted in Diagram 2, appears to correspond roughly with the sort of growth occurring at the point A in Diagram 1.

necessarily produce eight thousand in fifty years. This is sound enough arithmetic, but raises the whole question of the fertility of successive generations, or even successive children in large families. Several of the critics drew attention to the absence of heirs in old-established families, where heirs would be desired and the subsistence check absent. Booth suggested that there was a tendency for fecundity to decline with the distance from the parent stock.[1] Without accepting this view, it must be admitted that Malthus's arithmetic was sounder than his biology. The notion of a universal and constantly acting sex instinct, producing a steady increase in population apart from the operation of the Malthusian checks, however plausible it may strike one on first hearing, will not stand up to close analysis of the complex of factors involved.

THE MALTHUSIAN AUTHORITIES

If Malthus did not rely upon biological and analytical considerations, on what did he rely? The answer is, on the American increase.

'It has been said that I have written a quarto volume to prove that population increases in a geometrical, and food in an arithmetical ratio; but this is not quite true. The first of these propositions I considered as proved the moment that the American increase was related, and the second proposition as soon as it was enunciated. The chief object of my work was to inquire what effects these laws, which I considered as established in the first six pages had produced, and were likely to produce on society; a subject not very readily exhausted.'[2]

It must be admitted that Malthus's authorities for the American increase were very slender and incomplete. At the time of the first edition, the evidence appears to have been a pamphlet of Dr. Styles, quoted by Price in his *Observations on Reversionary Payments*. Subsequently other authorities were produced, but they do not make a very formidable array.

In addition to the authority already mentioned, reliance is placed on the following:

(1) 'According to a table of Euler, calculated on a mortality

[1] Booth (in Godwin, *On Population*, 1820), p. 288.
[2] *Essay*, 1806 edn., Vol. II, p. 520.

of 1 in 36, if the births be to the deaths in the proportion of 3 to 1, the period of doubling will be only $12\frac{4}{5}$ years. And these proportions are not only possible suppositions, but have actually occurred for short periods in more countries than one.'[1]

This amounts to very little, and is hardly honest. Euler had merely done the calculations for Süssmilch[2] and therefore his authority merely supports the accuracy of the calculations. Since the suppositions were for periods of doubling ranging from 250 down to $12\frac{4}{5}$ years, Malthus is bound to show why he has chosen the one most favourable to his hypothesis, but all he says is that these proportions have occurred for short periods in more countries than one. Thus certain short-period and unspecified increases are used to bring forward, with the illusory backing of Euler, a suggestion that population can double itself once in $12\frac{4}{5}$ years.[3]

(2) 'Sir William Petty supposes a doubling possible in so short a time as ten years.'[4]

[1] *Essay*, 1806 edn., Vol. I, p. 7.

[2] So far as can be discerned Euler was merely working out arithmetical calculations, and many of these were divorced from reality. It is possible to calculate how long it would take a man to run 100 miles on the assumption (quite correct) that he can do 100 yards in 10 seconds. Many of the calculations were of this nature—accurate enough arithmetically but of no relevance to real affairs.

[3] Süssmilch produces a calculation (p. 288) to demonstrate a doubling in $10\frac{7}{10}$ years. The assumptions are sufficiently extraordinary: a death rate of one in sixty, a marriage rate of one in sixty (that is two people out of every sixty marry) and five children per couple (which often happens in these days). The death rate and the marriage rate are taken from different areas: they could clearly not exist simultaneously without a divorce rate which would make Hollywood green with envy. Moreover, if this increase persisted for twenty years, three-quarters of the population would be under about twenty-one years of age—and still presumably, a marriage rate of one in sixty! The arithmetic doubtless is quite correct, but it takes no account of biological processes and the length of time a human being takes to rear. It is fair to add that, in spite of lapses, Süssmilch was not seriously deceived in his practical applications.

[4] The relevant passage is quoted, ante, p. 11 n., and is found in Hull, op. cit., p. 462. It involves every 'Teeming Woman' in a birth every two years and still a death rate of one in forty. To get out of the difficulty of the enormous range of possibilities extending from doubling in 1200 to this low figure of ten years, Petty strikes a kind of average at 360 years. His whole attitude is as cautious as that of Malthus is dogmatic.

Laconic, and wisely so, for 'supposes' is the correct word. Petty did not build anything on this particular supposition. Indeed the justification for the introduction of his authority is no greater than in the case of Euler.

These so-called authorities are obviously introduced in order to lend colour to the following remark.

'But to be perfectly sure that we are far within the truth, we will take the slowest of these rates of increase, a rate, in which all concurring testimonies agree, and which has been repeatedly ascertained to be from procreation only.'[1]

The assumption the reader is expected to draw is that Malthus is more modest in his estimates than either Petty or Euler, whereas Petty had decisively rejected any notion of a uniform increase of population, and Euler was probably only concerned with doing the 'sums.' Whose are the 'concurring testimonies' and where has such an increase been repeatedly ascertained to be 'from procreation only'? Surely a few more details, if available, would be worth far more than the doubtful authority of either Petty or Euler. But no, we glide on. 'It may safely be pronounced, therefore, that population when unchecked goes on doubling itself every twenty-five years, or increases in a geometrical ratio.'[2]

Godwin, in 1818, wrote to Malthus and asked for his authorities. Malthus's reply is quoted,[3] and he has now added the information contained in Pitkin's *Statistical View of America*, which contains the three censuses of 1790, 1800, and 1810, together with an estimate for 1749. But it would be tedious and outside our scope to go through all the criticism of the source of the American increase which was shown by these censuses.

Much of it has already been mentioned, but Ravenstone, Booth, Godwin, Sadler, Place, and Malthus all built much more on the figures than they could possibly bear. The critics doubtless over-estimated the amount of immigration. Place's argument that the shipping would have been insufficient to carry the supposed immigrants has a convincing ring. On the other hand, Malthus would appear to under-estimate, if not the volume of immigration at least its effects in adding to the community more than in proportion to its numerical importance.

1 *Essay*, 1806 edn., Vol. I, pp. 7–8.

2 Id., p. 8.

3 Godwin, op. cit., 1820, p. 122.

However that may be, Malthus clung tenaciously to the twenty-five-year period of doubling down to the end (whether through obstinacy or sheer regard for the truth is irrelevant), although it is not fundamental to his theory. A fifty-year term will serve as well, provided he can prove the constancy of the sexual urge in the reproduction of the species. He seems at times vaguely conscious that he has not made out his case and yet he has so much faith in his intuition that he cannot be persuaded to doubt, so he resorts to the tenacious holding of previously announced positions.

It would have been easy, he says, to have added many further illustrations, but the real facts, e.g. the numerical strength of the different checks, are not known. Thus there is no point in adding further to the 'very ample evidence of the only kind that could be obtained.'[1]

In the *Summary View*,[2] the American censuses are a 'prima facie' evidence of doubling in twenty-five years, and the onus of rebutting this conclusion is thrown on the critics. Malthus admits that he does not know the relevant figures of birth and death rates for the United States. All is speculation.

Rather oddly Malthus buttresses the American figures by appealing to the European,[3] but since the existence of checks in Europe is deduced from the supposed deficiency of increase there as against America, it is a little curious to find the rate of increase in Europe now brought forward with the assumption that, since it is there checked, the American rate of increase is likely. The same conclusion emerges: 'It may be safely asserted, therefore, that population, when unchecked, increases in a geometrical progression of such a nature as to double itself every twenty-five years.'

The footnote is illuminating: 'This statement, of course refers to the general result, and not to each intermediate step of the

[1] Preface, 5th edn. Cf. Appendix, 1806 edn., p. 520 n.: 'The principal fault of my details is, that they are not sufficiently particular; but this was a fault which it was not in my power to remedy. It would be a most curious, and to every philosophical mind a most interesting piece of information, to know the exact share of the full power of increase which each existing check prevents; but at present I see no mode of obtaining such information.' The hypothesis cannot be tested.

[2] *Summary View*, p. 11.

[3] Id., pp. 22–24.

progress. Practically, it would sometimes be slower, and sometimes faster.'[1] This is as near to giving up the thesis as Malthus could go without complete abandonment.

It has become usual to say that Malthus set no great store by the ratios, a statement presumably based on the way in which they are soft-pedalled in editions after the first. But the second edition is not independent of the first: it is a direct descendant; different in form, different in emphasis, different in tone; but fundamentally formed of the same materials. The premises may be implied rather than stated, but they still exist, and Malthus climbed to fame up the steps of the geometrical series.

Similarly, the preoccupation of the critics with this aspect of the matter is frequently scorned, but they knew what they were about. The ratios were 'the dazzling and showy part of the theory,' and it was the geometrical series that captured men's minds. It was as difficult to refute as Zeno's paradox, but while the latter was brushed aside as contrary to experience—Achilles can outstrip the tortoise—Malthus's paradox appeared no paradox at all to a people suffering from bad harvests, war, and a poverty which baffled all efforts to remedy it.

[1] *Summary View*, p. 25 n.

CHAPTER TWO

THE GROWTH OF SUBSISTENCE

THE ARITHMETICAL RATIO

POPULATION is necessarily limited by the means of subsistence. So runs Malthus's first proposition. This led to the accusation that he had written a quarto volume to prove that man could not live without food.

'It has been said that I have written a quarto volume to prove that population increases in geometrical, and food in arithmetical ratio; but this is not quite true. The first of these propositions I considered as proved the moment that the American increase was related, and the second proposition as soon as it was enunciated.'[1]

To which Ravenstone replies: 'These phrases, if they mean any thing, must mean that the geometrical ratio was admitted on very slight proofs, the arithmetical ratio was asserted on no evidence at all.'[2]

To avoid any ambiguity it must be emphasized that the term 'means of subsistence' for Malthus implies those actually in existence and not the potential means.

Whence does he derive the idea of an arithmetical ratio of increase for food? The answer is that it is an outside limit beyond which the most enthusiastic speculator cannot be expected to speculate.

Suppose that food and population are now equivalent, and population is ready to start off in the geometrical ratio: 1, 2, 4, 8, 16, 32, etc. Looking round this country, says Malthus, let us concede that for the first twenty-five years food could

[1] *Essay*, 1806 edn., Vol. II, p. 520 n.

[2] Ravenstone, op. cit., p. 152.

increase at the same rate as population, that is double itself. Surely no one would care to ask for more. Is it conceivable that this process could be again repeated? No. The most that could be imagined would be an equal actual increase, which is a smaller relative increase.

Thus the ratio 1, 2, 3, 4, 5 . . . for food represents not a strict fact but an outside limit.

Now this seems to be a most candid concession to the wildest claims of his opponents, but in reality, far from being a concession, it is a snare and a delusion. They can only claim their arithmetical increase of food if they are prepared to grant the geometrical increase of population. The more Malthus gives away, the more he has. The arithmetical ratio has no independent existence; Malthus has paid no more attention to the conditions of the growth of food than he did to those of population. Stripped of its mathematics we are back again at the old infinite series. Nothing can keep pace with a geometrical series whose factor is two. So far as the *Essay on Population* is concerned there is little more to it than that. It is true that there is an appeal to the known properties of the land; but clearly when acre has been added to acre, when the whole earth has been cultivated like a garden, the powers of population remain, while the powers of the earth are exhausted: that is the substance of it. This position had been clearly laid down by Wallace; the mathematics added by Malthus are entirely spurious.

It is obvious that the arithmetical ratio cannot have operated through all time, but when does it begin to operate? Again we are given no enlightenment.

What say the critics? They point to the waste land and the potentialities of the earth and are laughed to scorn. Man cannot eat potential food, only actual food. By subsistence Malthus means the actual food, not that which there might be.

It is vital to distinguish clearly two propositions of Malthus. None of the critics would deny that a population which continued to grow must stop somewhere—if not before, then when all the earth is cultivated. That is not the point. The question for them was not an academic one, but a practical one. Have the ratios begun to operate? Is the world full? The answer is, No. Then the common sense thing to say is, Why will not the cultivation of uncultivated lands allow population to expand as fast as children can be born? All that the people need do is to spread themselves.

Malthus has a reply: it is to shift his ground. A man is confined to a room even if he never approaches the walls.

'A man who is locked up in a room may be fairly said to be confined by the walls of it, though he may never touch them; and with regard to the principle of population, it is never the question, whether a country will produce *any more*, but whether it may be made to produce a sufficiency to keep pace with an unchecked increase of people. . . . In this country, it is not the question, whether by cultivating all our commons, we could raise considerably more corn than at present; but whether we could raise sufficient for a population of twenty millions in the next twenty-five years, and forty millions in the next fifty years.'[1]

To which Hazlitt replies:

'The case is really that of a man who has the range of a suite of rooms and who in a fit of the spleen, or from indolence, or stupidity, or from any other cause you please, confines himself to one of them.'[2]

The best answer then that Malthus can produce is this: that even if men do spread themselves the evil is only temporarily removed. The time will come when the earth will be full. The actual existence of waste lands means that the country is in the same position as if it possessed a smaller territory. Pressure there must be at all stages of growth, because of the difference between the two ratios. The only hope lies in the checks.

THE ALTERNATIVE VIEW

We have seen that there is no basis in fact for the arithmetical ratio.[3] It is a device to represent an outside limit, but it is not a legitimate device. If Malthus is going to talk of the tendency in all animated life to outrun the means of subsistence, he must surely realize that not only population but also food can increase in geometrical ratio; and moreover most animals and plants have in fact a quicker ratio of increase than has man.[4]

Consequently, a stricter expression of the laws of growth of

[1] 1806 edn., Vol. II, p. 298. [2] Hazlitt, *Reply*, p. 78.

[3] This was admitted by Malthus in the *Summary View*.

[4] Sadler, *Law of Population*, Vol. I, p. 93.

both population and food, if one accepts the Malthusian position, is this:

Population tends to increase in geometrical progression, unless checked by the results of shortage of food.

Food tends to increase in an even faster geometrical progression,[1] unless checked by what? The answer is a limited earth and a limited fertility.

Clearly therefore this view of the subject (and this was the view taken by the critics) does not give us any *a priori* information as to what the relative rates of increase may be at any particular time. And the existence of untilled land, and unoccupied countries would lead one to suppose, unless the contrary could be proved, that, until they were full, food and population might well keep pace with each other, as in fact they did in America. Therefore, although this has no bearing on the ultimate question of how many people the earth can hold, its immediate and practical bearing is that Malthus had not made out his case for the state of affairs at the time he wrote. The existence of a potential geometrical increase in wheat and animals; the existence of land untilled or unused both in England and in the world: these facts were a sufficient and necessary answer in regard to the existing situation. Yet the critics are regarded as being rather feeble-minded for advancing it; they are accused of misunderstanding Malthus. The fact is they were applying their minds to the contemporary state of the country; they had distinguished clearly between what might happen when the earth was full, and what was possible in the interim; and they refused to be dazzled by the prospect of long-term ruin into neglecting short-term possibilities.

Food they realize is produced like any other commodity in response to supply and demand.[2] A growth of population implies an increased demand, and it also implies an increase in the labour force wherewith to supply the demand. Malthus's view is of subsistence as a kind of gift of nature uninfluenced by the supply of labour; the opposite view is that, since the growth of population coincides with a growth in civilization and the extended division of labour, it is reasonable to suppose that subsistence will keep

[1] Purves, *Principles of Population and Production Investigated*, 1818, p. 58.

[2] E.g. Purves, op. cit., Book II, Chapter I.

pace with population growth. None of the critics expects to see in existence more subsistence than is demanded, not because it could not be produced and that quickly, but because food like any other commodity is produced only for a market.

THE LAW OF DIMINISHING RETURNS

It is at this point, of course, that most modern critics would call a halt. What, they would say, about the law of diminishing returns?

It is well to point out that Malthus's *Essay* was not based upon the law of diminishing returns, although it might be urged that some aspects of this law were present in his mind.[1] His principle was based on the arithmetical ratio, and to this the contemporary critics rightly addressed themselves. Nevertheless the law of diminishing returns was later substituted for the discredited ratio, and is specifically referred to by Senior; therefore it is well to look at the question from this angle, particularly as this law greatly strengthens the theory and gives it a much more plausible air.

[1] 'Of the three angles to the problem of diminishing returns—the historical taking up of poorer land, the exhaustion of the soil, and the failure of added doses of other factors applied to land to increase the output proportionately—Malthus seems to be consciously aware of only the first two. These would account for everything that he says about diminishing additions to the produce. In his mind the resort to inferior soils is the dominating idea; exhaustion of older lands comes second. The third aspect of the idea of diminishing returns, that of the lack of proportionality in the returns to added applications of labor and capital, is there only by implication. Malthus probably did not appreciate the significance of this idea, although he used it to good advantage' (Field, *Essays on Population*, 1931, p. 16).

But note Malthus, *Essay*, 1806 edn., Vol. II, p. 297: 'The French have already found their error in bringing under cultivation too great a quantity of poor land. They are now sensible that they have employed in this way a portion of labour and dressing, which would have produced a permanently better effect, if it had been applied to the further improvement of better land.' Nevertheless, he immediately proceeds on the next page to revert to the ratios.

Cannan draws attention to a passage (1806 edn., Vol. II, p. 282) and comments: 'Malthus little dreamed in 1803 that in less than three-quarters of a century a casual argument which he introduced with the word "particularly" would have been accepted as the foundation of the "Malthusian" theory of population, to the entire exclusion of the geometrical and arithmetical ratios on which he himself declared all his principal conclusions to have been founded' (*Theories of Production and Distribution*, 1903, p. 146).

It is important to bear in mind two considerations: (*a*) that the law is qualified by the caution, 'other things being equal,' (*b*) the question: 'diminishing returns of what?'

Ravenstone,[1] Godwin,[2] Edmonds,[3] and others pinned their faith in the progress of the division of labour and the advance of science. They seem to have had in mind vague ideas of a law of conservation of productivity, and the subsequent century vindicated their faith and belied the fears which the doctrines of Malthus contrived to spread. A modern writer says:

'It is unfortunate for Malthus's reputation as a sooth-sayer that the century following the publication of his *Essay* saw a phenomenal increase in food resources that he had not prophesied, but there is every reason to suppose that Malthus, duly informed of nineteenth-century progress in the discovery of new lands and the invention of new machines and processes, would have predicted fairly accurately the almost equally phenomenal increase of England's and the world's total head of population.'[4]

It is even more unfortunate that, although the critics of Malthus did forecast this very event, namely that population could both grow, and grow richer, their writings have been dismissed as negligible and those of Malthus revered. It is something to be said for a man's views that they lead to accurate predictions; rather more, in fact, than that subsequent events can be made to square with a theory. It is a noticeable feature of Malthus's theory that it is omnivorous; it can swallow and assimilate the most obstinate data.

So far other things have not been equal. The nineteenth century was one of progressive advance in numbers, civilization and well-being, and it is not a little strange that it should have been ushered in by such dismal and widely accepted forebodings of disaster. If all the arguments of the critics will not bear examination, it is something that they kept their heads, and wielded their pens, at a time when acquiescence in the prevailing philosophy might have proved more popular and congenial. Diminishing returns, as a world phenomenon, were to remain a dead letter for many years to come, and may for many more. The Malthusian theory can, of course, handle this situation. The ratios have not yet begun to operate. But if Malthus had any

[1] Op cit., p. 119, and p. 186. [2] *First Reply*, 1801, p. 67. [3] Op cit., p. 63.
[4] *Overpopulation*, P. Sargant Florence, 1926, pp. 4–5.

purpose in writing his book, it was to urge the imminence of disaster through overpopulation in a Britain of some ten million souls, and although the world may sooner or later be overpopulated, it seems clear that some more reliable guide than the 'principle of population' will be needed to forecast the event.

The second point to consider in examining the growth of subsistence is that the law of diminishing returns implies diminishing returns of something in particular. If we take one plot of ground and insist on growing carrots on it, it is perfectly obvious that sooner or later, sooner in fact rather than later, diminishing returns will set in. But why confine the land to carrots? The same area covered with glass would immediately yield rapidly increasing returns in tomatoes. The geometrical ratio diverging to infinity, and the law of diminishing returns converging to nothing—both alike can darken counsel.

Malthus's notion of man producing 'subsistence' with increasing difficulty, as though subsistence were as homogeneous as manna and as little under man's control, led to the conclusion that a man who was not starving would inevitably be breeding. There never emerged the notion of a standard of living. Fertility too was regarded as something inherent in the soil and comparatively unalterable, and followers of Malthus have too readily assumed that to increase the fertility of poorer soils must be the work of great expense and is the only source of greater food supplies. Man is pictured as a devouring animal eating a limited subsistence, much as a cow eats grass, with this exception. He is endowed with reason, the chief and only sensible use of which is to heed pleas for deferment of marriage.

A BROADER CONCEPTION NEEDED

This conception of man is too naïve, and overlooks too many traits of his character and too many of his activities and aspirations. It is true that more men, like more cattle, need more subsistence, but unlike the cattle men set to work to modify their environment so as to produce what they require. They are not doomed to try to live on the limited extra supplies of a given commodity which can be with difficulty raised on land already taxed to the uttermost; they have at their disposal all the resources which mark off man from the animals. The problem of human populations is essentially an ecological study.

'A true picture of the growth of human populations, from the biological standpoint, can no longer be gained by concentrating attention on those features in which human activities are supposed to resemble the activities of other animals. It involves the recognition that human life functions within a system of relationships with other organisms, constantly changing as the result of human effort, and constantly reacting upon the direction of human effort.'[1]

Man is an animal, but a tool-bearing animal, endowed with speech. This does not exempt him from his animal needs, but extends the ways in which he can satisfy them and the conditions compatible with survival. He can construct houses and he can make clothes to protect himself from adverse climatic conditions, thus widening his area of activity. He has at least three methods of survival:

(*a*) The elimination of competitive species,

(*b*) The improvement of chemical conditions governing the production of food,

(*c*) The modification of organisms in the ecological association of which he is the dominant species.[2]

It is early yet to say what developments are possible, but only the bold or the ignorant would care to assign limits to man's efforts at present. The elimination of the horse as a motive force makes more room for cows and pigs. Nitrates modify the rotation of crops, and these, formerly only obtainable from exhaustible deposits, are now obtainable from the atmosphere. Whereas formerly fats had to be used for illumination, today it is obtained from falling water. Exhaustible supplies of coal may soon be redundant through the use of atomic energy.

One is not here stating so much what will happen as rebutting the immature and premature setting of limits to what the earth can produce in accordance with some arbitrarily conceived law. By the rational control of his environment man has changed, and can change, the selective process. He can eliminate those species which injure him to make room for those which assist.

He can control the conditions of those species which satisfy his needs. Thus he not only stores food for himself but also for the animals he wishes to preserve and multiply. He can modify the

[1] Charles, *Menace of Under-Population*, pp. 2–3. [2] Id., p. 5.

chemical content of the soil and often at slight cost turn barren land into a fertile storehouse. By glasshouse and cloche culture he can make himself independent of the weather. He can stimulate winter egg production among fowls by means of artificial illumination.

He can eliminate competitors for his food supplies, such as weeds and pests, by using all the resources of science and industry at his disposal. The uses of chemical and parasitic controls are well known. The selection and breeding of immune strains bring about constant improvement.

Selection and breeding too have an important bearing not only on disease resistance but also on yield and time of maturing. Among plants there are early- and late-maturing varieties, hardy varieties, drought- and frost-resisting varieties, all extending the scope and yield of culture. Sex-linking among fowls leads to the early segregation and elimination of unnecessary cockerels. Artificial insemination has a big future.

Moreover there is much to be done in the field of nutritional studies. Subsistence is not merely the food available, but even more important the use made of it by the human body in satisfying the needs of life. The time will no doubt come when the crude yield of a crop will count for little beside its content of essential constituent food elements. There is a conservatism in food habits which has not yet been seriously challenged by scarcity but which would readily yield in the face of a threatened exhaustion of supplies.

It was the view of most of the critics that food could keep pace with the growth in numbers by the application of increased energy and improved knowledge and techniques. It is not contended that the earth could support an unlimited number of human beings, but it is contended that the limits to what can be produced are not defined by anything contained in the Malthusian theory.

Malthus did not prove his theory concerning the rate of growth of population. He hardly deigned to consider the growth of subsistence. He was convinced that the rate of growth of population must so outstrip that of food, that any serious attention to the latter was hardly worth while. On neither point, therefore, does his theory add anything of value to the stock of human knowledge.

CHAPTER THREE

THE RATIOS

THE IMPORTANCE OF THE RATIOS

IT is undeniable that the strength of the principle of population as enunciated by Malthus and promulgated by his supporters depended upon the ratios. It was not the demonstration of the geometrical increase of population, or indeed of the arithmetical increase of subsistence, but the juxtaposition of the two that won the minds of his readers. He was unquestionably right to draw attention to the fact that it is the relation between subsistence (or more correctly, output of all goods) and numbers which determines the wellbeing of the masses, although his work is seriously marred by his lack of interest in the question of maldistribution. But by setting his ratios one against the other he purported to have settled the issue once and for all in favour of a restrictionist attitude to population.

He laid down the ratios:

Population	1, 2, 4, 8, 16, 32, 64, 128, 256 . . .
Food	1, 2, 3, 4, 5, 6, 7, 8, 9 . . .

For anyone who had accepted his previous analysis uncritically the subject was closed.

'In two centuries the population would be to the means of subsistence as 256 to 9; in three centuries as 4,096 to 13, and in two thousand years the difference would be almost incalculable.'[1]

This sounds very impressive, and it was very impressive: it swept his readers off their feet. But reflection reveals that the appearance is deceptive. Since it is impossible to imagine the situation of the third term of the series, it is needless to go further.

[1] *Essay*, 1806 edn., Vol. I, p. 13.

If the numbers represent millions, how could four millions of people be sustained on the food of three? The answer of friends and foes alike would be—they cannot. Therefore, since the third term can never come into existence, all the subsequent terms are false. They serve to bewilder the reader; they serve to impress him with the overwhelming superiority of the power of population; but, since they do not represent fact, or even possibility, they obscure rather than illuminate the real problem. If Malthus was not himself deceived by them he does not appear to have mastered their full implications.

If food could only increase in arithmetical ratio, so could population. Man cannot live without food. Hence the two ratios would both be arithmetical. What then becomes of the geometrical series? It is reduced to the rate of food production in each period: more, its annual increase is reduced to the annual increase in food production. The invalidity of Malthus's ratios could never have escaped detection if he had stated the real series of increase and hence deduced all that it implied. Let us do it for him.

Period	*Amount of Food*	*Amount of Population*		*Amount of Check*
1	1	1	tends to become 2—becomes 2	0
2	2	2	tends to become 4—becomes 3	1
3	3	3	tends to become 6—becomes 4	2
4	4	4	tends to become 8—becomes 5	3
5	5	5	tends to become 10—becomes 6	4
6	6	6	tends to become 12—becomes 7	5
7	7	7	tends to become 14—becomes 8	6
8	8	8	tends to become 16—becomes 9	7
9	9	9		

This is a true tabulation of the results that may be expected whenever the Malthusian ratios are in operation, and they are sufficiently astonishing to make one pause and wonder. If there is anything fundamental in Malthus's theory, it is the geometrical growth of population. If there is anything dubious, it is the arithmetical increase of food, which was merely an outside limit. And yet when we analyse the theory in all its consequences we find nothing but arithmetic. The growth of food is in arithmetical ratio, and the loss of population due to the checks is in arithmetical ratio.

These consequences are worth investigation. In particular it should be noticed that the relation between the loss of population in each period, and the average number of living during the period, grows progressively bigger with each advance of population, even when it is held back to the level of food. Malthus can hardly have been aware of this when he said that he was no enemy of population when it followed its natural order. The future even under the dominion of the arithmetical ratio of increase grows steadily darker and darker, if there is any truth in his ratios. However, we shall return to this in our next chapter.

The trouble with the ratios is that the reader is never sure when they begin to operate. One gathers that Malthus thought they were in operation in most countries of the world at the time he wrote. In fact he goes so far as to say that we should be led into error if we supposed that food ever increased in geometrical ratio even in America, so that plainly he thinks that arithmetic is in charge during his own day. Nevertheless, as his contemporary critics complain, he is a difficult man to pin down, and if he had not contented himself with generalities he would have felt bound to explain certain anomalies to which his ratios gave rise.

RAVENSTONE'S ANALYSIS

Ravenstone, for instance, approaches the matter in this light. 'In examining Mr. Malthus's propositions, one cannot but be immediately struck with the want of fixity in his reasonings. At every attempt to handle them they elude the grasp. . . . It is owing to this slipperiness alone that the arithmetical ratio was not immediately rejected. Had any period been fixed at which the two ratios were to begin to operate, the absurdity of the scheme, its impossibility must have been directly perceived. If they are always to begin, if they are never to act but in futurity, the distinction between them is only in words; the first step of an arithmetical ratio is precisely the same as that of the geometrical. . . . The increase of men and of food will always for the next twenty-five years go on with equal rapidity. Their proportions will remain unaltered.'[1]

[1] Ravenstone, op. cit., p. 156.

But there is no reason why every generation cannot claim that theirs is the first link in the chain, and put off the evil day to the next. This in fact is the view of the majority of the critics, who refused to be terrified by prophecies of long-term disaster, and concentrated on short-term possibilities.

Another alternative is that the ratios are as old as the world. 'We are immediately encountered by a dilemma, one of whose horns it will be impossible to escape . . . either . . . the world abounded with the means of subsistence when there was none to consume them; every desert swarmed with the animal and vegetable productions convenient for the food of man; or if we allow, in conformity to history and experience, that food originally existed only in proportion to the wants of our first parents . . . we shall be compelled to admit that the actual inhabitants of the world must be suffering habitually and unknowingly all the horrors of famine. One thousand millions of people must according to this theory be living on a quantity of food which is only sufficient for 1,328 persons. . . .'[1]

If it be objected that this mode of reasoning ignores the operation of the checks, it is true. But to assume the checks is to beg the question. Malthus's success depends upon the way in which he adheres to general assertions and contrives to keep clear of details. But in reality the results are almost as astonishing on this reckoning.

'As the present inhabitants of the world amount to one thousand millions, the present stock of provisions must be equivalent to the wants of this number of people. But as this stock has only doubled arithmetically 166 times, there must have been, on this supposition, at the disappearing of the waters, a quantity equal to the subsistence of six millions of persons. The most unbounded plenty must, therefore, have been the lot of our first parents and their immediate descendants. . . . Amongst a people so situated property could have no existence, for who would seek to appropriate to himself that which was more than sufficient for all? . . . At the expiration of less than six centuries and a half the descendants of Noah will have increased to 200 millions. But here the operation of the geometrical ratio will have entirely ceased, its effects must have been at an end. Population will have overtaken subsistence. As the original stock of pro-

[1] Ravenstone, op. cit., p. 157.

visions will in the meantime have only doubled arithmetically twenty-six times, that which at first was sufficient for six millions of persons, will now only afford subsistence to 162 millions. At this early period, the most powerful of all the preventive checks, the want of food, must have acted with full force, and must have effectually hindered, in future, any rapid increase of numbers. . . . For the last 3,500 years the geometrical and arithmetical ratios have jogged on quietly, side by side. . . . Whenever population endeavoured to increase with too much rapidity, its efforts will have been immediately checked by a want of subsistence. Such is the conviction which must result from examining this system in detail. . . . But, unfortunately, when we have divested the geometrical ratio of all its terrors, we are no longer permitted to enjoy its milder charms. Facts immediately rose in opposition to the theory to which they obstinately refuse to accommodate themselves. If the arithmetical ratio be admitted for the growth of subsistence, we shall find that even after the very ample provision made for Noah and his children, a supply sufficient for six millions of people, the annual increase of the means of subsistence, will only afford a provision for 240,000 new inhabitants of the world. . . . But population cannot increase faster than the means of supporting its additional numbers. If then the annual increase of the means of subsistence be only sufficient to find food for 240,000 persons, 240,000 are all that, since the day when population overtook subsistence, can annually be added to the, at any time, existing population of the world. The number of its inhabitants cannot increase faster.

'This proposition must be somewhat startling to him who, with Mr. Malthus, believes that the United States, from procreation alone, add, in each year, more than this number to their population. . . .[1]

'The numbers of men certainly increase faster than is consistent with this theory; as we cannot controvert the fact we are forced to disbelieve the theory. The means of subsistence must increase in proportion to those who are to be subsisted. But the inhabitants of the world add to their numbers faster than is compatible with any belief in the arithmetical ratio. The theory of the arithmetical ratio, therefore, cannot be supported. It must fall to the ground; its existence is disproved by the experience of

[1] Ravenstone, op. cit., pp. 161–165.

all times; it is a mere non-entity; in vain shall he seek for its operation in any region of the world; it has no being but in the imagination of its author.'[1]

THE REAL ISSUE

It has been necessary to spend so much time on the ratios because it is impossible to understand the hold which the Malthusian theory gained on his generation without realizing that it depended upon their plausibility. If anyone suggested that improvements were possible within the near future, he was greeted with a pitying smile. He did not understand the ratios.

The real point at issue between those who supported Malthus and those who opposed him was this: Is subsistence the effective cause of population, or is population the effective cause of subsistence? Since it is a matter of observation that normally the two agree, the answer is not obvious on the face of it. It must be brought to some other test.

Weyland[2] believed that in some stages of society food was so plentiful as to encourage population growth; in others it was so scarce as to stimulate the population to extra exertions and hence bring about changes in technique and the structure of society. The answer to the question for him, therefore, depended very much upon circumstances. Most of the other critics, however, adhered to the view that food was produced in accordance with the ordinary laws of supply and demand, just as clothing or any other commodity, and that, as soon as the demand increased, the necessary amount of food would be forthcoming.

Malthus's view was that anything which enabled an increase of food to be produced, whether an improved technique or some fortuitous happening, would, by easing the burden of providing for a family, reduce the positive check, or relax the preventive check until such time as the old ratio of population to food was re-established.

Malthus argues continually as though the output of food were independent of the amount of human effort involved. This is implicit in many of his statements. Whereas his critics believed that an increased population by bringing improved methods

[1] Ravenstone, op. cit., pp. 166–167. [2] Op. cit., Chapters III–VII.

would promote an increased supply of food, Malthus appears to have thought that this increase could not be proportionate. Moreover, he also seems to have thought that, if some of the population were cut off by plague or war or some other reason, the survivors would be better off, which means, by implication, that the deceased were not in reality contributing to their support, or at least not covering the amount of it. These are questionable propositions, and if they had been pursued realistically, it would have been found that Malthus's notion is sometimes true and sometimes false. It might even have led to the concept of an optimum population.

How in fact does the increase of population cause an increased pressure on subsistence?[1] After the children are born nature has provided for their sustenance for approximately a year. Suckling in some tribes continues for as long as three. So far, unless we are to take into account the extra food which might be eaten by the mother, the pressure is not very heavy. Surely the father having this advance warning of a future liability has time to set about making provision for it. He will work the harder while the children are young in order that, when they become old enough to earn for themselves, he will reap the reward of some of their

[1] At this point it is of interest to look at Malthus's reply to an argument of Grahame: 'The apprehension that an increasing population would starve unless a previous increase of food were procured for it, has been ridiculed by comparing it with the apprehension that increasing numbers would be obliged to go naked unless a previous increase of clothes should precede their births. Now however well or ill-founded may be our apprehensions in the former case, they are certainly quite justifiable in the latter; at least society has always acted as if it thought so. In the course of the next twenty-four hours there will be about 800 children born in England and Wales, and I will venture to say that there are not ten out of the whole number that come at the expected time, for whom clothes are not prepared before their births. It is said to be dangerous to meddle with edged tools which we do not know how to handle, and it is equally dangerous to meddle with illustrations which we do not know how to apply, and which may tend to prove exactly the reverse of what we wish' (Appendix, 1872 edn., p. 521). The reader is referred to Sadler's reply (*Law of Population*, Vol. I., pp. 112–115) in which this is turned back to Malthus himself. An allowance of 10 in 800 is not sufficient for the twins that will be born. Which is cause and effect: do the parents have children because they have clothes, or do they procure clothes because they are going to have children? More to the point, is not the provision of the natural food for children made with even greater certainty than that of clothing?

surplus. It is a fact not without significance that, at the time Malthus was writing, many parents were dependent on their children and not children on their parents.

But the real test of precedence is whether the poor are as poor as they used to be; whether with the advance of civilization there is a relative advance in the standard of life of the people.

This was the issue on which Senior tried to pin Malthus in their correspondence, which has been previously discussed, and it is the crucial issue. As has been shown in this chapter the amount of check required by the ratios of Malthus grows steadily bigger and bigger as population advances, even if the people are to maintain the existing standard of living. It would appear, therefore, impossible to expect any substantial advances to be maintained in the long run. Yet as Senior points out, all over the world, and in many different countries, the standard of living in the various communities has shown considerable progress.

Malthus in reply attempts to evade the issue by referring to starts and oscillations due to food discoveries and the decimating effects of plagues, but his conclusion shows that he cannot or will not see the point.

'The main part of the question with me, relates to the cause of the continued poverty and misery of the labouring classes of society in all old states. This surely cannot be attributed to the tendency of food to increase faster than population. It may be to the tendency of population to increase faster than food' (p. 72).

Unfortunately the question is not the continued existence of poverty and misery, but whether in the natural order of social development the poor become relatively less numerous, less poor and less miserable. However, Senior patiently returns to the point.

'I mean, that if we look back through the history of the whole world, and compare the state of each country at distinct periods of two hundred or three hundred years, the cases in which food has increased during the preceding period of two hundred or three hundred years, in a greater ratio than population, will be found to be more numerous than those in which population has increased during the preceding period in a greater ratio than food. I admit that this increase has not been steady; it has been subject to the oscillations you have so well described. . . . Still I apprehend that, in the absence of disturbing causes, the retrogression would not be to the point at which food and population relatively stood, before the first improvement took place. . . . If we had always fallen back . . . we should still be ill-fed savages, earning a scanty subsistence by the chase' (pp. 73–75).

Further Senior defends his view that this is the natural course of human development. Premature mortality still exists, but the number of people who die in want is certainly less than it had been six hundred years before. Yet Malthus refuses to be empirical. It does not sound plausible to him. Despite the obvious facts brought forward by Senior he asserts: 'Repeated experience has shown that the facility of obtaining food at one period is not *necessarily* connected with the formation of more general habits of prudence subsequently' (p. 85). He still pins his faith in that sole salvation of the poor—'the improvement and right direction of their moral and religious habits' (p. 86).

Yet one must agree with Senior. The whole history of civilization has been one of a progressively improving standard of living. There have been ups and downs but the general trend has been undeniably upwards, and advances, which may have been the outcome of fortuitous events, have notwithstanding been consolidated and maintained. Far from improved circumstances leading to overbreeding and future disaster, they have in a large number of instances been the forerunners of great advance.

As Thompson states so well:

'Every advance made in the career of industry and comfort, has a tendency to engender habits of *prudence*, and instead of producing a superfluous population greater *in proportion to food and comforts* than the previous numbers under a smaller share of industry and comforts; their uniform tendency on the contrary is to produce a lesser proportion. A greater *absolute* population always follows increased industry and comforts; but as certainly a smaller *relative* population, a smaller population in proportion to the increased comforts and necessaries of life. It is by not attending to this distinction, not perceiving or wilfully confounding things so different as an absolute and relative increase of population, that much of error on this subject has arisen.'[1]

That ultimately is the answer to the ratios. The history of

[1] Thompson, op. cit., pp. 538–539.

civilization shows a growth in the absolute population of the world; but equally it shows that the relation of population to food is less than it has been formerly. It may indeed be higher than many reformers would like, but certain results clearly follow.

If the relative standard of living is improving, however slowly, then the pressure of population on subsistence must be lessening. Consequently all the other ameliorations to life resulting from improved agriculture, improved health services, and so on, are not necessarily doomed to futility as a rigid interpretation of Malthusian policy asserts.

The preaching of moral restraint may indeed be of benefit to the poor, but their progress is not entirely dependent upon it. Some progress at least had been made even prior to the publication of Malthus's *Essay*.

CHAPTER FOUR

THE CHECKS

MALTHUS'S POOR CLASSIFICATION

ALTHOUGH the ratios were the basis of Malthus's doctrine, they were designed to throw into relief the main purpose of the *Essay*, which was to enunciate and establish the need for the checks. Unfortunately the classifications he adopted in his survey of the checks serve as little to illuminate the subject as the ratios did in discussing the growth of population.

Malthus adopts the broad division of the checks into two categories—the preventive and the positive checks. So far the matter is reasonably clear. As Senior puts it: 'The first are those which limit fecundity, the second those which decrease longevity. The first diminishes the number of births, the second increases that of deaths. And as fecundity and longevity are the only elements of the calculation, it is clear that Mr. Malthus's division is exhaustive.'

There are nevertheless certain difficulties which arise even at this stage. The positive check is not the death rate, but the *premature* death rate whatever that may be. And the preventive check constitutes the difference in the numbers of those who would have been born had man behaved purely like an animal and exercised his maximum procreative powers, and the numbers actually born owing to the various motives, prudential, social, and otherwise, which restrict this 'natural' number to more modest proportions. Both checks, therefore, are a matter of judgment, and are incapable of being empirically determined. They involve a judgment as to what is a normal death rate and what is a normal birth rate, on neither of which did Malthus cast any considerable light.

Moreover these checks do not exist as independent alternatives, nor are the classifications as rigid as they at first appear. Infanticide, though nominally, one supposes, a positive check, is on all fours with abortion, which is a preventive check, so far at least as its effects on population are concerned. Nor is the preventive check really 'preventive,' since, according to theory, it is the existence of the positive check in full career which makes the use of the preventive check so urgent, and what is already in existence can hardly be said to have been prevented.[1] This may be regarded as no more than unfortunate terminology, but the Malthusian writings abound with this; and in spite of edition after edition Malthus so often appeals from his words to the spirit of his writings, that one is tempted to think that what cannot be clearly expressed cannot be clearly established.

The checks had, in the first edition, been announced as vice and misery; those practising the preventive check being either vicious or miserable. When, in order to soften his conclusions, Malthus added *Moral Restraint*, he broke up the original classification and left two conflicting versions of the checks.

As the acute writer in the *New Monthly Magazine* writes:

'Moral restraint is, no doubt, a subdivision of the preventive check; but, in the sense in which it is used by Mr. Malthus, it is a very small part of it indeed: and as to vice and misery, as he employs those words, they each of them embrace matters, that belong to both the preventive and corrective checks. *Actual* vice and misery is a sub-denomination of the latter. The apprehension of misery, and the necessity of committing vice, are portions of the former. The consequence of this confused distribution of his checks has been, that it is difficult to see whether his doctrine is, that the effects of the tendency are corrected *after* or prevented *before* they are produced. He indeed says, that moral restraint has *not* exercised much influence in times past, but that it is quite consistent with other things, included in the preventive check, having exercised the greatest. He also says, that vice and misery had been heretofore the most powerful in this operation; but he leaves us to guess whether they wrought these effects in their preventive capacity, or in their corrective.'[2]

It is unfortunate, but understandable, that Malthus should have created this confusion. He had other things in mind than a

[1] Hall, op. cit., p. 345. [2] *New Monthly Magazine*, 1821, Vol. I, p. 199.

scientific treatise on population growth. He was concerned to advocate social policy and his terms were chosen accordingly. Vice was reprehensible, misery almost unavoidable, moral restraint a remedy which (though a forlorn hope) came well from a clergyman anxious to vindicate the ways of God to man.

THE POSITIVE CHECKS

Vice and misery then are the chief positive checks, although vice is a very junior partner in the firm.[1] Misery, however, is quite capable of dealing with the human race if it tends to exuberance. The catalogue is set out: unwholesome occupations, severe labour and exposure to the seasons, extreme poverty, bad nursing of children, large towns, excesses of all kinds, the whole train of common diseases and epidemics, wars, plague, and famine.[2] Now it is obvious that not all these can be laid entirely at the door of the principle of population. The connection of some of them with shortage of food is decidedly tenuous.[3] Many of them are clearly more the result of human folly than of lack of subsistence.[4] Jarrold says: 'It would add considerably to the perspicuity of Mr. Malthus's reasoning, if he had made a distinction between the natural tendency to death, implanted in the constitution, and the acceleration of it by war and other calamities.'[5]

Hazlitt poses three questions on the same lines: What degree of vice and misery is due to human institutions and human nature, independently of the principle of population? Will the removal of these evils open the door to more vice and misery than ever? Is the tendency to excess the effect of a simple principle operating mechanically (i.e. inherent) or is it dependent on the state of society, public opinion, and a variety of other controllable causes?[6]

The answer of Malthus appears to be this. The principle of population dooms the excess of people born to starvation. There is a constant tendency to excess which can be reduced either by a reduction in the number of births or by a high death rate. Any reduction in births, any increase in the preventive check, renders

[1] Jarrold, op. cit., p. 67.
[2] *Essay*, 1806 edn., Vol. I, p. 19.
[3] Hazlitt, *Reply to Malthus*, 1807, p. 162.
[4] Jarrold, op. cit., p. 68.
[5] Id., p. 18.
[6] Hazlitt, op. cit., p. 151.

so many deaths unnecessary. Any deaths which occur from causes other than shortage of food render so many deaths from shortage of food unnecessary. Hence all causes of premature death, all positive checks, can justifiably be lumped together, as, with a given level of preventive check, the deaths must occur and deaths in one category of the positive check are mere substitutes for deaths in another.

At which Purves protests that to say that the cause of human distress is shortage of food, and then to say that actually famine is rarely necessary as other distresses answer a similar purpose in thinning the ranks, is to imagine a cause in theory, and to uncause it in practice.[1]

Everett too enters his plea: 'If the power of increase is subject by the laws of our nature to be checked by an accidental want of subsistence, resulting from the influence of moral and physical evil, before it is checked by a necessary want arising from the exhaustion of the resources of the earth, or any part of it, then it is necessary, in order to ascertain the rate of increase, for the purpose of comparing it with the possible resources of the soil, to take into view the effects of the prior and accidental check.'[2]

We are indebted, however, to Lloyd for probably the clearest exposition of this aspect of the subject. He distinguishes three rates of population growth.

(1) A theoretical rate supposing the absence, not only of scarcity of food, but of all causes which tend to diminish fecundity or prematurely to weaken or destroy the human frame.

(2) Another theoretical rate supposing only the absence of scarcity of food and not the other causes. Examples of this may be found.

(3) The actual rate which occurs in a country under its existing circumstances.[3]

The checks of Malthus comprise the whole of the difference between the first and third rates, and not that part only of the difference which depends on the scarcity of subsistence.

Of the positive checks, the chief and ultimate one, according to the theory, is famine. Yet, with the advance of civilization, famines become less severe, less frequent, and less widespread, and therefore the one check which could indubitably be assigned

[1] Purves, op. cit., p. 36. [2] Everett, op. cit., p. 60.
[3] Lloyd, op. cit., pp. 11–12.

to lack of subsistence makes rather a poor showing. Of the others, war and pestilence are certainly powerful checks to human numbers, although their connection with shortage of food is somewhat remote. Earlier writers than Malthus had discerned an underlying economic basis for war which, if not universal, was at least important. It is difficult to say the same of pestilence which is more connected with squalor, filth, and ignorance than with shortage of food.[1]

The operation of these checks appears to run as follows. There is a temporary and often considerable reduction in numbers due to the losses in war, the deaths through famine, or the numbers swept away by plague. The thinning of the ranks makes greater opportunities for those left behind and for the time being marriages are encouraged, the procreation of children is speeded up, and the comparative opulence enables more to be reared, until once again the numbers are equal to the subsistence available, and the stage is set for a further disaster. There is no doubt that such a theory encourages a certain equanimity and fortitude in the face of the disasters of others, and a certain callous indifference to depopulation.

Yet his analysis of the relevant statistics is not above suspicion as we shall see in the next chapter. Further, Jarrold attacks the supposed beneficial effects of plague on the grounds that, since the deaths are indiscriminate, grocers and customers, doctors and patients die in equal proportions, and opportunities are not thereby enlarged.[2] Ravenstone suggests that much of the recovery is due to the fact that the old and the weak are carried off prematurely during an epidemic, and population growth arises mainly from a slower subsequent death rate than from an enhanced birth rate.[3] Several writers, including Godwin, point out that the recovery is not so much due to any sudden impetus to marriage or procreation as to immigration from surrounding areas.

Malthus supposes that in many countries these visible and drastic checks are rendered unnecessary by the steady remorseless pressure of premature mortality operating continually. There is never enough food to go round and the result is that a large

[1] This was admitted by Malthus in the chapter on the American Indians (1806 edn., Vol. I, pp. 56–57).

[2] Jarrold, op. cit., p. 162.

[3] Ravenstone, op. cit., pp. 30–31.

number of people are compelled to live hard lives and die early deaths, not by any mismanaged institutions, but by the laws of nature. Children are the chief sufferers and there is nothing, short of the preventive check, which can be done about it.

There is much truth in this view, even if it is overstated, and the high infant mortality was a fact which many writers regarded as inevitable.[1] It was part of the natural order—the ordeal of infancy.[2] Grahame went so far as to approve of this positive check in so far as it is confined to infancy. He notes the higher infant death rate among the poor and regards it as proper. It is a faithful rehearsal of the difficulties which will confront the child in after-life and 'only that degree of strength will escape which can struggle with such difficulties.' The experience of Hall had made him wiser. After referring to the enormous death rate among the children of the poor, and giving a graphic description of the conditions leading to it, he writes:

'What renders this matter still more grievous is, that there are many more sufferers than those who die, from the same causes: many who have struggled with the difficulties, and escaped with their lives, have suffered greatly in the conflict, and continue ever after to suffer, from the injury their constitution received.'[3]

Ravenstone attributed the high death rate among the children of the poor to lack of attention. 'If the rich are more fortunate than the poor in rearing their offspring . . . it is not from any difference in their food,—it arises solely from more attention.'[4] And to the extent to which the rich employ the poor to look after their own children, to that extent the poor are prevented from having and rearing children of their own.

THE DILEMMA OF MALTHUS

In spite of these views it is undeniable that much infant mortality did arise from malnutrition either of parents or of the children themselves, and Malthus is correct in drawing attention to it. But the question still emerges: Is this due to the lack of the physical resources of the earth, or does it arise through defective institutions? It is at this point that critics point to unused acres and under-developed resources.

[1] Ravenstone, op. cit., pp. 41–43.
[2] Grahame, op. cit., p. 167.
[3] Hall, op. cit., p. 15 (1850 edn.).
[4] Ravenstone, op. cit., p. 26.

It is at this point too that Malthus finds that his doctrine lands him in a dilemma which was forecast by Hazlitt, who, after asking what degree of vice and misery is necessary as a check, observes: 'The vague, general term, "vice and misery," gives us no clue. It is mere cant; and applies equally to the best and worst of all possible governments. It proves either nothing, or it proves a great deal more than I conceive Mr. Malthus would in all cases wish to prove by it.'[1] It leads to the conclusion that any removal of vice and misery merely opens the room for its re-appearance at some other point.

Malthus himself vacillates as to where he shall draw the line. He is conscious of the dilemma and is now tough, now pliant. When discussing the poor laws he is toughness itself. The poor must be driven back on to their own resources. A mouthful given here means deprivation elsewhere. Does one suggest agricultural improvements, emigration, or ploughing waste land, or cutting down the dogs and horses of the rich? The relief will be only temporary and hardly worth upsetting the existing order. Waste lands are a useful reserve in a crisis. The luxury of the rich is a useful source of supply in grave emergency. As to emigration, the phial will soon be exhausted.[2]

Without the preventive check all efforts at human improvement and the eradication of disease will be in vain. 'Nature will not, nor cannot be defeated in her purposes. The necessary mortality must come, in some form or other; and the extirpation of one disease will only be the signal for the birth of another perhaps more fatal.[3]. . . If we stop up any of these channels, it is most perfectly clear that the stream of mortality must run with greater force through some of the other channels. . . .'[4]

The small-pox in spite of its ravages has not really reduced the population. 'The small-pox is certainly one of the channels, and a very broad one, which nature has opened for the last thousand years, to keep down the population to the level of the means of subsistence; but had this been closed, others would have become wider, or new ones would have been formed. . . . For my own part, I feel not the slightest doubt, that if the introduction of the cow-pox should extirpate the small-pox, and yet the number of marriages continue the same, we shall find a very

[1] *Reply*, 1807, p. 155.
[2] 1806 edn., Vol. II, p. 147.
[3] Id., p. 360.
[4] Id., pp. 362–363.

perceptible difference in the increased mortality of some other diseases.'[1]

He concludes modestly that there is hope that medical advances may not be entirely nugatory, if there is a start in agriculture, or if the doctrines of the *Essay* become widely accepted.

Simple adherents, having grasped this line of argument, proceded to apply it to the Slave Trade with Africa. Surely the removal of slaves from Africa could do the remaining African natives no harm. Rather would it be beneficial. Until the gaps in their ranks were filled again the natives would enjoy, if only for a short space, comparative ease and plenty.

Malthus is astonished. 'While the last sheet of this Appendix was printing, I heard with some surprise that an argument had been drawn from the Principle of Population in favour of the slave-trade.'[2] His answer nevertheless completely evades the point.

It thus becomes clear that, given the superior power of population over the powers of the earth to produce subsistence, the amount of the checks of all kinds is a constant. If one of the positive checks be removed, it is bound to be immediately replaced by some other to an exactly equivalent amount. The only way, therefore, to reduce the incidence of positive checks, of premature mortality, of vice and misery, is to increase the operation of the preventive checks. It is on these that Malthus is bound to pin his hopes, and to this end he directs the exhortations and plans of the *Essay*.

PREVENTIVE CHECKS

Promiscuous intercourse, unnatural passions, violations of the marriage bed, and improper arts to conceal the consequences of irregular connections, are preventive checks that clearly come under the head of vice and as such are not to be recommended. There remains moral restraint, rigidly defined as 'restraint from marriage, from prudential motives, with a conduct strictly moral during the period of this restraint.'[3] It is this check which Malthus advocates, although he does not think it has carried

[1] 1806 edn., Vol. II, pp. 366–367. [2] Id., p. 556.
[3] 1806 edn., Vol. I, p. 19 n.

much weight in the past. Prudential restraint, without sexual abstinence, makes a better showing, and meets with a strictly qualified approval.[1] Most of his proposals then are directed towards measures likely to lead to the deferment of marriage and consequently smaller families.

Most of the critics, when they feel driven to examine the checks, show a preference for moral restraint over the positive check, but many of them think that a growth in prudence arises automatically as society develops. There are, however, exceptions. Sadler denounces this check through many chapters. He regards the distinction between the preventive check and moral restraint as academic.[2] It is unnatural, injurious, unlawful, and wicked. It is unjust in that it is only prescribed for the poor. It is cruel, because a wife is a necessity to a poor man, as solace, companion, nurse, and servant. It is impolitic because early marriage is best for females. Moreover it will lead to more and earlier orphans who will be denied the right of support. And so on. The more temperate critics, however, generally regarded it as the best check, if check there must be, but with reservations.

Hall pleads for equality of treatment in the regulation of marriages.[3] Everett suggests that a lower age limit for marriage be set or lots drawn, apologizing for any absurdity in the suggestion by the absurdity of the hypothesis he is rebutting.[4] Thompson hints at birth control,[5] and Place wholeheartedly recommends it.[6]

For Malthus the preventive check means merely the postponement of marriage until there is a reasonable prospect of supporting a family, which involves the power in health of earning 'such wages, as at the average price of corn will maintain the average number of living children to a marriage.'[7] Elsewhere six children is the number mentioned,[8] but the whole notion of a reasonable prospect is absurd. One can imagine two labourers aged twenty mentally calculating their averages and deciding that they ought to defer marriage till thirty. The one takes a chance and as it turns out has only one child; the other prudently waits, and then runs into trouble by producing a child

[1] 1806 edn., Vol. II, pp. 537–538.
[2] Sadler, op cit., Vol. I, p. 317.
[3] Hall, op. cit., p. 334 (1805 edn.).
[4] Everett, op. cit., pp. 98–99.
[5] Thompson, op. cit., p. 549.
[6] Place, op. cit., pp. 165–166.
[7] 1806 edn., Vol. II, p. 537 (Appendix).
[8] Id., Vol. II, pp. 486–487.

per annum. Such instances as these would immediately discredit prudential restraint in the eyes of the labourers.

A further serious criticism is that under such a system the wrong men would increase. Those who are prudent and careful and who exercise forethought are the men who ought to multiply; the careless and improvident are plentiful enough; and yet it is just these latter who would continue to have large families and depress the general level of working conditions.

Malthus makes much of the lack of incentive to prudence in an equalitarian society, but the incentive is scarcely more marked under a system of private property. If Malthus is correct, a reduction in the number of labourers is the best way to an improvement in wages, but the incentive to any particular labourer to bring this about is slight indeed. Each man will feel the present privations of forgoing marriage and the joys of establishing a family. The effect, however, of his abstinence among a population of ten million is to raise the general level by so small an amount as to bring no corresponding reward. No man has any particular reason to think that he will be unlucky in the search for employment. He has only to face competition with other families like his own. If he is prudent he alone will not reap the benefit; if he is imprudent the loss too will be shared.[1]

As Lloyd says: 'A labourer obtaining good employment, with a prospect of its continuance during ten or twelve years, may marry upon that prospect without violating the rules of prudence.'[2] Moreover if all were to save they would counteract each other's expectations of advantage by withdrawing purchasing power from the market and so reducing the volume of employment.

Malthus's advocacy of the abolition of the poor laws, in order to spur men on to be self-dependent, arises from his projection of middle-class motives and fears into the minds of the poor. But the poor are not afraid of poverty, nor are maxims strong enough to oppose the strong laws of human nature. No man who has never been richer thinks himself too poor to marry.

The whole difficulty in which Malthus finds himself arises from his approach to the population problem. For him it is the question of checking some almost uncontrollable urge to procreate, which characterizes the human species. He addresses

[1] Lloyd, op. cit., pp. 27–29. [2] Id., p. 43.

himself to the poor, not because they are poor so much as because they are numerous. It was this dread of numbers which led otherwise sensible men to applaud the demolition of houses as putting obstacles in the way of marriage.

But there is a more rational way of looking at it. The tendency in population to increase faster than food is merely a disproportionate superiority of motives.[1] Senior was quite sure that the growth of population was accompanied in the main by an even greater growth in prudence.

As wealth increases, the luxuries of one generation become the decencies of their successors. The desire for additional comforts and conveniences, and a feeling of degradation in their absence become more and more widely spread. The increase of the productive powers of labour enables increased numbers to enjoy the increased comforts, and this appears to be the more natural course of events, namely, that the improved standard of living should not only accompany, but rather precede the increase of numbers.

'I speak of man as a rational animal, as having a tendency towards the ends, which he pursues through the intervention of forethought, as well as towards those which he pursues at the dictates of passion. In this sense I speak of any people as having a desire to increase their subsistence, (for that is what I mean when I speak of the tendency of subsistence to increase,) stronger than the desire which leads them to increase their numbers.'[2]

In the later stages of society many postpone marriage because they find life in the society in which they are placed more congenial than founding a family.

'The consequence is, that, in these stages of society, the addition to the population is kept within the limits of subsistence, not by premature mortality (as before observed), but by a diminution of the force of the "principle of population"; by which we are to understand, not the passion between the sexes in its coarser and more general import, but that modification of it, which induces men to marry; for we know it is *then alone* it increases population.'[3]

History, to which Malthus so frequently appeals, is against him. His theory reduces the growth of population to a function of

[1] Hazlitt, *Reply*, 1807, p. 111. [2] Senior, op. cit., p. 77.

[3] *New Monthly Magazine*, Vol. I, 1821, p. 204.

the food supply, and makes all material progress depend not on skill, knowledge or effort but on celibacy. Yet before he announced his doctrines, population, prudence and an improved standard of living had been developing side by side. And in the years during which he was making his most gloomy prophecies concerning the over-population of Great Britain and the dire results which would follow, its population was growing and the death rate was declining at the same time.

When these facts force themselves upon his notice, he belatedly murmurs about a *start* in agriculture instead of a response. The issue is invariably prejudged. The facts must fit the theory.

CHAPTER FIVE

THE ILLUSTRATIONS AND PROOFS

MALTHUS'S ILLUSTRATIONS

One of the most obvious differences between the first and second editions of the *Essay* was the enormous number of illustrations and proofs incorporated in the latter. Malthus makes a very necessary apology in his Preface. He fears he has been guilty of needless repetitions or of giving too much detail.

'In those parts of the inquiry which led to conclusions different from our usual habits of thinking, it appeared to me that, with the slightest hope of producing conviction, it was necessary to present them to the reader's mind at different times, and on different occasions. I was willing to sacrifice all pretensions to merit of composition, to the chance of making an impression on a larger class of readers.'

It is certainly a somewhat thankless task to follow Malthus on his tour of the world in search of vice, misery, and the preventive check. Hall thought two or three pages would have sufficed.[1] Sadler, however, observes: 'The human mind, thus assailed, generally declines the labour of an apparently useless examination, and naturally reposing some degree of trust in the authorities it consults, surrenders itself up to a settled conviction, which it is unwilling afterwards to have disturbed.'[2] In this Sadler and Malthus appear to be more or less in agreement.

One is tempted to wonder whether the sacrifice of pretensions to merit of composition did not arise from the difficulty encountered in drawing inferences favourable to the principle of population. It is difficult to see the wood for the trees, and the

[1] Hall, op. cit., p. 343.

[2] Sadler, op. cit., Vol. I, p. 14.

illustrations serve to perplex rather than instruct the mind.[1] After struggling through a few chapters the reader tends to assume that, since Malthus has been to such trouble, therefore his conclusions must be well founded. And yet, to quote Jarrold again: 'The research of the philosopher, extracting truth from doubtful evidence, does not appear; in place of it, I fancy I am reading the speech of a pleader, who is endeavouring to say all that is favourable of his friends, and all that is discreditable of his antagonists.'[2]

We have already seen, when considering the ratios, that Malthus used the authority of Petty and Euler in very dubious fashion.[3] It is as well, therefore, to follow him with caution into the realms where authorities are few, biased, and in many cases unreliable in themselves.

It is beyond our scope to criticize in detail his excursions into different lands in search of the checks. He is bound to find them. Unwholesome occupations, severe labour and exposure to the seasons, extreme poverty, bad nursing of children, great towns, excesses of all kinds, the whole train of common diseases and epidemics, wars, plague, and famine: it is impossible not to find several of these evils in any country one cares to investigate. It did not need the *Essay on Population* to convince mankind of the widespread nature of vice and misery. The preventive checks, promiscuous intercourse, and the rest coming under the head of vice, are also obvious in their manifestations, although that due to delayed marriage proves more intractable. But what is important is, not the existence of vice and misery and the other checks, but the quantitative effects of the different checks in repressing population, and their clear connection with lack of the means of subsistence. Viewed in this light, the illustrations and proofs do not show up so well.

The survey may be divided for convenience into two parts; (1) those countries where there is no statistical evidence, or practically none of any value; (2) those countries where statistics of births, marriages, and deaths of various degrees of imperfection exist, and which might therefore provide a surer basis for satisfactory conclusions.

[1] Jarrold, op. cit., p. 191.
[2] Id., p. 120.
[3] Ante, Book III, Chapter I.

PRIMITIVE TRIBES

The former group occupies most of Book I and includes savage tribes, American Indians, the South Sea Islanders, the ancient inhabitants of Europe, the modern pastoral nations, Africa, Siberia, Turkey and Persia, Indostan and Tibet, China and Japan, the Greeks and the Romans. All is speculation. The sources of information are records of voyages by Cook and others, missionaries' writings, and similar works. To the danger that these writings would concentrate on the unusual, the vivid and emotional aspects of the places and societies they purport to describe, is added the fact that Malthus himself naturally selected those incidents and facets which best seemed to him to support his theory.

One feels he has not been as critical as he might when one reads an account of the inhabitants of New Holland, who are 'neither tall nor well made. Their arms, legs, and thighs, are thin, which is ascribed to the poorness of their mode of living.' Yet these same natives climb the tallest trees after honey and flying-squirrels, 'by cutting a notch with their stone hatchets for each foot successively, while their left arm embraces [sic] the tree. Trees were observed notched in this manner to the height of eighty feet before the first branch, where the hungry savage could hope to meet with any reward for so much toil.'[1] Their arms, though thin, must have been passably long, and their efforts prodigious for a starving race.

The whole tone of these early chapters is definitely emotional. We are led to despise these creatures by the recounting of a mass of revolting details concerning their lives and habits, as the schoolboy is made to shudder at the thought of the French eating snails and frogs. Much of the detail concerning the sexual customs is probably quite true, but its connection with absence of food is not established.

THE NORTH AMERICAN INDIANS

When discussing the North American Indians the matter is left in a very confused state. We read in the same paragraph of the 'want of ardour' in the men towards the women, of the passion

[1] Seventh edn., 1872 (London, Reeves and Turner), p. 14.

between the sexes becoming 'more ardent,' and at the end 'the dissoluteness of their manners is sometimes excessive.'[1] This is gratuitously attributed to the varying degrees of hardship suffered. The women are held to be degraded and overworked, thus leading to low fecundity, the main causes of which are long suckling periods, the excessive labour already mentioned, pre-marital prostitution, and a certain amount of child murder. Under this rigorous treatment only the fittest survive.

Having passed through the dangers of childhood, other dangers scarcely less formidable await the Indian on his approach to manhood: indigestion, consumption, pleurisy, asthma, paralysis, smallpox, and malignant fevers. Deserted villages, skulls, and skeletons in huge numbers, all these complete the picture, that one is tempted to wonder how anyone survived.

Then the thought occurs to Malthus that when they have been thinned out enough, the age of plenty ought to dawn at least for the time being. But no! 'From their extreme ignorance, the dirt of their persons, and the closeness and filth of their cabins, they lose the advantage which usually attends a thinly peopled country, that of being more exempt from pestilential diseases than those which are fully inhabited.'[2]

Those who escape the dangers of infancy and disease are exposed to danger from war, mainly for the preservation of hunting grounds, and in the end even the ties of nature are loosened and 'a father will sell his son for a knife or a hatchet.'[3] We are not told in these circumstances what use the son is to the buyer, but possibly it is for food. At this point Malthus differs from Robertson, from whom much of his information is derived, in thinking that cannibalism must have had its origin in hunger and only more recently have become conventionalized. Nevertheless a diminution of numbers does not bring the greater plenty; it merely places each tribe at the mercy of stronger neighbours.

It is here that Malthus, like his readers, must have had some misgivings, which he relegates to a footnote, with which we may well leave this chapter of inconsistencies.

'These causes may perhaps appear more than sufficient to keep the population down to the level of the means of sub-

[1] 1872 edn., p. 19. [2] Id., p. 23. [3] Id., p. 24.

sistence; and they certainly would be so, if the representations given of the unfruitfulness of the Indian women were universally, or even generally true. It is probable that some of the accounts are exaggerated, but it is difficult to say which; and it must be acknowledged, that, even allowing for all such exaggerations, they are amply sufficient to establish the point proposed.'[1]

It is unnecessary to follow any further this chapter; and that on the South Seas can be readily dismissed. Successive accounts by travellers show that the population is now plentiful, now considerably reduced, and again Malthus admits that the accounts are probably not accurate. Nevertheless he retains the conclusion that 'great fluctuations must necessarily have taken place,'[2] the necessity being compliance with the principle of population. The best proof of these fluctuations which could have been advanced would have been changes in the age composition of the population, but he quotes no evidence from any of the sources on which he relies.[3]

NORTHERN EUROPE

In the next chapter attention is turned to the ancient inhabitants of Northern Europe, and Malthus proves to his own satisfaction, and with the aid of a quotation from Tacitus, that the successive waves of emigration from Germany were due to the principle of population which was capable of doubling the population of Germany in about twenty-five years. It is not at all clear why Germany should be singled out for this favoured treatment; why, when other tribes such as the North American Indians were in such dire straits, Germans should be capable of such expansion, even when their excellent habits are taken into account. Presumably the purpose is to show that an indefinite emigration can occur from a limited territory, owing to the departure of members making room for their successors.

There are gaps in the reasoning. In North America famine rarely if ever was succeeded by plenty; and the departure of emigrants from tribes consisting mainly of hunters does not seem to be such a manifest advantage. True there will be more game to be caught, but it still has to be caught, and without the most

[1] 1872 edn., p. 27. [2] Id., p. 40. [3] Ravenstone, op. cit., p. 76.

vigorous of the inhabitants who make up the larger part of the emigrants. Further it would be interesting to know by what checks the inhabitants were kept down prior to their taking up emigration, particularly in view of the striking contrast with the North American Indians. On these points the *Essay* is silent.

SOME OTHER CASES

In Southern Siberia the soil is of extraordinary fertility, some of it inexhaustible. Yet in spite of the possibility of plentiful subsistence many areas are sparsely populated. The reason for this is maldistribution of wealth and the small demand for labour. Corn will grow in abundance almost without attention, so the farmer can do all his work with the aid of his family and one or two hired men. The others 'are, in fact, as completely without the means of subsistence as if they were living upon a barren sand. They must either emigrate to some place where their work is wanted, or perish miserably of poverty.'[1]

This is sufficiently extraordinary. Here food is to be had without effort, yet the worker is condemned by the principle of population to starve. In New Holland he must climb eighty-foot trees to catch flying-squirrels, and still starve. The answer to this apparent conflict is, of course, that the causes of misery and poverty are many and are not all connected with the physical capacity of the earth to yield more, but with human institutions. Yet this is only fleetingly admitted by Malthus. Jarrold is more than just when he says: 'A fertile soil, as a check to population, does not come under the heads either of vice, misery, or moral restraint. In another edition of his work, Mr. Malthus will, doubtless, give it its proper place.'[2]

In Turkey it is clear that the main reason for the miserable state of the population is the corrupt and grasping nature of the government, and the depopulation is attributable to plague, epidemics, famine, and their consequences. In Persia the state of affairs is little better. Malthus ends the chapter with these words: 'The superior destruction of the plague, in Turkey, is perhaps nearly balanced by the greater frequency of internal commotions in Persia,'[3] a sentence which recalls vividly to mind

[1] 1872 edn., p. 83. [2] Jarrold, op. cit., p. 127. [3] 1872 edn., p. 92.

some words of Jarrold: 'There is something unpleasant, something that does not comport with the dignity of philosophy, to poise and balance sums of misery against each other. Nor does this mode of judging satisfy the mind. . . .'[1]

We therefore leave this section of the illustrations, pausing only to point out a misrepresentation of Plato's views. Having correctly outlined Plato's method of securing the quality and numbers of his guardians, he then asserts: 'From these passages it is evident that Plato fully saw the tendency of population to increase beyond the means of subsistence.'[2] Whereas anyone reading Plato's account will realize that he was not discussing this problem at all. His regulations are concerned solely to maintain the proper number and quality in the guardians of the Republic. So Plato joins Euler and Petty in being dragged forward to support a point which he did not contemplate.

THE STATES OF MODERN EUROPE

When Malthus turns to his survey of the states of modern Europe the investigation appears to offer more promise. There are a considerable number of statistics available, and although many of them are admittedly imperfect, it is not impossible that suitable treatment will produce results of value.[3]

The first country to be considered is Norway, which, being comparatively free from epidemics, and having a death rate of only 1 in 48, has been subject to small positive checks. It must therefore have suffered a considerable preventive check, and this is held to be evidenced by the low proportion of yearly marriages, i.e., 1 to 130 persons. Reasons are then assigned as to why this low proportion should exist.

[1] Jarrold, op. cit., p. 100.

[2] 1872 edn., p. 115.

[3] Cf. Ravenstone: 'We must be careful not to suffer our judgments to be misled by insulated facts, not to draw conclusions from the returns of a single town or a single parish. . . . As parts of a whole the returns will be very exact, though, when considered separately, they will exhibit results irreconcilable with any general principles. To these considerations, important as they are, Mr. Malthus has paid no attention; he has sought to find rather varieties than resemblances; rather to collect anomalies than to establish a general rule. His object was, to show population increasing in different countries in all possible varieties, according to the different checks which he supposes to impede its growth; this could be best effected by considering not the whole but each of its parts in detail. . .' (p. 78).

Further on Malthus examines the astonishingly high rate of marriages in Holland, viz., 1 in 64 persons, but the difficulty is solved when the mortality is found to be 1 in 22 or 23, as against 1 in 36 when the marriages are in the proportion of 1 in 108.

'The extraordinary number of marriages was not caused by the opening of any new sources of subsistence, and therefore produced no increase of population. It was merely occasioned by the rapid dissolution of the old marriages by death, and the consequent vacancy of some employment by which a family could be supported.'[1]

'A very curious and striking contrast to these Dutch villages, tending to illustrate the present subject, will be recollected in what was said respecting the state of Norway. In Norway the mortality is 1 in 48, and the marriages are 1 in 130; in the Dutch villages the mortality 1 in 23, and the marriages 1 in 64. The difference both in the marriages and deaths is above double. They maintain their relative proportions in a very exact manner, and show how much the deaths and marriages mutually depend upon each other; and that, except where some sudden start in the agriculture of a country enlarges the means of subsistence, an increase of marriages must be accompanied by an increase of mortality, and *vice versâ*.'[2]

This is not the case. If the average person lives to the age of 48, and the rate of marriages is 1 to 130 persons, then in a period of 48 years, in a stationary population, for every 130 people who are born, 130 people die and 96 are married. Therefore the percentage of the people who marry is about 74 per cent. Applying the same reasoning to the Dutch villages; in a period of 23 years, and again assuming a stationary population, for every 64 people who are born, 64 die and there are 23 marriages, i.e. the proportion of people who marry is $\frac{46}{64}$, that is 72 per cent.[3]

Malthus's error lies in using the crude rates. In a population with an average expectation of life of 23 years, the proportion of marriages must be high because their duration is so short. The number of marriages will be high, the number of married people few. In a population with an average expectation of life of 48 years, the proportion of marriages must be low, because the

[1] 1872, edn., p. 156. [2] Id., p. 157.

[3] This rough statement ignores the effect of second and subsequent marriages, but there is no point in refined analysis of these figures.

divisor is swollen by the existence of such a large number of older people, married and unmarried. Malthus has mistaken a statistical phenomenon of crude rates for a factual phenomenon which supports his theory.

Actually it is not possible to determine the extent of the preventive check in this way. The same rates could obtain for various ages of marriage, and before the Norwegian rates can support his theory he must show not fewness of marriages, but also lateness, and this he cannot do. What is important in showing a preventive check is not the rate at which marriages occur, but the number which co-exist at the same time, which depends on their duration.

Malthus pursues this fallacy further, by comparing rates in the same places at different periods of time.

'In the town of Leipsic, in the year 1620, the annual marriages were to the population as 1 to 82; from the year 1741 to 1756 they were as 1 to 120.

'In Augsberg, in 1510, the proportion of marriages to the population was 1 to 86; in 1750 as 1 to 123 . . .'[1]

And so on; which ratios he takes to show that, as places and facilities become more difficult to obtain, the rate of marriages declines. The simple and obvious explanation of an improvement in longevity diluting the crude figures is passed over. We feel that there is much truth in the statement he makes: 'All general proportions however of every kind should be applied with considerable caution.'[2]

SWITZERLAND

Malthus prefaces his chapter on Russia with the remark that it is impossible not to receive the figures 'with a considerable degree of suspicion.' Sharing that suspicion, we pass on to consider Switzerland. We are told it 'is in many respects so different from the other states of Europe, and some of the facts that have been collected respecting it are so curious, and tend so strongly to illustrate the general principles of this work, that it seems to merit a separate consideration.'[3]

The peculiarity in question is the fact that M. Muret, minister of Vevay, had investigated and confirmed a decline in the

[1] 1872 edn., pp. 157–158. [2] Id., p. 159. [3] Id., p. 163.

population, which had been deplored in the Transactions of the Economical Society of Berne, and regarded as a fact 'so obvious as not to require proof.' Malthus investigates the figures and arrives at a figure of 22,536 for the Swiss population in contrast with Muret's total of 18,512. Without following him in his calculations there is some justice in Jarrold's remark: 'It is scarcely possible a people should increase from 18 to 22,000 and not to be conscious of it: the old inhabitants must have witnessed the building of houses, the inclosing of waste lands, the general increase of accommodations over the country, the extension of manufactories; and what they had seen they would speak of; but the very reverse was their testimony: they lamented the decay of towns and villages, the declension of the arts, the languid state of agriculture and commerce, the frequency of emigration; in short the face of the country indicated a declining population.'[1]

Malthus considers in detail the parish of Leyzin and is taken to task by Ravenstone in his analysis. The average expectation of life was 61 years, and the equal numbers of births and deaths proved, says Malthus, that there had been no emigration and that the resources of the parish for the support of population had remained stationary. The inference drawn is that there is a powerful preventive check due to late marriages.

'It is evident that a very large proportion of the subsisting marriages would be among persons so far advanced in life, that most of the women would have ceased to bear children; and in consequence the whole number of subsisting marriages was found to be to the number of annual births in the very unusual proportion of 12 to 1. The births were only about a 49th part of the population; and the number of persons above sixteen was to the number below that age nearly as 3 to 1.'[2]

Ravenstone challenged the whole analysis.

'That the population of a grazing parish should always remain nearly stationary, that its births should be unusually few, is not peculiar to Leizin. The registers shew the same fact in every parish under similar circumstances. It is always in towns the increase of population takes place, it is there that the surplus population of the country finds employment.'[3]

Figures do not bear out the existence of a large preventive

[1] Jarrold, op. cit., pp. 146–147. [2] 1872 edn., p. 168.
[3] Ravenstone, op. cit., p. 80.

check. If the births are 1 to 49 of the population and 1 to 12 marriages, then about half the population are married.

'If the marriages were contracted at so late a period of life as materially to limit the number of births; if, for instance, women, one with another, did not marry till forty, the number of the single women must greatly exceed that of the married, they must be as three to one; but, in this parish, the number of married and unmarried is nearly equal.'[1]

Actually the facts point to comparatively early marriage.

'Nor is it possible to conceive that the circumstances which are supposed to prevent early marriages can ever continue to operate for any length of time. Such preventive checks may make a good figure on paper, they can never have any real existence. . . . If one generation were to defer marriage till a late period of life, they would be ready to quit the world before their successors would be fit to enter into it; the next generation as it rose to manhood would find all the places unoccupied. If women do not marry till forty, one with another, they will not survive the birth of their children more than eighteen years. As, according to this system, a marriage will take place wherever there can be found the means of subsistence, the marriages of the children would be as much earlier as those of their parents were later; the delay of the fathers would quicken the speed of the sons.'[2]

The result would be violent oscillations of population, and considerable changes in its age composition, but the registers of Leyzin show no such results.

The real explanation is that the young emigrate, contract their marriages elsewhere, and most of their children are born elsewhere. At the death of the father one will return to occupy the farm, but he is probably already married and many of his children are already born. Any other explanation leads to absurd statistical results.

'Mountainous districts are, from the very nature of things, breeding countries; they do not furnish their neighbours with cattle only, but likewise with men; they are continually and necessarily sending forth a part of their population; their deaths will, therefore, always bear a small proportion to their births; of those who are born with them, many die elsewhere.'[3]

[1] Ravenstone, op. cit., p. 80. [2] Id., p. 81.
[3] Id., p. 83.

Whatever may have been the strength of the preventive check in some parts, when Malthus reached Lac de Joux he heard a different story, for his landlady complained of the poverty and misery round about. She asserted that 'boys and girls were marrying who ought still to be at school; and, that, while this habit of early marriages continued, they should always be wretched and distressed for subsistence.' He was also delighted with a Swiss peasant who 'appeared to understand the principle of population almost as well as any man I ever met with.'[1] This man denounced early marriages as *le vice du pays*, and advocated a law prohibiting men from marrying under the age of forty and then only with *des vieilles filles*. Malthus was so struck with his perspicacity that he did not even dissent from this last proposition.[2] Indeed his conversations with the Swiss peasantry led him to believe that it would be no difficult task 'to make the common people comprehend the principle of population, and its effect in producing low wages and poverty.'[3]

THE BRITISH ISLES

When Malthus approaches a study of England he has apparently more materials to work on. He first of all outlines the prevalence of the preventive check by means of practical observations. Men of liberal education fear to fall several rungs down the ladder; tradesmen and farmers must defer marriage till they are established; the single labourer hesitates before sharing his pay among four or five; domestic servants are reluctant to quit comparative luxury. Proof is adduced of the check, with the same force as the proof already considered in the case of Norway, in that the annual marriages are to the population as 1 to about 123. He then considers the returns of births and deaths which are admitted to be deficient, but by means of a series of 'corrections' he reduces the average mortality from 1 in 49 to 1 in 40. A similar adjustment of the baptisms gives a proportion of births to population of 1 in 30. The defects in the registers are admitted and the problem of reconciliation is difficult, but one feels that

[1] 1872 edn., p. 173.

[2] Cf., p. 316. 'I am indeed most decidedly of opinion that any positive law to limit the age of marriage would be both unjust and immoral.'

[3] Id., p. 175.

probably the soundest part of the chapter is the conclusion, namely that we should be 'extremely cautious in applying the proportions which are observed to be true at present to past or future periods.'[1]

Later when he has the results of the census of 1811 to hand he betrays astonishment at the accelerated rate of increase of population, a 'striking instance of the readiness with which population starts forwards, under almost any weight, when the resources of a country are rapidly increasing.'[2] This is a substantial admission from the prophet of doom of 1798. The figures are difficult to reconcile with those of 1801, but prove more tractable when he adds one-sixth to the births and one-twelfth to the deaths. At all events we get a new table, and 'whether the new table be right or not, the old table must be wrong.'[3] All again is speculation, for which it would be unfair to blame Malthus, except insofar as he insists on building such a comprehensive theory on such doubtful evidence.

He is only certain of one thing. The rapid increase in population cannot continue since it would double the number of the inhabitants in less than fifty-five years. So much for prophecy![4]

In 1825 he returns to the figures again, there having been a third census of population, but we reach the rather depressing conclusion that 'if we can put any trust in our enumerations, no reliance can be placed on an estimate of past population founded on the proportions of the births, deaths, or marriages. The same causes which have operated to alter so essentially these proportions during the twenty years for which we have enumerations may have operated in an equal degree before.'[5]

With this sad conclusion concerning the motherland it would be heartless to follow him to Scotland. By this time he fears he has already tired the patience of his readers and from the acknowledged omissions in the registers, few just inferences can be drawn.[6] The proportions of births and deaths 'are so extraordinary that it is difficult to conceive that they approach near

[1] 1872 edn., p. 206 [2] Id., p. 206. [3] Id., p. 212.

[4] Id., p. 215. The actual figures for the Population of England and Wales were: 1801, 9,168,000*: 1851, 17,928,000; 1911, 36,070,000.

(* Corrected figure from Talbot Griffith: *Population Problems of the Age of Malthus.*)

[5] 1872 edn., p. 219. [6] Id., p. 219.

the truth.'[1] With regard to marriages it is 'still more difficult to form a conjecture.' As to Ireland the growth in population is due to the potato, the checks are chiefly positive. The chapter concludes with the significant words that 'information, however much to be desired, is unattainable.'[2]

PREMATURE SPECULATION

It may seem that in surveying these points we have been unfair to Malthus, and that one ought to be more tolerant towards a man wrestling with inadequate material in an effort to draw inferences and conclusions. This view could be accepted if Malthus had been really approaching the subject with an open mind, bent only on eliciting the truth. But one gets the overwhelming impression that he is almost blind to what does not fit in with his hypothesis, and much of his labour is to build conclusions on foundations not meant to bear their weight. His method too, frequently noticed above, of writing a chapter full of hints of this check and that which support his view, so that the mind feels to some extent sympathetic toward him, and then at the end, when the seed has been sown, disarmingly to admit that all is speculation—this method, though doubtless useful in obtaining converts, does not enhance the book as a work of science.

The correct scientific approach is not to wrest data to fit conclusions, but to test them scrupulously before admitting hypotheses. Most of the speculations were premature. The state of knowledge of births and deaths at his time did not permit of any but the roughest conclusions being drawn, and it is to be feared that the figures were used not so much to find out what could be discovered as to give an air of scientific accuracy to what was at most only an unsupported hypothesis.

MISQUOTATION OF SÜSSMILCH

Before finally leaving the illustrations we must take up one more point, namely the extract he quotes of a Table of Süssmilch which purports to illustrate the huge increase in marriages which occurs after a plague has swept away large numbers of the population. Malthus draws pages of conclusions favourable to his

[1] 1872 edn., p. 220. [2] Id., p. 229.

viewpoint from this table, but even a cursory glance reveals that his copy of the table completely misrepresents the position.[1] (See pp. 270–271.)

It is clear that the figure for 1711 includes the marriages for the two years 1710 and 1711, as nowhere else is it matched or nearly matched, and it is difficult to see what justification there can be for such a mishandling of the figures.[2] A careful writer anxious only to ascertain the truth would have broken down this figure, which would still have given his case a little support, but Malthus does not do this. Instead he retains the figure long after he must have realized its falsity. Indeed in a footnote he says:

'It is possible that there may be a mistake in the table, and that the births and marriages of the plague years are included in the year 1711; though as the deaths are carefully separated, it seems very strange that it should be so. It is however a matter of no great importance. The other years are sufficient to illustrate the general principle.'[3]

If an error of 100 per cent. or so is of no great importance, one wonders that he should have taken so much trouble with the minutiæ of his calculations in other fields. However, the attitude is clear. A striking figure such as that of 1711 may well convince the flagging reader, who will be only too pleased to skip the rest of the chapter and proceed to the 'General Deductions' which immediately follow.

Actually the marriage rate seems to have remained high in the three years 1710–1712 and then fallen sharply to a lower level more in keeping with the decimated population. Probably a large proportion of these marriages may be accounted for by the re-arrangement of marital relationships which would inevitably occur. There would be many widows and widowers who would naturally remarry, as well as younger persons marrying for the first time, and a period of two years might well elapse before these arrangements had sorted themselves out and a return

[1] Cf. Sadler's discussion, op. cit., Vol. II, pp. 191 et seq.

[2] It was probably not deliberate misrepresentation, but more probably an error in the figures as supplied to him by another. We have seen that Booth thought Malthus did not consult the Censuses himself, though that seems hardly likely. Nevertheless this instance lends colour to the view that some of the statistical work was done for him. Examples such as these cast doubts on either his ability or his intellectual honesty.

[3] *Essay*, 1872 edn., p. 246 n.

Ein und zwanzigste Tabelle.

Liste vom Königr. Preussen und Herzogth. Litthauen.

Jahre.	Getraute Paare.	Getaufte.	Gestorbene.	Verhältniß der Getrauten zu den Getauften.	Verhältniß der Gestorbenen zu den Getauften.
1693	5799	18757	16881*		
1694	5910	19294	14918		
1695	5937	20946	14964		
1696	5540	19903	12786		
1697	5551	19678	14761		
S. 5 J.	28737	98578	74310		10: 13
					oder
Mittelz.	5747	19715	14862	10: 34	100: 132
1698	6191	21803	17091*		
1699	6225	22680	14121		
1700	6105	23929	15165		
1701	5831	26330	13761		
1702	5998	25819	12732		
S. 5 J.	30350	120561	72870		10: 16
					oder
Mittelz.	6070	24112	14574	10: 39	100: 165
1703	5787	25752	14936		
1704	6031	27521	15766		
1705	5669	28068	15362		
1706	6058	27920	16575		
1707	5722	26835	17155*		
1708	7230	25281	18789*		
S. 6 J.	36497	161377	98583		10: 16
					oder
Mittelz.	6082	26896	16430	10: 44	100: 163
1709	5477	23977	59196 } Pest		
1710	⸗ ⸗	⸗ ⸗	188537 } Pest		
		Sum.	247733		
1711	12028	32522	10131		
S. 3 J.	17505	56499			

E 2

Portion of Table XXI, from Süssmilch, *Die Göttliche Ordnung*, Fourth edn., Vol. I, p. 83 of the Tables.

Annual Average.	Marriages.	Births.	Deaths.	Proportion of marriages to births.	Proportion of deaths to births.
5 years to 1697 5 years to 1702 6 years to 1708	5747 6070 6082	19715 24112 26896	14862 14474 16430	10 : 34 10 : 39 10 : 44	100 : 132 100 : 165 100 : 163
In 1709 and 1710	a plague	number destroyed in 2 years.	247733		
In 1711 In 1712	12028 6267	32522 22970	10131 10445	10 : 27 10 : 36	100 : 320 100 : 220
5 years to 1716 5 years to 1721 5 years to 1726 5 years to 1731 4 years to 1735	4968 4324 4719 4808 5424	21603 21396 21452 29554 22692	11984 12039 12863 12825 15475	10 : 43 10 : 49 10 : 45 10 : 42 10 : 41	100 : 180 100 : 177 100 : 166 100 : 160 100 : 146

Portion of Malthus's Table IV, purporting to be taken from Süssmilch See *Essay*, 1872 edn., p. 245.

Notes.

In Süssmilch's Table the brackets connecting the years 1710 and 1711 are quite clear, thus demonstrating that the figures 12,028 and 32,522 denote the sum of the marriages and births for the two years.

The matter is clinched beyond dispute by the last line, where the totals 17,505 and 56,499 are specifically stated to be the sum of the three years.

to normal had been established. However it is not our object to reopen the question of the effects of plagues here. Sadler drew up a parallel table showing the number of marriages occurring in healthy and unhealthy years respectively, and also of marriages occurring in the year succeeding each unhealthy year,[1] and the results do little to encourage belief in Malthus's viewpoint.

The matter serves mainly to show that Malthus can use data in any way which suits his purpose, and is a glaring instance of his habit of making statements in the main body of the text, and then, when he subsequently finds them in error, leaving them alone and qualifying them by an obscure or unobtrusive footnote.

[1] Sadler, op. cit., Vol. II, p. 202.

BOOK FOUR

THE APPLICATION OF THE THEORY

CHAPTER ONE

APPLICATION TO PERFECTIBILITY

THE ATTACK ON GODWIN

THE first application of the principle of population was to refute the doctrines of Condorcet and Godwin, particularly the latter, concerning the perfectibility of man by the gradual extension of the reign of reason. And this application was so successful that, slowly at first, and then with increasing rapidity, Godwin and his doctrines faded completely out of the picture, while Malthus climbed quickly into the ascendancy.

The spectacle is sufficiently extraordinary. It can hardly be said to be due to the strength of the argument: rather it would appear that men were willing to believe what they desired to believe. The doctrine of population appeared to show that the lofty aims at an improved society were doomed to frustration. The excesses of the French Revolution made former supporters glad of an excuse to withdraw their allegiance. To the conservatives the theory showed what they had all along believed to be true—that it was only the existing institutions which preserved an already suffering humanity from even greater degradation and ruin. If we add to these considerations the general difficulties of the period, which have already been alluded to, the success of the doctrine is seen to be due, not to any inherent strength, but to its timely appearance.

Godwin barely sensed the danger as his polite and generous reply of 1801 shows. He regards it as 'obvious and glaring . . . that the reasonings of the *Essay on Population* did not bear with any particular stress upon (his) hypothesis.'[1] Nevertheless these reasonings converted vast numbers of his supporters.

[1] Godwin, *First Reply*, 1801, p. 55.

Malthus adopts the arguments which Wallace had put forward against a hypothetical Utopia of his own contriving. Under a perfect government the difficulties of having and rearing a family would be so slight, that, in spite of occasional plagues and epidemics, the population of the world would reach such a level that the earth would be overstocked and unable to sustain its inhabitants.[1]

But Malthus goes further and expresses his astonishment that the difficulty should have been treated as being remote. Far from it: it is imminent and immediate. 'At every period during the progress of cultivation, from the present moment, to the time when the whole earth was become like a garden, the distress for want of food would be constantly pressing on all mankind, if they were equal. Though the produce of the earth might be increasing every year, population would be increasing much faster; and the redundancy must necessarily be repressed by the periodical or constant action of misery or vice.'[2] The reason for this point of view is the ratios.

'If the proportion between the natural increase of population and food, which I have given, be in any degree near the truth, it will appear, on the contrary, that the period when the number of men surpass their means of subsistence, has long since arrived; and that this necessary oscillation, this constantly subsisting cause of periodical misery; has existed ever since we have had any histories of mankind, does exist at present, and will for ever continue to exist, unless some decided change take place, in the physical constitution of our nature.'[3]

As for Condorcet's proposal for a social security fund to provide for the aged, the widows and the orphans, it may sound all

[1] Wallace, *Various Prospects of Mankind, Nature and Providence*, p. 114.

[2] First edn., pp. 143–144. Cf. the subsequent modification of this (1806 edn., Vol. II, p. 78) where the checks are moral restraint, vice and misery.

[3] First edn., p. 153. This statement depends on the arithmetical ratio. It is not as he suggests universally true. In the short run, so long as there is uncultivated land, as there always has been, and so long as produce can grow in geometrical ratio if land is available, the rate of growth of produce can equal that of population. If it does not do so, the check is not obviously due to any fundamental ratio which can be deduced, but to circumstances as they exist. Malthus is stressing a point of view which at times may be important, but he constantly blurs and falsifies his statement by adherence to the ratios, and by confusing the long-term and short-term views.

right on paper, but it is quite impracticable. Labour, asserts Malthus, would not be performed without the goad of necessity,[1] and population would rapidly increase if the rising generation were freed from the 'killing frost' of misery.

He makes nonsense of Condorcet's view that human life might be prolonged indefinitely. There is no evidence of such an extension. He draws careful analogies with developments in sheep breeding and horticulture where, although progress is made, there are limits which, though ill-defined, clearly exist. 'In all these cases therefore, a careful distinction should be made, between an unlimited progress, and a progress where the limit is merely undefined.'[2] He then leaves what might have been developed into a promising discussion of eugenics[3] for a barren attack on Godwin.

Godwin's system of equality is most beautiful and engaging, but it is doomed to frustration by 'the grinding law of necessity; misery, and the fear of misery.' His main error is in attributing vice and misery to human institutions. If this were the case there would be hope of amelioration, and reason would be the correct instrument of progress, but alas! human institutions are mere feathers on the surface; deeper seated causes 'corrupt the springs, and render turbid the whole stream of human life.'[4]

The beautiful picture painted by Godwin is far from being a possible reality, for, even if perfectibility were achieved, such a society would be immensely favourable to the growth of population. Nearly every woman of twenty-three would have a family. Even if we grant such a population the power to double within twenty-five years, and to maintain its food supply by ploughing up grazing land and cultivating it with manure, there will soon be an end to land, manure, and surplus population. Twenty-eight millions of people trying to live on food for twenty-one![5]

Alas, what a disaster! Provisions no longer flow in to support the mother with the large family. 'Benevolence yet lingering in a few bosoms, makes some faint expiring struggles, till at length self-love resumes his wonted empire, and lords it triumphant over the world.'[6] And no human institutions are to blame.

If the reader is still doubtful, let him try a few more doubling

[1] Following Townsend.
[2] First edn., p. 167.
[3] The story of Maud, the Milk-maid, p. 171.
[4] Id., p. 177.
[5] Id., p. 189.
[6] Id., p. 190.

periods, and before the conclusion of a century 'the population would be one hundred and twelve millions, and the food only sufficient for thirty-five millions, leaving seventy-seven millions unprovided for.'[1]

Of course, he says, 'I am sufficiently aware that the redundant millions could never have existed.'[2] The population would be kept down to the level of the food supply by vice and misery. The perfect state would probably have to re-establish the institutions of property and marriage. Property would be redivided among individuals, and thereafter children who were born into a world already appropriated, would be 'the unhappy persons who, in the great lottery of life, have drawn a blank.'[3] Labour would be ill-paid, the rearing of families would be checked by sickness and misery, and a society founded on benevolence would degenerate into a society divided into a class of proprietors and one of labourers, 'with self-love for the mainspring of the great machine.'[4] Not thirty years would elapse before the complete destruction of Godwin's system from the simple principle of population.

Actually it would never be established. The causes which would destroy it if it were set up would see to this. There has been no progress towards the extinction of the passion between the sexes, and Godwin overrates the power of reason. Voluntary acts are preceded by decisions of the mind, but bodily cravings influence such decisions, and often lead men into unreasonable actions.[5] There is no future whatever for equality: of that let there be no slightest shadow of a doubt.

'Were I to live a thousand years, and the laws of nature to remain the same, I should little fear, or rather little hope, a contradiction from experience,[6] in asserting, that no possible sacrifices or exertions of the rich, in a country which had been long inhabited, could for any time place the lower classes of the community in a situation equal, with regard to circumstances, to the situation of the common people, about thirty years ago, in the northern States of America.'[7]

Thus he bids farewell to the idea of progress!

[1] *Essay*, First edn., p. 192.
[2] Id., p. 193.
[3] Id., p. 204.
[4] Id., p. 207.
[5] Id., pp. 252–254.
[6] So much for prophecy based on this principle. Compare Godwin at the end of the present chapter.
[7] Id., p. 277.

THE REPLY OF HAZLITT AND GODWIN

Yet this extraordinary doctrine carried the day. This, probably more than any other single cause, brought about the eclipse of Godwin. It appeared to Hazlitt like a 'refinement on absurdity' to assert that men would be '*bad*, in proportion as they were *good*; that their excellence would be their ruin.'[1] And yet that is what the first *Essay* did assert. It granted Godwin a state of perfectibility in which individual interests were subordinated to the general good, in which reason governed the whole of men's actions and their relations with one another, and then asserted that it would be brought down by the unrestricted and unreasonable operation of a single passion; and that, having reached such a state of well-being, the inhabitants would be utterly indifferent to or ignorant of the conditions of its continuance, or incapable of carrying such conditions into effect.

To quote Hazlitt again:

'Against whatever other scheme of reform this objection might be valid, the one it was brought expressly to overturn was impregnable against it, invulnerable to its slightest graze. Say that the Utopian reasoners are visionaries unfounded, that the state of virtue and knowledge they suppose, in which reason shall have become all-in-all, can never take place, that it is inconsistent with the nature of man and with all experience, well and good—but to say that society will have attained this high and palmy state, that reason will have become the master-key to all our motives, and that, when arrived at its greatest power, it will cease to act at all, but will fall down dead, inert and senseless before the principle of population, is an opinion which one would think few people would choose to advance or assent to without strong inducements for maintaining or believing it.'[2]

The introduction of the check of moral restraint into the second and subsequent editions of the *Essay* effectively destroys any claim which the first *Essay* had to be an answer to Godwin. As the latter says, in his *Reply* of 1801, the preventive check operates considerably among the middle classes even under the existing system.

'Will there be less of virtue, prudence and honourable pride

[1] *Reply to Malthus*, 1807, p. 49.

[2] Hazlitt, *Spirit of the Age*, World's Classics, p. 147.

in such a condition of society, than there is at present? It is true, the ill consequences of a numerous family will not come so coarsely home to each man's individual interest, as they do at present. It is true, a man in such a state of society might say, if my children cannot subsist at my expence let them subsist at the expence of my neighbour. But it is not in the human character to reason after this manner in such a situation. The more men are raised above poverty and a life of expedients, the more decency will prevail in their conduct, and sobriety in their sentiments. . . . Where a man possesses every reasonable means of pleasure and happiness, he will not be in a hurry to destroy his own tranquillity or that of others by thoughtless excess.'[1]

THE FALLACY OF THE MALTHUSIAN REASONING

Malthus is of the opinion that the best guarantee of the operation of the preventive check is to insist on each man supporting his own children under all circumstances, and to make the fear of having a large family and of being unable to provide for it the main obstacle to an early marriage. But this form of reasoning is hardly likely to become prevalent among the poorest, as was shown by Lloyd. No man can advance his wages by such an expedient. He will forgo the pleasures of marriage and so reduce the future labour supply by rearing less children, but the resulting improvement in wages which will arise from one man's abstinence will be shared by all, including those who marry early. Benefit will accrue to all only when all, or nearly all, defer marriage and so reduce the supply of labour. To expect this to occur in an individualistic society is as Utopian as the scheme of Godwin.

In a state of equality, action which advances the common good will be more easily seen and more easily enforceable. If this indeed be the only way of raising wages, then it will also be seen that all ought to share in bringing about this desirable state of affairs, by equally abstaining from marriage until the adjustment is achieved. Every man will understand the interests of the community, and be master in outline of its political state. Moreover he will realize that his own happiness depends on the institutions which prevail, and public opinion will powerfully

[1] Godwin, 1801, pp. 73–74.

reinforce any action which makes for the maintenance of such institutions. A man 'will not be able to live without character and the respect of his neighbours, and no consideration on earth will induce him to forfeit them.'[1]

To preach moral restraint to the poor, as Malthus does, is to preach something which has nothing to do with the institutions of society, which has no backing of public opinion, and which can yield little results to the individual workman. He will not have a wife and family to support but he will lose all the comforts of home life, and the blessings of a home however poor. His wages will still be at the mercy of his fellow workers who have married early and are glutting the labour market with their children; and if unemployment becomes inevitable for some, he may find that he suffers on the ground that those who have the biggest families are most in need of work and wages.

There is a further consideration, pointed out by Cannan:

'It must also be remembered that though under present conditions prudence frequently counsels man against matrimony, it often, and perhaps almost equally often, counsels woman to marry. Marriage may be a lottery, but there are at any rate some prizes. Spinsterhood, except among the rich, provides nothing but blanks.'[2]

Wallace, faced with the supposed dilemma of a redundant population, runs over the various expedients which might be adopted: restraints on marriage, the cloistering of women, celibacy of priests or of members of other professions, the institution of eunuchs, child exposure, euthanasia, and so on, but ends by lamenting:

'Alas! how unnatural and inhuman must every such expedient be accounted! The natural passions and appetites of mankind are planted in our frame, to answer the best ends for the happiness both of the individuals and of the species. Shall we be obliged to contradict such a wise order? Shall we be laid under the necessity of acting barbarously and inhumanly?'[3]

This is strange language when, if such an eventuality ever came about, all that is required is to establish a minimum age of marriage for all, which would be easily agreed when all are

[1] Godwin, 1801, p. 75.

[2] Cannan, *Economic Review*, Jan. 1892, p. 85.

[3] Wallace, *Various Prospects of Mankind, etc.*, 1761, pp. 118–119.

affected in the same manner by existing circumstances, and are equally interested and equally inclined to submit to rules calculated to remove the common evil.[1]

Yet Malthus, like his mentor Wallace, regards such a suggestion with abhorrence.

'But who are the persons that are to exercise the restraint thus called for, and either to marry late or not at all? . . . As all would be equal and in similar circumstances, there would be no reason whatever why one individual should think himself obliged to practise the duty of restraint more than another. The thing however must be done, with any hope of avoiding universal misery; and in a state of equality the necessary restraint could only be effected by some general law. But how is this law to be supported, and how are the violations of it to be punished? Is a man who marries early to be pointed at with the finger of scorn? is he to be whipped at the cart's tail? is he to be confined for years in a prison? is he to have his children exposed? Are not all direct punishments for an offence of this kind shocking and unnatural in the last degree?'[2]

His own remedy appears to him far less shocking and unnatural. The poor are to marry late or not at all, in spite of the increased temptations to which their bad housing and squalid conditions expose them, and the defective education which opens up little in the way of a constructive life beyond the rearing of a family. The relative strength of public opinion behind the law in the two states has already been discussed. As to the finger of scorn and other punishments so emotionally presented, they are to be replaced by the 'natural' doom of starvation. Man, wife, and children, after the appointed day, and having been duly warned and admonished, know where they stand. 'If he cannot support his children, they must starve.'[3]

By such expedients he hopes to bring men to see reason and control their passions, a feat impossible to the perfect inhabitants of Godwin's Utopia, for as Malthus adds:

'However powerful may be the impulses of passion, they are generally in some degree modified by reason. And it does not seem entirely visionary to suppose that, if the true and permanent cause of poverty were clearly explained and forcibly brought

[1] Cf. Hall, op. cit., p. 334, and Everett, op. cit., p. 98.

[2] *Essay*, 1872 edn., pp. 285–286.

[3] Id., p. 404.

home to each man's bosom, it would have some and perhaps not an inconsiderable influence on his conduct.'[1]

With which it seems that Malthus has sufficiently answered himself.

MISPLACED SENTIMENT

It was suggested to Malthus, prior to the publication of his 1817 edition, by persons for whose judgment he had a high respect, that he should throw out his criticisms of Wallace, Condorcet, and Godwin. He ignored their better judgment, partly through sentiment, since such an attack had been the original object of the work, and partly because he thought there ought to be 'somewhere on record an answer to systems of equality founded on the principle of population.'[2]

For what it is worth then it remains, though one cannot but agree with the anonymous author in the *New Monthly Magazine* that the reply to Godwin's perfectibility on the grounds just mentioned is no more worth recording than any other. Why not assume an alteration in this principle as well as in any other principle of man?

'If Mr. Malthus will, to fit man for such a state, undertake to restrain selfishness, ambition, avarice, pride, and vanity, or to reduce to one unvarying similitude those actual differences in human character, such as differences in talents, application, self-controul, which must always produce differences in the circumstances of individuals, we pledge ourselves to modify and restrain in the same way, and by the same means, the principle of population. If he will tell us how to throw salt on the bird's tail, we shall tell him how the bird is to be caught.'[3]

Yet in his day Malthus triumphed, though it is interesting to note that, while he was prophesying poverty and misery at the dawn of the greatest industrial expansion, Godwin the visionary was looking ahead, in the felt presence of broad truths:

'I cannot so despair of the virtues of man to submit to the most obvious rules of prudence, or of the faculties of man to strike out remedies as yet unknown, as to convince me that we ought to sit down for ever contented with all the oppression, abuses and inequality, which we now find fastened on the necks, and withering the hearts, of so great a proportion of our species.'[4]

[1] 1872 edn., p. 404.
[2] Id., p. 281.
[3] Loc. cit., p. 197.
[4] Godwin, 1801, pp. 76–77.

CHAPTER TWO

APPLICATION TO WAGES

THE SUBSISTENCE THEORY

THE implications of the theory of population with regard to improvements in wages were very sombre. Practically nothing was possible. There is at any particular time a fund appropriated to the maintenance of labour, namely the aggregate quantity of food possessed by the owners of land beyond their own consumption.[1] If the demands on this fund were great, wages would be low, men would offer to work for a bare subsistence, and the rearing of families would be checked by sickness and misery. If on the other hand the numbers of workers were comparatively small, or the fund were increasing relatively quickly, wages would be above the level of subsistence, men would live in ease and comfort, and would be able to rear larger numbers of healthy children. In this way, whether wages were above or below subsistence, they would always be tending towards that point, and, except in unusual circumstances, would never for long be far away from the bare level of subsistence.

'On the state of this fund, the happiness, or the degree of misery, prevailing among the lower classes of people in every known state at present, chiefly depends; and on this happiness or degree of misery depends principally the increase, stationariness, or decrease of population.'[2]

The poor are thus, always tending to breed themselves into misery, or die their way back to comparative comfort.

Not content with this general principle, however, Malthus sets out to prove that if the rich were to give to the poor, or to

[1] *Essay*, 1872 edn., p. 280. [2] Id., p. 280.

increase their wages, it would not only be the height of folly, but quite useless in effecting an improvement in their standards.

'Suppose that by a subscription of the rich, the eighteenpence or two shillings which men earn now were made up to five shillings, it might be imagined that they would then be able to live comfortably, and have a piece of meat every day for their dinner.'[1]

It would indeed appear to tend in that direction, but this, we are told, is a false conclusion.

'The transfer of three additional shillings a day to each labourer would not increase the quantity of meat in the country. There is not at present enough for all to have a moderate share. What would then be the consequence? The competition among the buyers in the market of meat would rapidly raise the price from eightpence or ninepence to two or three shillings in the pound, and the commodity would not be divided among many more than it is at present.'[2]

Nevertheless it must be admitted that the tendency would be for the poor to get rather more than before, and Malthus in other respects is a great man for tendencies.

'When an article is scarce, and cannot be distributed to all, he that can show the most valid patent, that is, he that offers the most money, becomes the possessor.'[3]

In this respect again the condition of the poor would seem to be improved: their patents would be somewhat the better and those of the rich somewhat the worse. And if the poor could not get more meat, they might get a little more of some other kind of food.

'If we can suppose the competition among the buyers of meat to continue long enough for a greater number of cattle to be reared annually, this could only be done at the expense of the corn, which would be a very disadvantageous exchange; for it is well known that the country could not then support the same population, and when subsistence is scarce in proportion to the number of people, it is of little consequence whether the lowest members of the society possess two shillings or five. They must at all events be reduced to live upon the hardest fare, and in the smallest quantity.'[4]

In spite, therefore, of the improvement of their patents, they are no better off. But he hastens to meet another objection.

[1] *Essay*, 1872 edn., p. 294.
[2] Id., p. 294.
[3] Id., p. 294.
[4] Id., pp. 294–295.

'It might be said perhaps that the increased number of purchasers in every article would give a spur to productive industry, and that the whole produce of the island would be increased. But the spur that these fancied [sic] riches would give to population would more than counterbalance it; and the increased produce would be to be divided among a more than proportionably increased number of people.'[1]

All of which is very bewildering. There is no more food available, nor can there be. Food goes to those who have most money, yet if the poor have relatively more money, they will get relatively no more food. Yet, if by any chance the rise in prices does provoke an increased productivity, the spur of these *fancied* riches would *more than* counterbalance the increased production.

The object of this farrago is then made clear.

'No possible sacrifices of the rich, particularly in money, could for any time prevent the recurrence of distress among the lower members of society, whoever they were. Great changes might indeed be made. The rich might become poor, and some of the poor rich; but while the present proportion between population and food continues, a part of the society must necessarily find it difficult to support a family, and this difficulty will naturally fall on the least fortunate members.'[2]

Malthus here omits to allude to the advantage which the rich would now enjoy of adding the practice to the precept of moral restraint, but the argument runs on.

'If the rich were to subscribe and give five shillings a day to five hundred thousand men without retrenching their own tables, no doubt can exist that as these men would live more at their ease and consume a greater quantity of provisions, there would be less food remaining to divide among the rest; and consequently each man's patent would be diminished in value, or the same number of pieces of silver would purchase a smaller quantity of subsistence, and the price of provisions would universally rise.'[3]

HAZLITT'S ANSWER

Hazlitt, captious, vitriolic, at times unfair, but always writing with deep feeling, and, we believe, sincerity, dealt with this as it deserved.

[1] *Essay*, 1872 edn., p. 295. [2] Id., p. 295. [3] Id., pp. 295–296.

'Wealth is nothing but the power of securing to yourself the fruits of the earth, or commanding the labours of others.'[1] To say that a redistribution of income would not mean that the good things of life would be shared more equally is flat nonsense. 'It is true that the lowest members of the community will still live upon the hardest fare, and in the smallest quantity: but their fare will be less hard and in larger quantities than it used to be, *in proportion* to the advance in the price of labour.'[2]

A rich man who gives money to a poor man must necessarily cut down the quantity of food or other things consumed in his own house. It does not matter to the community who spends the money; the only difference is between the individuals. If giving the poor more money would not enable them to command a greater proportion of the food, 'there could be no room for competition, nor for an increase in the price or the demand.'[3]

Malthus never makes up his mind whether he intends the rise in wages to be real or nominal, but if the rich did hand over a portion of their wealth to the poor, 'it must be proportionably beneficial. . . . It must throw a greater quantity of the necessaries or comforts of life into the hands of those who most want them, and take them from those who are oppressed with their superfluities.'[4]

Given a stock of goods of all kinds, a fixed quantity of money, and a transfer of money from the rich to the poor, then the rich must retrench somewhere. If they buy less food, then there is more food for the poor. If they cut down on other things, the poor will have the same food, but can buy extra conveniences of some other kind. There would be the same purchasing power, but a shift in the nature of employment.[5]

'The rise of wages would certainly take from the pomp and luxury of the rich, and it would as certainly and in the same proportion add to the comforts of the poor. I am not here recommending such a change. I only contend that it would follow the distribution of wealth; and that it is absurd to say that the poorer a man is, the richer he will be.'[6]

[1] *Reply*, 1807, p. 309. [2] Id., p. 310. [3] Id., p. 313. [4] Id., pp. 323–324.

[5] This is recognized by Malthus when he discusses the remission of taxation (see 1872 edn., pp. 314–315). If the national debt were extinguished the increased spending power of the taxpayers would be offset by the loss of demand of the fundholders and the government. As usual he can argue both ways.

[6] *Reply*, 1807, p. 326.

MALTHUS ANSWERS HIMSELF

However, in another context and at a later date, Malthus answered himself in his *Observations on the Effects of the Corn Laws.*[1] Here he is not admonishing the poor but concerning himself with bounties and duties as affecting the landed interest (although he disclaims all partiality). The connection between the price of corn and that of labour is not now so intimate. Corn is only a portion of working class expenditure, and there is a time lag between changes in price and adjustments in the working population sufficient to change the direction of the flow of capital.[2] If the real price of corn were unchangeable, agriculture would be exempt from the operation of the principle by which capital flows from one employment to another according to the changing needs of society.

'It will follow, that the growth of corn, has at all times, and in all countries, proceeded with a uniform unvarying pace,[3] occasioned only by the equable increase of agricultural capital, and can never have been accelerated, or retarded, by variations of demand. It will follow, that if a country happened to be either overstocked or understocked with corn, no motive of interest could exist for withdrawing capital from agriculture in the one case, or adding to it in the other, and thus restoring the equilibrium between its different kinds of produce. But these consequences, which would incontestably follow from the doctrine, that the price of corn immediately and entirely regulates the prices of labour and of all other commodities, are so directly contrary to all experience, that the doctrine itself cannot possibly be true; and we may be assured, that, whatever influence the price of corn may have upon other commodities, it is neither so immediate nor so complete, as to make this kind of produce an exception to all others.'[4]

Readers of the *Essay on Population* would unfortunately have gathered just that idea—that, while other commodities were responsive to the laws of supply and demand, food, and particularly corn, was governed by the arithmetical ratio which is now disowned. It is gratifying to learn that agricultural capital

[1] Quotations from 3rd edn., 1815.
[2] Id., pp. 7–8.
[3] In an arithmetical ratio.
[4] Id., p. 9.

can be accelerated and retarded, and with it presumably the output of corn; provided, and Malthus seems to regard this proviso as important, the stimulus of an increased price arises from a bounty on export, and not from a distribution of wealth in favour of the poor.

'Let us suppose, for instance, an increase in the demand and the price of corn, occasioned by an unusually prosperous state of our manufactures and foreign commerce—a fact which has frequently come within our own experience. According to the principles of supply and demand, and the general principles of the *Wealth of Nations*, such an increase in the price of corn would give a decided stimulus to agriculture; and a more than usual quantity of capital would be laid out upon the land, as appears obviously to have been the case in this country during the last twenty years. According to the peculiar argument of Adam Smith, however, no such stimulus could have been given to agriculture. The rise in the price of corn would have been immediately followed by a proportionate rise in the price of labour, and of all other commodities. . . . And thus it would appear, that agriculture is beyond the operation of that principle, which distributes the capital of a nation according to the varying profits of stock, in different employments; and that no increase of price can, at any time, or in any country, materially accelerate the growth of corn, or determine a greater quantity of capital to agriculture.'[1]

So we leave the argument with the feeling that after all an increase in wages might not be ineffective. If the rich curtailed their expenditure on other things than food, and, in consequence of the increased price of food due to the increased demand, new capital flowed into agriculture, there might perhaps be hope.

But no modification of the original argument occurs in subsequent editions of the *Essay*. A rise in the price of corn to the farmers is one thing: a rise in wages is quite another.

[1] Loc. cit., pp. 10–11.

CHAPTER THREE

APPLICATION TO THE POOR LAWS

DENUNCIATION OF THE POOR LAWS

ALTHOUGH the chief object of the first *Essay* was an attack upon Godwin, the main practical application soon shifted to the poor laws. Most of Malthus's contemporaries admitted that the provision for the poor was extremely defective, both in conception and administration, but they addressed their minds to discovering ways of improving it. Malthus, on the other hand, attacked the poor laws, not on the ground of their imperfection, indeed he has words to say in defence of their administrators, but on the ground of the utter impracticability of making such provision. The notion of poor relief for him is inherently unsound, and the defects flow not from faulty conception or faulty administration, but from the impossibility of the amount of provisions keeping pace with the growing numbers of the poor.

He admits that there has been some alleviation in certain cases, but this has been merely at the cost of forcing up the price of food to all consumers, and thus of spreading the misery more widely among the remainder of the poor. Benevolent though the laws are in intention, they have merely subjected the common people to 'grating, inconvenient, and tyrannical laws, totally inconsistent with the genuine spirit of the constitution.'[1] The business of settlements, contradictory to the ideas of freedom, aggravates the situation by impeding the mobility of labour, but the remedy does not lie in reform; it lies in abolition. The evils of the system are irremediable, and the tyranny of churchwardens and overseers, where it exists, arises not from their own characters, but from the nature of the system they administer.

[1] 1872 edn., p. 305.

'I feel persuaded that if the poor-laws had never existed in this country, though there might have been a few more instances of very severe distress, the aggregate mass of happiness among the common people would have been much greater than it is at present.'[1]

The basis of this forthright assertion is the principle of population, and once again we are confronted by the ratios. Wages express the demand of society for population; low wages imply that there are too many people, and that the size of families should be reduced. High food prices are the sign that population is increasing faster than food, but the poor laws prevent price from exercising its natural function of rationing provisions and enforcing economy by compelling the poor to adopt cheaper substitutes for wheat.

If a man is sure of the means of provision for his children, if his income grows with the size of his family, as under the Speenhamland system of administration, we are led to expect an alarming growth in the numbers of the poor.[2] Furthermore, it follows from the idea of the wages fund that the extension of poor relief, by raising prices, would in the first instance lower the real value of the money held by all other consumers, the rest of the poor and the rich alike.[3]

The poor laws do not relieve the poor; the law of population will not be denied; and the greater spreading of misery, the high death rate in workhouses and among pauper apprentices, all serve to level the population with the food supply. In fact, 'it may be asserted without danger of exaggeration, that the poor laws have destroyed many more lives than they have preserved.'[4]

THE REAL REMEDY

The remedy for poverty is not a system of poor laws, but moral restraint; otherwise natural and moral evil are unavoidable.

[1] 1872 edn., p. 305.

[2] When he observes (1872 edn., App., p. 503 and p. 504 n.) that the facts do not support the theory, and that the poor laws have not actually encouraged population, he still retains the argument by blaming the shortage of cottages.

[3] That agriculture would be stimulated is not worth taking into account, because of the ratios.

[4] Third edn., 1806, Vol. II, p. 184. Later withdrawn.

The two chief desires of man are for food and the passion between the sexes, and the normal effect of these desires is to produce more children than food.[1] 'If these two tendencies were exactly balanced, I do not see what motive there would be sufficiently strong to overcome the acknowledged indolence of man, and make him proceed in the cultivation of the soil.'[2]

If it be thought that a much smaller disproportion between the two ratios would have sufficed, if it be thought that Providence has rather overdone it, 'if the question be merely a question of degree, a question of a little more or a little less strength, we may fairly distrust our competence to judge of the precise quantity necessary to answer the object with the smallest sum of incidental evil.'[3]

The strength of the populating force must be adequate in all circumstances. 'To effect the apparent object without any attendant evil, it is evident that a perpetual change in the law of increase would be necessary, varying with the varying circumstances of each country.'[4] This notion Malthus brushes aside with scant ceremony as inconsistent with other parts of nature.

Hence he arrives at the conclusion that the preventive check is essential. 'It is clearly the duty of each individual not to marry till he has a prospect of supporting his children; but it is at the same time to be wished that he should retain undiminished his desire of marriage, in order that he may exert himself to realize this prospect, and be stimulated to make provision for the support of greater numbers.'[5]

This doctrine is aimed at the poor, and it is fair to say that this is inevitable in view of their numerical importance, but it is

[1] Some of the critics seem to have thought it rather odd that Providence should have ordered the growth of population and food on such dissimilar scales, but Malthus hastens to the defence of the Deity. Diseases are not the inevitable inflictions of Providence, but an indication that we have offended against the laws of nature. 'If we are intemperate in eating and drinking, our health is disordered; if we indulge the transports of anger, we seldom fail to commit acts of which we afterwards repent; if we multiply too fast, we die miserably of poverty and contagious diseases. The laws of nature in all these cases are similar and uniform' (1872 edn., p. 390).

[2] 1872 edn., p. 395.

[3] Id., p. 395.

[4] Id., p. 395. There does not seem to be any reason to reject this hypothesis out of hand unless one is committed to the geometrical ratio.

[5] Id., p. 396.

nevertheless unfortunate that, in thus placing the burden of remedial measures on the poor, he goes out of his way to exonerate the rich, not only from the need of moral restraint, but also from the evils arising from their luxurious spending.[1]

STARVING THE POOR INTO MORAL RESTRAINT

Having decided on moral restraint as the remedy for poverty, the next question is that of the motives whereby this remedy is to be made effective, and, like his precursor Townsend, Malthus relies on fear and hunger, preferably fear. Fear of want, rather than want, is the best stimulus.[2] The threat of starvation is essential to industry.

'Hard as it may appear in individual instances, dependent poverty ought to be held disgraceful.'[3] The poor always live from hand to mouth; they seldom think of the future. Even when they have the opportunity to save, they seldom do; and the poor laws, in addition to impoverishing the workers as a class, have destroyed both the power and the will to save.

As a remedy for poverty, starving the poor into moral restraint wears an appearance of novelty, but it is one further instance of Malthus's lack of understanding of the working-class mind, so clearly revealed by Place.[4] Malthus insists on projecting middle-class motives and ideals into the minds and habits of the poor, and draws the most astonishing conclusions. Thus he proceeds: 'No man whose earnings were only sufficient to maintain two children would put himself in a situation in which he might have to maintain four or five, however he might be prompted to it by the passion of love.'[5]

Then he remembers sadly that it is women who bear children and notes that late marriages are principally confined to men who usually marry young wives. If only, he sighs, women could be persuaded to defer marriage.

'If they could look forward with just confidence to marriage at twenty-seven or twenty-eight, I fully believe that if the matter

[1] 1872 edn., pp. 384–385. [2] Id., p. 382. [3] Id., p. 303.

[4] Place (op. cit., Himes's edn.), pp. 151–156.

[5] 1872 edn., p. 397. If this is anything at all, it is an argument not for deferred marriage, but for continence within the marital relation after the maximum number of children have been born, but this is not what Malthus advocates.

were left to their free choice, they would clearly prefer waiting till this period to the being involved in all the cares of a large family at twenty-five.'[1]

Few actions tend so directly to diminish the general happiness as to marry without the means of supporting children, and consequently, he who does this offends against the will of God, violates his duty to his neighbours, and must put up with the proposed treatment.[2]

Having now propounded the remedy, moral restraint, which he has not the folly to imagine will be universally or even generally practised, in which he clearly has little faith, but which is necessary to remove any imputation on the goodness of the Deity, Malthus announces his sanctions. If a man follows his instructions, he will reap the 'full fruits' of his action, whatever may be the number of others who fail. If he disobeys:

'If he cannot support his children, they must starve; and if he marry in the face of a fair probability that he shall not be able to support his children, he is guilty of all the evils which he thus brings upon himself, his wife, and his offspring.'[3]

Thus the remedy for poverty lies in the hands of the poor themselves, and in the hands of no one else. They must refrain from marriage until they have 'struck the double average between a day's wages and the quartern loaf.'[4]

There is no salvation in increasing the food supply, for as fast as food multiplies, population more than keeps pace with it; it is

[1] 1872 edn., p. 399. This might be true of middle-class women with a larger range of cultural and other interests, but it has little validity for the poor, for whom the pleasures of a family are the limit of their horizon.

[2] Id., pp. 401–402. But, as Hall points out, practically no working man can marry and be sure of being able to support a family.

[3] Id., p. 404. This notion of a fair probability worries Malthus, although he does not give it the attention it deserves. The poor man must wait 'till by industry and economy he is in a capacity to support the children that he may reasonably expect from his marriage.' When wages are only sufficient to maintain two children and a man marries and has five or six, 'it never enters into his head that he can have done anything wrong' (p. 405). Note the extraordinary language about 'king and country' which might have been replaced by a statement as to what age a man might safely marry and be sure not to have more than two children.

[4] Ensor, op. cit., p. 204.

like setting the tortoise to catch the hare.[1] The remedy is to reduce the supply of labourers,[2] the method the abolition of the poor laws.

THE MALTHUSIAN PLAN

A regulation should be made 'declaring that no child born from any marriage taking place after the expiration of a year from the date of the law, and no illegitimate child born two years from the same date, should ever be entitled to parish assistance.' To impress this strongly on the minds of the lower classes 'the clergyman of each parish should, after the publication of banns, read a short address, stating the strong obligation on every man to support his own children.' In this way the poor man would have 'fair, distinct, and precise notice' of what to expect. To marry without the prospect of being able to support a family, while an immoral act, should not be forbidden. 'When nature will govern and punish for us, it is a very miserable ambition to wish to snatch the rod from her hands, and draw upon ourselves the odium of executioner. To the punishment therefore of nature he should be left, the punishment of want.'[3] He should be denied all parish assistance and left to private charity. He should be taught that he has no claim of right to the smallest portion of food beyond what his labour will buy.

With regard to illegitimate children they too should be left to private charity. 'The infant is comparatively speaking of little value to the society, as others will immediately supply its place. Its principal value is on account of its being the object of one of the most delightful passions in human nature—parental affection.'[4] If the parents do not supply this, society has no call to interfere, save to punish the parents. At present the child goes to a

[1] 1872 edn., p. 407.

[2] Here Malthus answers three objections: (*a*) *An understocked labour market.* The rich must not be stupid. To abolish poverty the poor must have higher wages, and to complain of this is the 'act of a silly boy who gives away his cake and then cries for it.' (*b*) *Diminution of population.* This would only occur till food and population were on a level. Then they could progress together in arithmetical ratio. (*c*) *That vice would be encouraged.* Poverty itself is the most prolific source of vice, and thus an attack on poverty is the best way to attack vice.

[3] 1872 edn., p. 430.

[4] Id., p. 431.

foundling hospital and probably dies in the first year; and the loss, though the same, 'passes as a visitation of Providence instead of being considered as the necessary consequence of the conduct of its parents, for which they ought to be held responsible to God and to society.'[1]

If it appears hard that a mother and her children should suffer thus, it is in accordance with the Ten Commandments. The sins of the fathers are visited upon the children (but not, under the Malthusian scheme, unto the third and fourth generation).[2]

THE INFLUENCE OF MALTHUS ON THE POOR LAWS

It was this application of the doctrine of population which provoked a great deal of the controversy, much of which has already been outlined. Bonar writes: 'Of all the applications of the doctrines of Malthus, their application to pauperism was probably, at the time, of the greatest public interest. . . . Malthus is the father not only of the new poor law, but of all our latter-day societies for the organization of charity.'[3]

And this view was shared by Malthus's contemporaries. Bishop Otter writes, in his Memoir of Malthus:

'The Poor Laws Amendment Bill has been framed and passed into a law; and a great experiment is now making throughout the country under its authority, upon the result of which, the due and harmonious adjustment of the relations between the rich and the poor will hereafter mainly depend. But this act is founded upon the basis of Mr. Malthus' work. The *Essay of Population* and the Poor Laws Amendment Bill, will stand or fall together. They have the same friends and the same enemies, and the relations they bear to each other, of theory and practice, are admirably calculated to afford mutual illumination and support.'[4]

No less a man than Samuel Whitbread, in his speech in the House of Commons in February 1807, asserted:

'No one ever ventured to surmise that the system itself was radically defective and vicious. . . . One philosopher in particular has arisen amongst us, who has gone deeply into the causes

[1] 1872 edn., p. 431. [2] Id., p. 433.

[3] Bonar, *Malthus and His Work*, pp. 304–305.

[4] Malthus, *Principles of Political Economy*, 1836 edn., *Memoir* by Bishop Otter, p. xix.

of our present situation. I mean Mr. Malthus. His work upon Population has, I believe, been very generally read; and it has completed that change of opinion with regard to the poor laws, which had before been in some measure begun. . . . This philosopher has delivered it as his opinion, that the poor laws have not only failed in their object, but that they have been productive of much more wretchedness than would have existed without them. . . . Many persons, agreeing in this position, have wished that the whole system was well expunged from our statute book; and perhaps I should not go too far in saying, that such is the prevailing sentiment.'[1]

THE LONG ROAD TO REFORM

Malthus made a host of converts. The *Edinburgh Review* was with him from the start. The *Quarterly Review*, at first hostile, was gradually converted. Of the many who did not go all the way with him, most paid due deference to his views and the prestige they enjoyed. But if Malthus was the father of the new poor law of 1834, the period of gestation was more than thirty years. The existing poor law was liked by no one. The rich saw in it merely a rapidly mounting burden which did not achieve its objective, which was inequitably distributed, oppressive, often crushing in its local incidence, aggravated by the law of settlement which hindered the mobility of labour. Nor were the poor better pleased. Faced with rapidly rising prices, the spread of enclosures, and the clog on migration, they contrasted the insufficiency of the relief with the growing national wealth.

'Without opportunity for securing a foothold on any ladder of advancement; without margin for effective saving; virtually bound hand and foot to the few local farmers, who in many parishes suspended his wages whenever frost or rain, or the winter pause in agricultural operations, enabled them for a few days or weeks to dispense with his services, and summarily ejected him from the hovel that was his home as soon as he showed any sign of independence, it was inevitable, even apart from the Allowance system, that the rural labourer should for the most part, be driven to Poor Relief whenever sickness or the

[1] Abridged quotation taken from Webb: *English Local Government—English Poor Law History*, Part II, Vol. I, pp. 24–25.

infirmity of old age, or the mere failure of employment for a week or two, deprived him of his exiguous and always precarious wage.'[1]

Yet, in spite of this general dissatisfaction with the position, a period of forty years elapsed from the food riots of the late nineties to the Reform Act of 1834. The terror of the French Revolution made an impression on this country which took a long time to fade. The Napoleonic Wars absorbed the attention of the nation up to 1815, and there was a spirit of unrest, leading to sporadic explosions, which not only thwarted the abolitionists but held up the more moderate reformers. The poor laws were largely a local concern, and even though they had become a national scandal, the Government at Westminster was loath to take any action which would upset the established expectations of the masses.

There were abortive efforts in 1796 by Pitt and eleven years later by Whitbread. The peace in 1815, which brought a spate of replies to Malthus, brought also a rapidly rising poor rate and a Committee in 1817 under Sturges Bourne, which, while producing no remedy, publicized the abuses and stimulated the pamphleteers.

Two streams of thought had by this time coalesced and were accepted by the Committee: (1) that pauperism was a social disease, and that public relief as distinct from private charity was degrading; (2) that poor relief, by virtue of the doctrine of the wages fund and the principle of population, was not only no cure but rather an irritant.

The first stream of thought begins in our period with Townsend, whose work has already been adequately dealt with. It regards poverty as essential to industry, as the main-spring of effort. Hunger is the driving force; it 'will tame the fiercest animals, it will teach decency and civility, obedience and subjection, to the most brutish, the most obstinate, and the most perverse.'[2] But Townsend's work was too early. The era of the French Revolution was no time to abolish the poor laws. Chalmers regarded the poor laws as a bungling attempt to do by legislation what had better be left to Nature and Christian charity. The connection between Townsend and Malthus has

[1] Webb, op. cit., pp. 5–6.

[2] *Dissertation*, op. cit., pp. 407–408 (McCulloch's edn.).

already been demonstrated, and the attitude of Malthus in this respect needs no further elaboration. Another writer of note was Thomas Walker, who characterized the principle of poor relief as 'Moral Pestilence.'[1]

It is obvious to even a cursory inspection that there is a strong religious element in the approach to the question, and many of the pamphlets and books were the work of clergymen or ministers of religion, including Townsend, Chalmers, and Malthus. In addition to attacking the poor laws and the abolition of compulsory provision, they were constrained to descant on the virtues of private charity. Thus Townsend:

'Nor in nature can anything be more beautiful than the mild complacency of benevolence, hastening to the humble cottage to relieve the wants of industry and virtue, to feed the hungry, to clothe the naked, and to soothe the sorrows of the widow with her tender orphans; nothing can be more pleasing, unless it be their sparkling eyes, their bursting tears, and their uplifted hands, the artless expressions of unfeigned gratitude for unexpected favours.'[2]

Malthus quotes this passage of Townsend with approval, and adds much of his own. Discussing voluntary charity, he says:

'The person who receives it is made the proper subject of the pleasurable sensation of gratitude; and those who do not receive it cannot possibly conceive themselves in the slightest degree injured. Every man has a right to do what he will with his own, and cannot, in justice, be called upon to render a reason why he gives in the one case, and abstains from it in the other.'[3] No man should look upon charity as a fund on which he may depend. The key text, equally a law of nature as a saying of St. Paul is this: 'If a man will not work, neither shall he eat.'[4]

This idea of natural law, so characteristic of the *laissez-faire* philosophy, runs through the whole of the literature we are discussing, and the natural law is made to embody all the man-made law which happens to suit its adherents. Thus it includes the private ownership of land and of capital, but excludes such public provision as statutory relief of the poor, and later on the Factory Acts and similar legislation. When the exponents of this

[1] Webb, op. cit., pp. 7–21.
[2] Quoted by Malthus, 1806 edn., Vol. II, pp. 431–432.
[3] *Essay*, 1806 edn., Vol. II, p. 433.
[4] Id., p. 435.

view were confronted with a logical dilemma, they got round it in some fashion. Thus Chalmers justifies the whole of the property law as the result of natural law, and even when 'the original mode of acquisition is lost sight of, all that a man has retained by long and undisturbed possession, is felt and acknowledged to be his own also. Legislation ought to do no more than barely recognize these principles, and defend its subjects against the violation of them.'[1]

Malthus pursues the same strain in the *Summary View*.

'Allowing, then, distinctly, that the right of property is the creature of positive law, yet this law is so early and so imperiously forced on the attention of mankind, that if it cannot be called a natural law, it must be considered as the most natural as well as the most necessary of all positive laws.'[2]

So we see the case building up. Public provision for the poor is ruinous to the rich and degrading to the poor. It hinders the exercise of charity which engenders the most beautiful sentiments in all concerned. It is unnatural and anti-Christian. What more is needed? But one more nail in the coffin—the Principle of Population!

Wallace had announced it; Townsend had developed it in some degree; Malthus perfected it, and to him must go the credit. The poor laws were ruinous, degrading, unnatural, anti-Christian—and USELESS. They could not achieve their object. No wonder Bonar says: 'Without the discussions raised by the *Essay on Population* it is very doubtful if public opinion would have been so far advanced in 1834 as to make a Bill drawn on such lines, at all likely to pass into law. The abolition of Outdoor Relief to the able-bodied was nothing short of a revolution. It had needed a lifetime of economical doctrine, reproof, and correction to convince our public men, and to some extent the nation, that the way of rigour was at once the way of justice, of mercy, and of self-interest.'[3] This was the triumph of Malthus.

'Except as to medical attendance, and subject to the exception respecting apprenticeship hereinafter stated, all relief whatever to able-bodied persons or to their families, otherwise than in well-regulated workhouses . . . shall be declared unlawful, and shall cease, in manner and at periods hereafter

[1] Quoted in Webb, op. cit., p. 19. [2] *Summary View*, 1830, p. 72.
[3] Bonar, *Malthus and His Work*, p. 317.

specified; and that all relief afforded in respect of children under the age of sixteen, shall be considered as afforded to their parents.'[1]

The principle of less eligibility was established, 'Every penny bestowed, that tends to render the condition of the pauper more eligible than that of the independent labourer, is a bounty on indolence and vice.'[2]

This was the system which was to operate during the rest of the century during which the workhouse was an ever-present threat to the old or the unfortunate. Seventy-four years were to run before the Webbs wrote *The Break-up of the Poor Law*; one hundred and twelve before National Insurance embraced the whole nation.

The poor law reform of 1834 was the victory of Malthus, and we need not grudge him the verdict of his biographer: 'There is scarcely any other instance in the history of the world of so important a revolution effected in public opinion, within the compass of a single life and by a single mind.'[3]

THE ALTERNATIVE PLAN OF SIMON GRAY

The problems of 1834 were not those of the twentieth century, and it is idle to try to reverse the judgment of history, but since we are mainly concerned with the critics, it is worth while to state the other view. It has been touched upon in the chronological survey, let it be gathered together in the words of Simon Gray.[4]

Almost everyone in a populous community can earn a competency, provided that his health remains good and he encounters no unfortunate circumstances. Nevertheless, since income depends on health, and a man who is out of work is still faced with necessary expenditure, and since in a rich country frugal habits and rigid economy are scarcely to be expected from all, there is no margin provided for illness, unemployment or old age. The public must, therefore, make up the deficiency, and in this it has no grievance.

[1] *Poor Law Report*, 1834, p. 262. [2] Id., p. 228.

[3] Otter's *Memoir*, loc. cit., p. xvi.

[4] References are to *The Principles of Population and Production Investigated, etc.*, by George Purves, L.L.D., London, 1818. (The author is obviously Gray.)

It is the poorer classes who provide the riches of the higher, who produce the most children and thus enrich the community. Consequently, in making provision for the poor, 'the middle and higher ranks are only paying back a part of the wealth which they have received from that mass, as well as making some return for the various comforts which they derive from its labours. The claim of the distressed poor for the contributions of the richer, is a claim not merely of humanity, but of justice. It is a claim of strict right' (p. 422).

Malthus says that the poor have no right to support, but there are natural rights, social rights, and legal rights. 'When a natural right is also warranted by the good of society, it becomes a real social right; and is strictly indefeasible. Its value, or reality, does not depend on the authority of any positive law, or of any declaration from those possessing power; but on the arrangements of nature. A legal right is something that has been acknowledged and authorized by the community' (p. 423). Legal rights may be set aside, but they cannot turn a real social right into an unreal one, and if they attempt to do so, they are contrary to the unalterable laws of justice.

The poor have at present a legal right which might be rescinded, but this right 'is grounded alike upon the good of the community and of the individual. The well-being of both requires its admission' (p. 424). It is both instinctive and Christian.

Malthus seems to think that pauperism springs chiefly, if not wholly, from marriage, but 'no man, who depends upon his own labour or the chances of employment, can be said to have such a prospect of being able to support a family, as would justify him in marrying, if he were debarred of all prospect of assistance from others or the public, in case of accident or misfortunes. A week after marriage the most healthy prudent man, at the time well employed, may meet with an accident which may either lame him or so affect his health as to prevent him from earning a livelihood' (p. 425).

Prudence is desirable, and is widespread. Rashness punishes itself. 'The English mode of supporting the poor, with all its faults and inconveniences, does credit to the country; that it is the source of relieving a vast amount of misery, and effecting a vast amount of comfort. I hesitate not to affirm, that this very system of supporting the poor, which has been of late attacked so violently by so many, forms a portion of the brightest glory of England' (p. 427).

The great increase in the amount has frightened many people, but 'contributions for the poor, like other taxes, are not really paid by the nominal payers. They are charged on the general fund, or form part of the price which each circulator charges for the articles in which he deals' (p. 429).

It is true that supporting the poor in a generous humane way may be abused; it may make for less frugality, but it tends to diminish the fears of poverty which are inseparable from a condition of dependency on wages, and a knowledge of this is a source of hope and comfort to the poor, even if they never need it. It is a sound principle to employ the poor, but not so as to undercut the normal market by selling at lower prices. The system of settlements is savage and inhuman, and should be abolished, and schemes should cover counties rather than parishes to obviate the inequitable burdens, since wealthy parishes may have no poor. By thus equalizing the charges, the general rate would be lower.

Gray concludes with a sketch of a National Poor's Fund, which bears contrast with the Malthusian scheme and comparison with modern ideas. 'It seems to me, that a plan, which should make the poor pay for themselves, by contributions towards a national poor's fund, would remedy many of the faults of the present system' (p. 434). It would rescue the deserving from the degradation of feeling paupers.

The fund should be a national one, but for greater convenience the business might be done in counties, where there should be a central office for receiving contributions and making disbursements to the parishes.

'The tax, or contribution, must be compulsory under the authority of the legislature.[1] There should be different rates, according to which for contributing a larger or smaller sum, each person should be entitled to draw a larger or smaller weekly allowance.[2] But there must be a minimum calculated on what is necessary to supply the wants of the poor.[3] This amount

[1] This is the basis of current legislation.

[2] Although a flat rate has been adopted in this country, others, e.g. the United States, have rates varying with earnings.

[3] Cf. Beveridge Report, Cmd. 6404 (1942), p. 76, para. 193.

at least, every one, above a certain age, possessing a separate income, must contribute, and for this he or she will be entitled to draw according to a settled rate. The various offices should also have a power to receive gifts and legacies, to form a permanent fund, to be applied to the purposes of the institution' (p. 435).

'The lower ranks would have to pay this tax directly, but it would operate to produce a rise in their wages to cover it; and as the object of it is expressly to relieve them from distress, and make a provision for them in old age, it would probably soon cease to have the unpopularity of a tax' (p. 435).[1] The middle and higher ranks might even pay more than the fund required, and since such persons would rarely draw benefits, their contributions would swell the general amount available. 'A percentage might be taken on the amount of the whole, to form an accumulating fund, to meet particular exigencies arising from seasons of sickness, or of scarcity real or pretended' (p. 435). The surplus interest should also be placed to reserve, and in times of deficit there should be a temporary increase of contributions.

Disbursements should be made during sickness, inability to work, or in times of insufficient earnings, and an opportunity should be given to lay something aside for old age. 'Some of our economists and justices seem to calculate the life of the poor, as that of beasts of burden. While a man is able to work at all, he ought, according to them, to be forced to work' (p. 436). This is disgusting. At seventy a man should have a pension for life according to his contributions, and it should be left entirely to himself whether he worked or not.[2] Such earnings should be an extra, but he should have enough to live on in his usual style independently of working. Such a pension should be held neither disgraceful nor dishonourable, but as his own property arising out of his own earnings. 'On this poor's fund might be ingrafted schemes for pensioning widows and orphans' (p. 437).[3]

Friendly societies could be exempt from contributions, and members be exempt from the tax on producing a certificate of membership. But, after the introduction of the scheme, the

[1] If Gray did not solve, at least he was well aware of the problem of incidence.

[2] Cf. National Insurance Act, 1946.

[3] This was a later development.

legislature might decide not to exempt such persons, but allow them to contribute to both types of scheme.

In this way did Gray foreshadow, not only the main outlines, but much of the detail and many of the problems of the modern approach to the provision of social security. That is not to say that the scheme he laid down was practicable in his own day, but the current might have begun to flow in the right direction. Instead, the views of Malthus triumphed, and social insurance was put back for nearly a century.

It is ironical, therefore, to read in Otter's eulogy of Malthus: 'After all it must be allowed that the great, we had almost said the only, fault of Mr. Malthus with the public was that his opinions were in advance of his age.'[1]

Of that posterity is competent to judge.

[1] Otter's *Memoir*, loc. cit., p. xlviii.

CHAPTER FOUR

APPLICATION TO EMIGRATION

MALTHUS ON EMIGRATION

No survey of the Malthusian period would be complete without some mention of emigration, and the position of Malthus can be shortly stated.[1]

Although emigration would not be practicable in an equalitarian world society such as Godwin envisaged, yet, in view of the irregular development of the different lands of the earth, it seems obvious that emigration should take place from highly developed and populous areas to those which are uncultivated or thinly peopled. But while this seems to be an adequate remedy for overpopulation, experience suggests that it is but a slight palliative. The dangers and difficulties encountered by early settlers appear to be so great that economic motives alone are not sufficient to encourage people to emigrate, only the more powerful passions, 'the thirst for gain, the spirit of adventure, and religious enthusiasm,' being strong enough to enable the first adventurers to overcome the formidable obstacles. And even in these cases the moral worth of the conquerors is often inferior to the race which has been enslaved or extirpated.

Malthus surveys the fate of many early expeditions whose members were either destroyed by savages or Indians, decimated by famine and disease, or reduced in some way to a miserable remnant, only too glad to return home at the earliest opportunity. One of the reasons for such failure is the unsuitability of the habits and methods of home life for the conditions which obtain in a newly-settled land. Another reason is that, at the outset, the arrivals exceed the produce available, and must

[1] 1806 edn., Book III, Chapter IV.

suffer unless they are supplied from the mother country. 'The frequent failures in the establishment of new colonies tend strongly to show the order of precedence between food and population.'[1]

Obviously the type of man who is subject to distress from a rapidly rising population at home would not have the resources to establish himself in a new colony abroad, and, unless leaders of the requisite ability and substance were forthcoming or support were available from the home government, no matter what degree of misery men suffered at home, they would be unable to take possession of the uncultivated land in other parts of the world.

When once a colony is established, subsequent arrivals find difficulties diminished, but even then they need some resources. How far the government should provide these is an open question, but it presumably would not do so unless the proposed emigration promised some colonial advantages.

He hastens to defend people who do not wish to emigrate. Is a man to blame if he feels an attachment to his friends and his native land? The great plan of Providence seems to require emigration on occasions, but it is none the less painful because essential. Besides the poor have just grounds for fear. The promises held out to them may be deceptive, and, if they are assisted to depart, they are well aware that they can expect no such assistance to return.

If it were imagined that a tract of land could be suddenly annexed to a country, the effects would be great and striking; but the gain would be of short duration.[2] The geometrical ratio would soon fill up the land to the same density as before. 'It is evident therefore, that the reason why the resource of emigration has so long continued to be held out as a remedy to redundant

[1] 1806 edn., Vol. II, p. 141. There is a contradiction here. Malthus normally understands by the means of subsistence those actually in existence at a given time. In that sense the argument is true and population exceeds subsistence. But, if we use the same meaning for the mother country, then clearly the emigrants are not leaving owing to lack of the means of subsistence in this sense; otherwise there would be no possibility of supplying them from the mother country. It is this shifting of meaning which seems to make the doctrine of population so universally applicable, by making poverty and a physical shortage of the means of subsistence synonymous.

[2] Cf. Evidence before the Emigration Committee, Third Report, 1827, Qs. 3350 et seq.

population is, because from the natural unwillingness of people to desert their native country, and the difficulty of clearing and cultivating fresh soil, it never is or can be adequately adopted.' If it could be, the phial would soon be exhausted and 'every hope from this quarter would be for ever closed.'[1]

As a permanent solution, therefore, emigration is quite inadequate, but as a partial and temporary expedient, it seems to be both useful and proper. Hence, if governments do not encourage, they ought not to prevent it. The fears of depopulation are ill-grounded. The *vis inertiæ* of the common people is so strong that they will not be driven to emigrate unless the country is in such a state as to benefit by their departure. If the level of wages in a country is satisfactory, the people will not leave; if it is not, they should not be prevented.

Such were the early views deducible from the principle of population, and, since England was then at war with Napoleon, it was hardly to be expected that the subject would be very much alive, or the notion of a drain of men very popular. But in 1815, at the end of the war, the position was radically altered. English life was in an unnatural condition. The war, which had stimulated the growth of and the demand for population, gave way to peace which had very different requirements. The demand for war materials dried up, and about half a million soldiers were released. Disaster overtook agriculture. So, writing in 1817, Malthus was constrained to add the following:

'If for instance, from a combination of external and internal causes, a very great stimulus should be given to the population of a country for ten or twelve years together, and it should then comparatively cease, it is clear that labour will continue flowing into the market with almost undiminished rapidity, while the means of employing and paying it have been essentially contracted. It is precisely under these circumstances that emigration is most useful as a temporary relief, and it is in these circumstances that Great Britain finds herself placed at present.' If emigration does not take place the population will conform itself to the new facts, but the suffering will be great. 'The only real relief in such a case is emigration; and the subject is well worthy the attention of the government, both as a matter of humanity and policy.'[2]

[1] 1806 edn., pp. 146–147.

[2] *Essay*, Book III, Chapter IV.

PRACTICAL STEPS

The government did in fact turn its attention seriously to the matter in 1820, and in that and the following years many debates were held in both Houses of Parliament to discuss its value as a remedy for the social distress in which the country found itself. The culmination of these discussions was the appointment of a select committee, under the chairmanship of Wilmot Horton, which reported in 1826 and 1827.

Meanwhile something was being done. In 1816, at the instance of the War Office, Lt.-Col. Cockburn persuaded a number of British soldiers, whose period of service expired while they were in Canada, to take up land between the St. Lawrence and Ottawa rivers. Plots of land were given to the men, varying from 100 to 1,200 acres, according to their rank, and they were provided with rations while preparing the land for cultivation. They were joined in 1820 by a group from Lanarkshire, but the difficulties proved so great that by 1823 most of the settlers had deserted their plots.

Other emigrations occurred almost annually from various parts of the United Kingdom, and parliamentary grants were made in 1819, 1821, 1823, 1825, and 1827. That of 1819 was used to send some 3,659 people, out of a total of 90,000 applicants, to South Africa, where, after many hardships and with the aid of further government and charitable assistance from home, they were eventually satisfactorily settled. In 1823, Mr. Peter Robinson, a Canadian, conducted an experimental colonization, recruiting mainly from the County of Cork, and sending to Bathurst some 568 people. The total cost was £12,593 3*s.* 0*d.* which ran out at about £22 1*s.* 6*d.* a head, or £88 6*s.* 0*d.* per family. He also supplied cattle, utensils, buildings, seed corn, and other necessaries. A further scheme on a larger scale was carried through in 1825, under the same leadership and again from Ireland, when about 2,024 emigrants were chosen from over 50,000 applicants. The success of these schemes was a matter of conflicting opinion, and Parliament refused to vote the necessary funds for a third effort until after the Emigration Committee had reported.

THE EMIGRATION REPORT, 1826

The gist of the report of 1826 is as follows. Extensive districts in Ireland, and also districts in Scotland and England have redundant populations, as a result of which there is widespread misery, a deterioration of working-class standards, and a reduction of wages below subsistence level. On the other hand, in British North America, the Cape of Good Hope and Van Diemen's Land there is fertile land which is unappropriated. The unemployed man at home consumes more than he produces; if transplanted abroad he could produce more than he would consume. Consequently the national wealth would be increased if the colonies were considered as an extension of the nation and the question of emigration is worth serious attention. It should, however, be voluntary on the part of the emigrants and relate to that part of the community which is in a state of permanent pauperism, and, as a general rule, any grants made to emigrants should be repaid. In England the poor fund could be made applicable to the repayment of the expense of emigration. In Scotland and Ireland no such funds are available, and voluntary contributions should be sought, and would probably be forthcoming if benefit could be proved. Successive emigrations should prove less and less costly.

Only a peep into the Minutes of Evidence is possible, but even that is instructive.[1] Mr. Chambers, a police magistrate of the Borough of Southwark, appears to agree with Malthus to the extent that 'the only good law against emigration is that which nature has engraven on every heart' (p. 87). Edward Jeremiah Curteis, an M.P. and a Sussex magistrate, states that one-quarter of the emigrants return, their object in emigrating being idleness, and not the expectation of a better livelihood through hard work (p. 115). Sir John Sebright, M.P., frankly admits that he would gladly emigrate certain families, if he could select them himself. 'The first class of persons I would select would be persons having large families, the next would be men of bad character, and families of bad character. . . . My first object would be, and perhaps with me it would be a greater object even

[1] *Report from the Select Committee on Emigration from the United Kingdom*, May 26th, 1826. Minutes of Evidence.

than getting rid of the redundant population, to send away those families' (p. 124). William Gabbett, a gentleman of Limerick, after noting the pulling down of cottages, says he would prefer to pay a tax to keep men at home rather than a tax for their emigration (p. 131). Thomas Law Hodges of Kent thinks that emigration would improve wages provided cottages were pulled down; otherwise improved conditions would lead to early marriage (p. 140). Thomas Spring Rice, one of the members of the committee, thinks 'it might become a question whether, if the waste lands were brought into cultivation, and if the population now concentrated in the poorer arable districts were dispersed throughout the country, the population would be considered as redundant' (pp. 210–211).

It is important to remember that the main background to the reports was not so much the problem of England as that of Ireland. There the wage level was lower than in England, and the Irish were living in squalor and poverty on a staple diet of potatoes. It was feared that if this state of affairs continued, the potato-fed population of Ireland would soon drag down to its own level the wheat-fed population of Great Britain.[1] If the emigration of Englishmen were fostered, the vacuum would soon be filled by the Irish, and therefore, although emigration was applicable to overpopulated parishes in England, it should be applied primarily to Ireland. The report is overshadowed with this dread of the 'Malthusian' vacuum.

THE EXPERT WITNESS

The third report of 1827 is of even greater importance in that Malthus himself was the chief witness. He appeared before it on May 5th, 1827, and Wilmot Horton was in the chair. The report speaks thus of his evidence:

'The testimony which was uniformly given by the *practical witnesses*, who appeared before Your Committee, has been confirmed in the most absolute manner by that of Mr. Malthus; and Your Committee cannot but express their satisfaction at finding that the experience of facts is thus strengthened throughout by general reasoning and scientific principles.'[2]

[1] See *History of Emigration*, S. C. Johnson, 1913, p. 54.

[2] Third Report, 1827, p. 9.

Wilmot Horton got the assent of Malthus to many arguments in favour of emigration; it would increase the wealth of the Empire;[1] it would furnish a valuable market for British goods;[2] it would help to prevent secession or conquest.[3] But it is clear that the main preoccupation was with redundancy, with the principle of population and with poor relief. By means of leading questions the relevance of the principle of population to the subject was elicited.

If a thousand labourers, for whose labour there is no demand, were to die, the wealth of the country would not be diminished.[4] Even the removal of men who were out of work would not improve wages, although the removal of a portion of those in work would do so.[5] It becomes then a matter of the relative cost of emigrating the men or maintaining them, since they are useless anyhow, although humanity is allowed to peep through the clouds by the frequent insertion of phrases such as 'removal with benefit to themselves and their families.'[6]

If men could be emigrated at less cost than they could be maintained at home it would be a good thing, and even if the expense were the same, it would still be legitimate,[7] and government assistance might be justified if the expenditure were not likely to recur.[8] Further, emigration might pave the way for the abolition of the English poor laws, and Malthus insists that no improvement is possible without denying the legal claim of the poor to support.

'If a system of emigration could be adopted with benefit to the labourer emigrating, do you think that it might justify the enactment of a positive law, removing all claim upon the part of an able-bodied pauper for assistance or for work under circumstances of his being in a state of destitution?—As I should say so independently of the question of emigration, I must say so still more strongly when coupled with the remedy proposed.'[9]

Other remedies were considered only to be rejected, Malthus opposed the view that the cultivation of waste lands offered a solution, and when a parallel was attempted between overseas colonies and the addition of a contiguous territory, he

[1] Third Report, 1827, Q. 3294.
[2] Q. 3295. [3] Q. 3299. [4] Q. 3238. [5] Q. 3259.
[6] Q. 3246. [7] Qs. 3246–7. [8] Q. 3277. [9] Q. 3257.

strenuously resisted the analogy.[1] It was impossible not to consider the question of expense and the strong human feelings against leaving the motherland. The cultivation of inferior lands within the country must end in failure.[2] Public works, though offering a temporary relief, in the long run made matters worse. It was suggested that cheap pamphlets might be delivered to the poor and the doctrines taught in the schools, but Malthus was no more than lukewarm.[3]

The remedy, if remedy there be, is emigration, but here the situation of the Irish presents a problem. The habit of the Irish of living on potatoes naturally encourages population.[4] Potatoes lead to famine. If the Irish lived on wheat, they could resort to rye, barley, oats, or potatoes in times of scarcity.[5] This is in fact the principal distinction between the English and the Irish—their staple food.[6] There is a constant threat to reduce England to a potato economy, and even if districts of England and Scotland were partially reduced by emigration, the vacuum would tend to be filled by the immigrant Irish.[7]

Thus, if emigration is to succeed, it must be applied first to Ireland, and here an analogy is drawn with English conditions. In England, where the poor laws exist, the chief check to population is the shortage of houses.[8] If, therefore, half a million people were to be emigrated from Ireland, the vacuum would soon be filled by the Irish themselves, unless the landlords changed their system of management, altered the distribution of the land, and pulled down the hovels of those who went abroad.[9] Over and over again this question of housing crops up, and he thinks it is not a bad suggestion to tax landlords who build cottages.[10] Emigration, without demolition, is doomed to failure.[11]

The committee then suggest that there is hope of an improvement in Irish habits which will depend mainly on the introduction of education of the right kind, but the first step towards any improvement is the reduction of the present redundancy, without which reduction the situation is hopeless. Even then emigration alone is not sufficient. 'If without any pressure with regard

[1] Third Report, 1827, Qs. 3350–3353. [2] Q. 3342.
[3] Q. 3377. [4] Q. 3203. [5] Q. 3238.
[6] Q. 3406. [7] Qs. 3222, 3395. [8] Q. 3361.
[9] Q. 3231. [10] Qs. 3366, 3325. [11] Q. 3253.

to expense you could effect a constant emigration to a large extent, you would no doubt keep the population in a better state; but if such a current of emigration were to stop at any time, you would have a still greater tendency to a redundancy.'[1] Nevertheless, in spite of all the qualifications and provisos, Malthus concludes by saying: 'I think that a judicious system of emigration is one of the most powerful means to accomplish that object,' namely the improvement of conditions in Ireland.[2]

The committee duly reported its findings, but the Irish question of emigration was being solved by the Irish themselves, and the only point which remained for decision was whether Great Britain was to be the host and be deluged with poverty and wretchedness by the equalization of wages in the two countries, or whether the stream should be turned in the direction of the American colonies. Two different standards of living could not permanently co-exist side by side, and therefore either the Irish should be raised to the standard of the English, or the English would be lowered to the standard of the Irish. Battle would be joined between potatoes and wheat.

Though the report influenced public opinion, the recommendations of the committee were not implemented. Two bills, introduced into Parliament by Wilmot Horton to allow the mortgaging of the poor rates, were thrown out. A short-lived commission, which was dissolved in 1832, contented itself with the dissemination of information, but some statutory provision was made for the borrowing by parishes from the Treasury in 1834. Meanwhile emigration grew enormously in proportions, reaching its peak in 1832, when more than 100,000 left these shores for Canada, the United States, and the Colonies of Australia and New Zealand.[3] We can follow the story no further.

We have already noticed, in earlier chapters, the views of the critics of Malthus regarding emigration where they were relevant to the principle of population. Actually emigration occupies a smaller position in the discussion than most other issues, because in this case both sides were talking about the same thing. The critics concentrated in the main on the short-term position, and here they were in agreement with Malthus

[1] Third Report, 1827, Q. 3382. [2] Q. 3434.

[3] Johnson, op. cit., p. 344.

that emigration would provide immediate relief. Notable exceptions were Cobbett and Sadler, who opposed it bitterly, but it would not advance our present purpose to follow them into the fields of controversy. Our aim has been merely to demonstrate one more aspect of national policy where the name and the doctrines of Malthus wielded a great influence.

CHAPTER FIVE

BIRTH CONTROL

THE PREVENTIVE CHECK

ONCE the ratios had captured the minds of his contemporaries, the need for the checks was regarded as axiomatic. The only questions which remained to be discussed were the nature and extent of the various manifestations of the checks, the relative importance to be attached to each, and the method, by which the most desirable, or perhaps the least undesirable, checks might be fostered and encouraged.

The early checks, vice and misery, were naturally enough very unpopular, especially among those who might be held to fall within their scope. But these checks were alternatively classified as positive and preventive, and in spite of the unsatisfactory and blurred nature of this classification, majority opinion soon settled for the preventive species. Godwin and Hall regarded infanticide as preferable to unmitigated misery, if that were the real choice. Sadler attacked fiercely and at length the preventive check, but he did not support the positive variety: rather he relied on his own theory of population as denying the need for either. Grahame stated his case for preferring the positive check, when it was confined to infancy, on the grounds (mistaken, as Hall demonstrated) that such a check provided a eugenic device for selecting those fitted for survival in the station of life to which they were born. Of the rest of the critics, those who accepted the ratios, and hence the need for some form of check, seem invariably to have plumped for prevention, preferably moral restraint.

Malthus himself set the tone. The second *Essay* came down heavily in favour of this check. He advocated moral restraint and devised what he thought was a satisfactory scheme for encouraging the preventive check. It is true that he did not expect much from moral restraint as such, but this was compatible with a much greater faith in the efficacy of the preventive check, which for him meant abstention from or postponement of marriage.

Wallace, when faced with the problem, ran over the various possibilities, only to reject them all. Malthus had in mind not only the proposal of a hypothesis, but the establishment of a remedy, and this remedy was the preaching of restraint to the poor. Theoretically, restraint ought to have been preached to rich and poor alike, but in practice the admonitions were addressed in the main to the poor. Nor is this illogical in that they are the more numerous, and therefore no scheme which does not touch them could possibly succeed. The rich were urged to reform their drawing-room etiquette;[1] the poor were to be deprived of the benefit of the poor laws.

Other writers, particularly the equalitarians, proposed that the solution to the dilemma, if and when it arose, would be a

[1] It has been said that Malthus never stooped to the grossness and coarseness of his critics, but it is difficult to like the following passages: 'It is not enough to abolish all the positive institutions which encourage population; but we must endeavour, at the same time, to correct the prevailing opinions, which have the same, or perhaps even a more powerful effect. . . . The matron who has reared a family of ten or twelve children, and whose sons, perhaps, may be fighting the battles of their country, is apt to think that society owes her much; and this imaginary debt, society is, in general, fully inclined to acknowledge. But if the subject be fairly considered, and the respected matron weighed in the scales of justice against the neglected old maid, it is possible that the matron might kick the beam. She will appear rather in the character of a monopolist, than of a great benefactor of the state. If she had not married and had so many children, other members of the society might have enjoyed this satisfaction; and there is no particular reason for supposing that her sons would fight better for their country than the sons of other women. She has therefore rather subtracted from, than added to, the happiness of the other parts of society' (1803 edn., pp. 549–550). 'It is perfectly absurd as well as unjust, that a giddy girl of sixteen should, because she is married, be considered by the forms of society as the protector of women of thirty, should come first into the room, should be assigned the highest place at table, and be the prominent figure to whom the attentions of the company are more particularly addressed' (Id., pp. 551–552). It is true these unhappy passages disappeared in the next edition, but that they dwelt with him long enough to warrant being inserted gives some insight into his habits of thought.

minimum age for marriage, calculated so as to restrict population to the required level; but Malthus would have none of this. Like Wallace before him, he was horrified at the idea. If marriage without fair prospects was an immoral act, to fix a minimum age verged on the criminal.

REASONS FOR THE REJECTION OF THE PREVENTIVE CHECK

Now clearly Malthus's plan was bound to be rejected. It was impossible for long to maintain that the remedy for poverty lay with the poor and with them alone, and that postponement of marriage was the solution. As a remedy it was inappropriate, because, in the first place, marriage, for the poor man, offered an immediate prospect, not merely of sexual gratification but of genuine comforts, which far outweighed the prospect of future ills. A wife to such a man was not a liability, but in many cases a real asset.

In the second place, as Malthus admitted, the restraint he proposed was not likely to be moral. So far as we are concerned with a check to population this is not of the utmost importance, but it was well known that in practice amongst the poor, celibacy and immorality were almost synonymous. It was not to be expected, therefore, that opinion would settle down to the theory that vice was preferable to misery without some attempt to explore further possibilities.

In the third place, as was pointed out by many writers, and by none more ably than Lloyd, the motives leading to the preventive check among the poor were hopelessly inadequate. A poor man who abstained from marriage would suffer the whole of the deprivation of comforts, while the rise in wages due to such abstinence would be infinitesimal. Yet Malthus, who, in his argument with Senior, defended his ratios by urging the superior strength of the motives towards sexual gratification as against the weaker ones making for the production of food, now proposes a solution which pits the whole of the forces making for the desirable state of marriage against small and problematical gains to the whole community.

In the fourth place, even if a poor man did abstain from marriage until such a time as he could reasonably hope to maintain a family, the result might belie the expectation. A wife of unusual fertility would soon reduce him to squalor and want. The most he could do would be to make a prudent start: the rest would have to be left to providence.

Lastly, it must be noted that the widespread adoption of this check would have an adverse effect on the quality of the population. The prudent would be few in numbers, while those who were heedless of caution would grow and multiply, insofar as they escaped the positive check.

THE SOLUTION—BIRTH CONTROL

In view of these and such considerations the completeness with which the Malthusian diagnosis was accepted was the measure of the dissatisfaction with the proposed remedy. Some critics, like Weyland and Sadler, sought refuge in alternative theories of population growth. To escape the conclusions they denied the premises. Others attacked the ratios in the short run, and left the long-run problem to solve itself when it arose. But for those who accepted the Malthusian analysis the situation called for a remedy, and for something superior to that put forward by the master himself.

It has been pointed out already that Malthus did not sufficiently distinguish between fertility and fecundity. He noted the difference, but did not pay adequate attention to its significance. The whole of his admonitions were directed towards postponing the age of marriage. After the event children must come along as they will, and this fact alone invalidates the solution.

When he says: 'Every act which was prompted by the desire of immediate gratification, but which threatened an ultimate overbalance of pain, would be considered as a breach of duty; and consequently no man whose earnings were only sufficient to maintain two children, would put himself in a situation in which he might have to maintain four or five, however he might be prompted to it by the passion of love,'[1] he is talking nonsense. This might be true if he were advocating continence within the marriage relationship, but the next few lines show that he was not. As it stands the statement postulates that a man before marriage can determine the number of children he is likely to have, which is absurd.

[1] 1806 edn., Vol. II, pp. 321–322.

No, not absurd! That is if the notion of birth control be accepted. The whole of the Malthusian thesis leads as inevitably to the solution of birth control as though it had been devised for the purpose; yet it cannot be too strongly emphasized that Malthus himself refused to countenance it. In his first edition he deplored the check mentioned by Condorcet. He was indignant with Grahame when he thought that Grahame had charged him with supporting such a check. Yet the solution was put before him in no uncertain terms by Place, whose criticism was on the whole friendly; and one would have thought that the logic of the situation would have led Malthus to embrace, however reluctantly, the only way of reconciling fecundity and food.

Place was under no illusions. The son of a dissolute father, he was reared in poverty, and early fell into vicious habits. He was rescued by his marriage at nineteen to a girl of seventeen years, but the price of his rescue was some fifteen children. He was no man to preach continence, for, as he wrote to Ensor, it 'has served so well in the instances of you and I—and Mill, and Wakefield—mustering among us no less I believe than 36 children . . . rare fellows we to teach moral restraint.'[1]

Reason and experience alike led Place to the open advocacy of birth control after marriage. James Mill had earlier made guarded references to it. Thompson a little later proposed it, but again in somewhat vague terms. Carlile, at the outset indifferent and even hostile, passed by degrees to full support. Sadler, on the other hand, noted in 1830 the spread of the practice and of its preaching with disapprobation.

This is not the place to trace the history of the birth control movement.[2] We are merely concerned with its connections with Malthus in the period we have considered, and in our opinion the movement is correctly named 'Neo-Malthusian.' No doubt birth control of a sort goes back long into history in the form of tribal customs as to cohabitation, suckling, periods of intercourse, abortion, child exposure and the like devices; no doubt crude techniques for preventing conception had been known in this country to the few for some time; but the real pioneer in its

[1] Himes, Introduction to *Place on Population*, p. 10.

[2] See the works of Himes; Field, *Essays on Population*; and the many writers to whom they refer.

open advocacy was undoubtedly Francis Place, and the connection with Malthus is clear and acknowledged.

The full fruits were to come later, after the Bradlaugh–Besant trial had given enormous publicity to the movement, but to Place goes the early credit of exposing himself first to the obloquy which resulted from the propaganda.

REASONS FOR MALTHUS'S REJECTION OF BIRTH CONTROL

Why then did Malthus not adopt the solution so ready to his hand? That it was a solution there is no doubt whatever. The decline in population which is threatened as a result of the trend of the birth rate since 1877 has led to the problem being posed as the 'Twilight of Parenthood.' Here, brought to his notice, was a means of reconciling early marriage with a reasonable number of children. It was likely to reduce vice by permitting early monogamy instead of promiscuous intercourse. It could emancipate the race from the geometrical ratio, and the rate of growth and size of families could be controlled by individual parents. Why, one asks, did Malthus, in so many respects the utilitarian, turn his back on this solution and accept the traditional morality?

Place thought it was fear of public opinion, and, as a contemporary of Malthus, Place's view carries some weight.

'Mr. Malthus seems to shrink from discussing the propriety of preventing conception, not so much it may be supposed from the abhorrence which he or any reasonable man can have to the practice, as from the possible fear of encountering the prejudices of others.'[1]

There may be some substance in this charge. Malthus made enemies by his *Essay on Population*, but he also made friends, allies, and a reputation. Moreover, even if this was incidental, the doctrines he propounded were such as fitted in with the notions of influential men of his day. His shafts were aimed mainly at the poor, even if in their real or supposed interests, and he could reverse engines when it came to advocating corn laws. The agitation for birth control came late in his life, at a time when he had other interests than the principle of population, when his

[1] Op. cit., p. 173. See also Himes's comment on pp. 297–298.

reputation was established, and his views orthodox.[1] He had every reason, and few would blame him, for turning away from the new remedy.

In addition, he seems to share with, or to have imbibed from Wallace, a fear of interfering with marriage. When his opponents proposed fixing a minimum age below which no one should marry, he regards such a proposal as repugnant. Whether this was merely an old orthodoxy which he could not shake off and refused to question; whether it was a reaction to the views of Godwin on marriage (for Godwin was his first opponent, and the *Essay* never really rid itself of the effects of its controversial origin); or whether he feared that to countenance such a policy would be subversive of the established social customs; these are matters of speculation. Malthus was a staunch believer in private property and in the main structure of the society of his day. He could not but have viewed with concern so radical a proposal as that put forward by Place.

Perhaps, however, there is another more plausible explanation. Malthus learned much from Townsend, and not least the supposed effects of hunger as a driving force. 'Hunger,' said his mentor, 'will tame the most savage beast.' And it was by the pressure of want, brought about by the abolition of the poor laws, that Malthus proposed to tame the poor. He believed firmly in the 'acknowledged indolence of man,' and that the disproportionate growth of population and food was the essential spur to industry.[2]

'Even if from passions too easily subdued, or the facility of illicit intercourse, a state of celibacy were a matter of indifference, and not a state of some privation, the end of nature in the peopling of the earth would be apparently liable to be defeated.'[3]

Consequently man should not marry until he could maintain his family, but at the same time he should preserve his desire for marriage in order to stimulate him to exertions.[4] Here more than in the other reasons already given, may be the clue to Malthus's ignoring the proposed remedy.

[1] See Correspondence with Senior, who regards himself as attacking the 'received opinions.'

[2] *Essay*, 1806 edn., Vol. II, p. 316.

[3] Id., p. 317.

[4] Id., p. 318.

Be that as it may, the logical conclusion *was* drawn, by Place and others; the diabolical handbill was circulated; one writer after another took up the theme. The movement spread, and it only needed the prosecution of Charles Bradlaugh and Annie Besant to publicize the possibilities in all the corners of the land. The rest of the story is found in the statistics of births for the past seventy years.

CONCLUSION

Our survey of the Malthusian era has been so extensive that it would involve needless repetition to attempt a complete summary of what has gone before. Our purpose has been to rescue the contemporary critics from an ill-deserved neglect, and for that reason it has been found desirable, by extended quotation, to allow them to speak for themselves—the more so because there has been a tendency to belittle the standard of the criticism offered. The traditional view is to extol Malthus, even if some minor blemishes are admitted, and, because he was so successful in his own day, to ignore contemporary criticism as of little account. But since population theories seem almost inevitably to be coloured by the circumstances of the time when they are enunciated, and since the Malthusian monster raised its head in a modified form in the twenties of this century, and there are even now the premonitory rumblings of its further approach, it is well to remind ourselves that, even when he was writing, there was criticism, sufficient in volume and acuteness, to have made an impartial reader doubt the validity of the principle of population. Moreover, the intervening years have justified the critics and falsified the theory attacked.

It is generally agreed that Malthus was not original in his views, and our first book has shown the completeness with which his main points had been earlier brought forward by other writers. Wallace and Townsend, the latter a contemporary, left between them little to be added. But Malthus's *Essay* was the book of the hour. It caught the tide; and as Godwin's star began to wane, that of Malthus rose to the ascendancy. Across the channel property was threatened; and Malthus was the apostle of private property. Within the country the rich saw, in the poor laws, an intolerable burden; and Malthus appeared to show that they were both ill-conceived and fruitless. The industrial revolution was bringing with it a feeling of uncertainty and unrest; institutions were in a state of flux; and Malthus preached that the old order was sound, its laws, if not natural laws, at least the most natural of positive laws, and departure from them the sure road to disaster. The times made him a prophet.

Yet his triumph was not quite complete. Voices were raised against him, and although they were not strong enough to turn the tide, their influence must have been substantial in the long run. A careful perusal of Book II will reveal not a series of disjointed attacks, but a steady development of thought. The earlier critics were inclined to hit out in all directions; there is an element of desperation in their writings; but gradually later writers were able to discern which lines of attack were to prove the more fruitful. Malthus could purport to ignore Godwin, but he was driven to answer Booth. Place accepted the fundamentals of the principle of population but his advocacy of birth control was the beginning of a movement which can completely nullify the geometrical or any other ratio. The Malthus of the *Summary View* was a very cautious, one could almost say chastened writer, and although his political significance was still great, his intellectual hold had begun to weaken. Senior tried his best to get a restatement from him, but in vain. He was either too prejudiced, too set in his ideas, or, as at times it appears, too little interested to change his mind. Yet in spite of the development of the controversy during its passage through time, it is surprising to note how much of the more mature and scholarly criticisms of such men as Senior and Lloyd were foreshadowed in the earlier trio: Hall, Jarrold, and Hazlitt.

As for the theory itself it has two aspects. The first, derived mainly from Wallace, was that the power of population so exceeded any possible rate of growth of food supplies that sooner or later the world would be full and famine would level the two. To this theory Malthus added the ratios which, unfortunately, so captured his mind that he visualized the history of man as divided into consecutive twenty-five-year periods during which population proceeded to grow in geometrical and food in arithmetical ratio. The result of this analysis was that the pressure was not remote but constantly operating, except when there were agricultural 'starts,' which presumably began a new set of ratios. However, he never developed this part of the theory in detail or with any accuracy, and when the critics attacked it, he abandoned the mathematics but retained the advantage of the impression he had created. In fact, whenever he was hard pressed, as in the correspondence with Senior, he relied in the most clumsy fashion on the ratios he had so nearly disowned.

The ratios were never proved, and rested on the slenderest foundations. The basic assumption was a constantly operating passion between the sexes; yet although differential fertility rates in different strata of society were apparent even in his own day, Malthus drew no clear distinction between fecundity and fertility. The supposed period of doubling was deduced from the very doubtful American statistics, and, although a twenty-five-year term is not fundamental to the hypothesis, yet its practical advantages were so great that he clung tenaciously to it throughout his lifetime. If he had paid less attention to defending the precise period of doubling chosen, and more to attempting to establish its operation elsewhere, he would have done more to advance the status, if not the acceptance of his theory, but in fact he found that all the other countries were exceptions to this rate of growth. This led him to enunciate the theory of the checks, which were ill-defined as vice, misery, and moral restraint, and alternatively classified as positive and preventive.

The latter is the more accurate, though still defective classification, representing as it does the amount of the premature deaths and the reduction in the possible births, but it is still necessary to show the extent of these divergences and that he completely failed to do. In connection with the other classification, no one doubts that vice, misery and prudence will be found in a greater or lesser degree throughout the world, but to prove the Malthusian thesis something more is required: they must be shown to be a function of the deficiency in the food supply, and this again he was unable to do. Throughout he begged the question. The checks were assumed from the slower rate of growth in old countries; the superior power of population from its rapid growth in America, where admittedly food was keeping pace with it. It would have been in order to state that, if one population is growing at a slower rate than another, this must be due to a reduced number of births or a greater number of deaths or both, and these might well have been called checks. Even so, having established their existence, their cause and their necessity have still to be shown.

The arithmetical ratio is nonsense: it never had any foundation at all. If the geometrical ratio does represent the ratio of growth of populations of living things, then it is clear that most kinds of food can multiply even more quickly than mankind. Thus the question returns to the position of Wallace—sooner or later the earth will be full. But the critics were not at all concerned with Wallace, they were concerned to deny that the ratios were operating in Great Britain at the beginning of the nineteenth century in such a way as to stultify all efforts at improvement and to compel them to accept the remedies proposed by Malthus. Leaving aside, therefore, the question of what will happen when the earth is full, we find them advocating the development of waste lands, colonization, the adoption of improved methods of cultivation, and so on. Yet, although these remedies were dismissed as naïve and useless, this is certainly not the case unless one admits the validity of the arithmetical ratio, the most doubtful part of a dubious structure.

It was really never more than a figure of speech, but it was made to do the job of a valid series. Malthus was forced to admit that, so long as there was vacant land, food too could grow in geometrical ratio, as indeed it must have done in the United States. Therefore in advancing these remedies for existing troubles the critics were on sound ground, and the Malthusian tenets offered no information as to the possibilities of advance. Indeed, Malthus's erroneous forecasts as to what could happen in the next hundred years strengthen the view that the principle of population has no bearing on the short-term possibilities.

Neither the geometrical nor the arithmetical ratios were soundly based. The former was a mere hypothesis which has already been criticized in great detail. A father whose son weighed seven pounds at birth, might weigh him at the age of six months and find that he weighed fourteen pounds. Reasoning on Malthusian lines he would deduce that the boy would weigh a hundredweight at the age of two and approximately twelve and a half tons at the age of six. Like Malthus, he would be convinced that shortage of house-room was a likely check to population growth. But the population of cells which forms the body does not grow according to such a ratio; nor is there any reason to suppose that a population of human beings does so. We are not aware of the mechanisms and influences which determine the rates of population growth, and so far they have only been observed in a world where further food production was still possible; therefore without specific evidence we are not bound to accept the geometrical ratio even as an abstract tendency. Pearl has examined carefully the growth of a *Drosophila* population in a closed universe, and he finds that its growth can be depicted by a logistic curve. While it is true that human beings are not fruit flies, neither are they terms in a geometrical series and those who lay down such a series must show the ground on which they rest, and it must be something more solid than the Malthusian demonstration already examined.

With regard to the growth of food the arithmetical ratio contributed nothing, although in places Malthus argued more accurately as to the real conditions of growth and seems to have had a fair idea of the law of diminishing returns. Yet he never connected population and food supply with any degree of accuracy. Whenever population advances in a way inconsistent with his theory, he never doubts the theory, but murmurs of an agricultural 'start.' In this way he is enabled to inaugurate a new series and begin again. But a theory which asserts that population and food grow in certain ratios, and then admits that quite frequently, and for no discernible reason, they do not, can only be expected to produce such erroneous forecasts as those actually made by Malthus himself. Yet Malthus did not investigate these so-called starts. To do so might have been to find out that his theory would need to be inverted, so that whenever the pressure of population reached a certain point, the volume of food would be increased to meet it.

The existence of checks, in spite of the voluminous apparatus of 'proofs,' was assumed rather than demonstrated. It is true that he showed the existence of vice, misery, and prudence, but he did not succeed in connecting them with his principle in any convincing way. If he does not find the population being decimated by famine, he asserts that it is the existence of the other evils which act as prior checks and so prevent this happening. Thus we reach the conclusion that the existing volume of vice and misery is a constant (for moral restraint is a dead letter and degenerates into the prudential check, synonymous with vice).

He swallows with difficulty the implications. Medical science is unavailing. Cure one disease, and you extend the dominion of another. The only hope is for an agricultural 'start,' which the geometrical ratio will soon dispose of. Truly we are driven to believe that the principle of population is *the* discovery of the age.

Having thus brought mankind to its knees he was bound to offer a solution—'moral restraint,' or, failing that, the prudential check. Having denied to the rational inhabitants of Godwin's Utopia all ability to control their sexual impulses, he proceeds to recommend to the uneducated poor of England 'moral restraint.' The grounds on which he hopes for success are that in a state of private property a man's individual interest will lead him to moral restraint. This point of view was demolished by Lloyd who showed that the individual's motives to restraint are hardly greater in a system of private property than in one of common property, and, since the general standard of social awareness would be greater in the latter state, Malthus's remedy makes a very poor showing. If Godwin's society would breed itself back to ruin, the poor of England could hardly be expected to win salvation through celibacy.

It was here that Place carried the Malthusian theory to its logical conclusion by advocating birth control, and it is noteworthy that, just as Malthus's predictions of the turn of future events proved false, so subsequent generations have reversed the practical consequences of his policies, and declared in favour of the main tenets of the critics. Malthus opposed birth control, yet it has become so widespread that where it is practised the notion of a geometrical ratio can have no validity at all. In older countries the problem is not one of stemming the flood of people, but of preventing a decline, of unbalanced age-structures and differential fertility rates. Far from dooming infants to starve, there is a concerted attack on infant mortality so that the wastage shall be as low as possible. Instead of abolishing the poor law, or severely restricting its application, the gradual development of social insurance has lead to the establishment of the firm principle of the right of a man to a minimum income, even when he is unable to work. Malthus denied the possibility of the welfare state. He has not yet been proved wrong, but the whole trend of the last fifty years has been towards that end, and only a bold man today would prophecy total failure. He asserted that wages would always hover about subsistence level, whereas the modern concept is that of an adequate standard of living, and the word 'optimum' tends to replace the word 'minimum' in current discussions of social policy.

If the immediate future declared against Malthus, what of the more distant prospect? Although he asserted that he was no enemy of population when it followed its natural course, this is mere verbiage. He left the clear impression that each growth of population carried the human race so much the nearer disaster, and even when, in the early days of the nineteenth century, population in England was both growing, and growing healthier, he was busy forecasting an end to the process in imminent poverty and misery. If there is a long-term menace in the theory, we constitute, at a hundred and fifty years' distance, the posterity on whom it should fall, and not infrequent rumblings of disaster continue to be heard.

Alarm is felt at the growth of world population based on the same irrational foundations bequeathed to us by Malthus, but there is another view of the subject. While population is growing it shows that there is room for it. If world population is growing it cannot be because food is short, it must be because longevity is increasing and health improving. A population whose standards are below subsistence level must decline, in accordance with Malthus's first postulate, and if the world were really short of food, population could not grow: children would die in the cradle, and the rates of infant and adult mortality would increase —yet growth is what we observe. A growing population, instead of being a thing to deplore, is a sign that, for the time being at all events, conditions are easier and health is better.[1] It is this irrational fear of a full world, the legacy of Malthus, which scatters alarm, leads to gloomy forebodings, and hinders a rational approach to the problems of population growth and the standard of living.

[1] This is strictly true of a population hovering on the subsistence level. Where a country has a high standard of living a growing population might reduce it, but this is not necessarily to be deplored. Material standards are not the only ones, and it is possible to hold that life itself is more than the raiment. If such a country dropped to subsistence level, it would then cease to increase in numbers. Generalizing in this field is dangerous, but all things considered, a growing population is a good rather than a bad sign. The wise economist will, however, look to other indices for guidance.

It is right that man should look to the future and conserve resources, but the indices to watch are not the figures of population but the rates of mortality, and particularly those of infant mortality. A population which is reducing these must be improving, and the appropriate course of action is not that of starving or frightening people into celibacy, but the vigorous application of human ingenuity to improving medical science and applying it more widely, to stimulating productivity and all other things which are conducive to human welfare and happiness.

The Malthusian preoccupation with shortage of food, which has captured the imagination because everyone eats, has its counterpart in the fears that coal, oil, and timber supplies will soon be exhausted; and yet up to the present time the ingenuity of man has overcome the obstacles as they confronted him. Malthus regarded food as the cause of population. His critics regarded it as the consequence of the efforts of man to feed himself. If Malthus is correct subsequent generations should enjoy little if any advancement in comfort, whereas the recorded history of civilization is one of progressive improvement in the standard of living of the lowest sections of the population. Whether this be due to prudence or to the advance of knowledge or whatever cause, the broad facts of history have not supported the Malthusian theory, and Senior was right in asserting that the increase in population tends to lag behind the increase in supplies.

Malthus has been credited with being a pioneer in the inductive method in economics, but with regard to the subject of population this is a very superficial estimate. Although his illustrations and proofs have a first appearance of careful inductive work, the basis of all his ideas is the postulate of the geometrical ratio which he does not find in practice. Thus he does not go to work to test a hypothesis so much as to bolster up a theory. He uses his illustrations to show the existence of checks, but, since his classification of the checks is unscientific and defective, the method is neither useful nor instructive. He is unable to assign to them any quantitative details, and he leaves the reader with the impression that he is carefully selecting all the favourable material and overlooking that which is difficult to assimilate. He discovers his checks the world over but he is quite unable to evaluate their incidence, or even in many cases to connect them with numbers at all.

Nor is his statistical work of any considerable value. He is attempting to prove a thesis rather than develop methods, and, instead of welcoming the work of Booth and Ravenstone, who relied on age-group analysis to achieve results, he grudgingly acknowledges it, accuses Booth of being unable to apply his own methods, and ends by showing that, in spite of all, the geometrical ratio remains intact. Actually, with the inferior data at their disposal, these two critics probably did as much as was possible, but one is inclined to regret that they wrote so little as much as one regrets that Malthus wrote so much. At all events their method of concentrating on the group of women between menarche and menopause, and of analysing populations by means of age groups and mortality rates, brings them closely into line with the current methods of treatment. Without belittling Malthus's influence on the age in which he lived, and this has already been adequately dealt with, it remains true to say that the *Essay on Population* is mainly of historic interest, with the first edition as the most interesting specimen. The nearest approach he makes to the truth is in the restatement in the *Encyclopædia Britannica*, reprinted as the *Summary View*.

Bonar writes: 'He took the public into partnership with him, and made every discussion a means of improving his book. This gives the *Essay on Population* a unique character among economical writings. It leads the author to interpret his thoughts to us from many various points of view, leaving us, unhappily, often in doubt whether an alteration of language is or is not an alteration of thought.'

This is a doubtful compliment, if it is intended as such, but there is much truth in it, although it is difficult to see how increasing obscurity can improve a book if its main doctrines are clear. But the *Essay* throve on obscurity, and we have already seen that, whatever inconsistencies these frequent changes of language involved him in, Malthus could and did always fall back on the ratios as a final defence. Meanwhile it was impossible to criticize him without going to inordinate length.

Malthus did not enter into controversy with many of his critics, but we have examined such replies as he did vouchsafe. He gave as his reason for not replying, that their criticisms were not worthy of it, but, if the standard of the replies he actually did make is any criterion of his powers of controversy, in silence was wisdom. He could rarely refrain from allegory, and in almost every case it either misled his readers, roused their ire, or, in some instances, proved the very reverse of what he had intended.

We began with a quotation from Hazlitt in which he said of Malthus: 'He has not left opinion where he found it; he has advanced or given it a wrong bias.' By provoking a ferocious controversy Malthus invested the subject with immense importance, and to that extent he advanced it. As for his own work, he gave it a wrong bias. Which of the two outweighs the other is perhaps a matter of opinion, but, if there was any profit in controversy, then the works of his critics are worthy of consideration.

We end, as we began, with another quotation from the same writer, for whom this question was one of burning importance:

'We think he had the opportunity and the means in his hands of producing a great work on the principle of population; but we believe he has let it slip from his having an eye to other things besides that broad and unexplored question.'[1]

[1] *Spirit of the Age*, O.U.P., p. 153.

BIBLIOGRAPHY

This is not a complete bibliography of the relevant literature, but is compiled merely to facilitate the following of references made in this book.

BACON, FRANCIS. *Essays* (W. Aldis Wright's Edition). 1865.

BEER, MAX. *History of British Socialism.* 1920.

BONAR, JAMES. *Letters of David Ricardo to Thomas Robert Malthus.* 1887.

—— *Theories of Population from Raleigh to Arthur Young.*

—— *Malthus and His Work.* London, 1885. Second Edition. 1924.

BOOTH, DAVID. *A Letter to the Rev. T. R. Malthus, M.A., F.R.S., being an Answer to the Criticism on Mr. Godwin's Work on Population, which was inserted in the LXXth number of the 'Edinburgh Review,' etc.* London, 1823.

—— *Dissertation on the Ratios of Increase in Population, and in the Means of Subsistence.* (Incorporated in GODWIN, *Of Population.* London, 1820.)

CANNAN, EDWIN. *A History of the Theories of Production and Distribution in English Political Economy from 1776 to 1848.* Second Edition. London, 1903.

CHARLES, ENID. *The Menace of Under-Population.* London, 1936.

CUNNINGHAM, W. *The Growth of English Industry and Commerce in Modern Times—The Mercantile System.* Cambridge, 1925.

DARWIN, CHARLES. *On the Origin of Species by means of Natural Selection.* London, 1921. (Watts & Co.)

EDMONDS, THOMAS ROWE. *An Enquiry into the Principles of Population, exhibiting a System of Regulations for the Poor; designed immediately to lessen, and finally to remove, the evils which have hitherto pressed upon the Labouring Classes of Society.* London, 1832. (Published anonymously.)

ENSOR, GEORGE. *An Inquiry concerning the Population of Nations: containing a Refutation of Mr. Malthus's Essay on Population.* London, 1818.

EVERETT, A. H. *New Ideas on Population, with Remarks on the Theories of Malthus and Godwin.* Boston, 1823 and 1826.

FIELD, JAMES ALFRED. *Essays on Population and other Papers*. Chicago, 1931.

FLORENCE, P. SARGANT. *Over-Population*. London, 1926. (Kegan Paul.)

FRANKLIN, B. *Observations concerning the Increase of Mankind, Peopling of Countries, etc.* Pennsylvania, 1751. (Reprinted in McCulloch's Selection of Scarce and Valuable Tracts, listed below.)

GODWIN, WILLIAM. *An Enquiry concerning Political Justice, and its influence on general virtue and happiness*. London, 1793, 1797, and 1798.

—— *The Enquirer, Reflections on Education, Manners and Literature*. London, 1797.

—— *Thoughts occasioned by the Perusal of Dr. Parr's Spital Sermon, preached at Christ Church, April 15, 1800: being a Reply to the attacks of Dr. Parr, Mr. Mackintosh, the author of 'An Essay on Population,' and others*. London, 1801.

—— *Of Population. An Enquiry concerning the Power of Increase in the Numbers of Mankind, being an answer to Mr. Malthus's Essay on that subject*. London, 1820.

GRAHAME, JAMES. *An Inquiry into the Principle of Population: including an exposition of the causes and the advantages of a tendency to exuberance of numbers in society, a Defence of Poor-Laws, and a Critical and Historical View of the doctrines and projects of the Most Celebrated Legislators and Writers, relative to Population, the Poor, and Charitable Establishments*. Edinburgh, 1816.

GRAY, ALEXANDER. *The Socialist Tradition—Moses to Lenin*.

GRAY, SIMON. *The Happiness of States: or An Inquiry concerning Population, the modes of subsisting and employing it, and the effects of all on Human Happiness: in which is developed The New or Productive System of Statistics*. Second Edition. London, 1819.

—— *The Principles of Population and Production investigated, etc.* (Published under the pseudonym of PURVES. See below.)

GRIFFITH, G. TALBOT. *Population Problems of the Age of Malthus*. Cambridge, 1926.

HALE, MATTHEW. *The Primitive Origination of Mankind, considered and examined according to the Light of Nature*. London, 1677.

HALL, CHARLES. *The Effects of Civilization on the People in European States*. London, 1805. (Reprinted in the Phœnix Library. London, 1850.)

—— Appendix to above: 'Observations on the Principal Conclusion in Mr. Malthus's "Essay on Population."' London, 1805.

HAMMOND, J. L. and B. *The Village Labourer*.

HAZLITT, WILLIAM. *A Reply to the Essay on Population, by the Rev. T. R. Malthus. In a series of letters. To which are added, Extracts from the 'Essay,' with notes.* London, 1807.

—— *Political Essays, with sketches of Public Characters.* London, 1819.

—— *The Spirit of the Age or Contemporary Portraits.* (Oxford, World's Classics, 1947 Reprint.)

HOWLETT, JOHN. *An Examination of Dr. Price's Essay on the Population of England and Wales; and the Doctrine of an Increased Population in this Kingdom, established by Facts, etc.* Maidstone, 1781.

HULL, C. H. (Ed.). *The Economic Writings of Sir William Petty, together with the Observations upon the Bills of Mortality more probably by Captain John Graunt.* Two volumes. Cambridge, 1899.

HUME, DAVID. *Essays Moral, Political, and Literary.* Edited by Green and Grose. Two volumes. London, 1898.

JARROLD, THOMAS. *Dissertations on Man, Philosophical, Physiological and Political; in answer to Mr. Malthus's 'Essay on the Principle of Population.'* London, 1806.

JOHNSON, S. C. *History of Emigration.* London, 1913.

KEYNES, J. M. *Essays in Biography.* 1933.

LLOYD, W. F. *Two Lectures on the Checks to Population, delivered before the University of Oxford in Michaelmas Term, 1832.* Oxford, 1833.

MCCULLOCH, J. R. *A Selection of Scarce and Valuable Economical Tracts, from the Originals of Defoe, Elking, Franklin, Turgot, Anderson, Schomberg, Townsend, Burke, Bell and others, with a Preface, Notes, and Index.* London, 1859.

MACLEAN, C. M. *Born under Saturn.*

MALTHUS, T. R. *An Essay on the Principle of Population, as it affects the Future Improvement of Society, with Remarks on the Speculations of Mr. Godwin, M. Condorcet, and other Writers.* London, 1798. (Bonar's Edition. London, 1926.)

—— *An Essay on the Principle of Population; or, A View of its Past and Present Effects on Human Happiness; with an inquiry into our prospects respecting the future removal or mitigation of the evils which it occasions.* A New Edition, very much enlarged. London, 1803.

—— *The Same.* Third Edition, two volumes. London, 1806.

—— *The Same.* Fifth Edition, three volumes, with important additions. London, 1817.

—— *The Same.* Seventh Edition, one volume. London, 1872. (Reeves and Turner.)

—— *A Letter to Samuel Whitbread, Esq., M.P., on his proposed bill for the amendment of the poor laws.* Second Edition. London, 1807.

MALTHUS, T. R. *Observations on the Effects of the Corn Laws, and of a Rise or Fall in the Price of Corn on the Agriculture and General Wealth of the Country*. Third Edition. London, 1815.

—— *The Grounds of an Opinion on the Policy of Restricting the Importation of Foreign Corn; intended as an appendix to 'Observations on the Corn Laws.'* London, 1815.

—— *Additions to the Fourth and Former Editions of an Essay on the Principle of Population, etc*. London, 1817.

—— *A Summary View of the Principle of Population*. London, 1830.

—— *Principles of Political Economy considered with a view to their practical application. Second edition with considerable additions from the author's own manuscript and an original memoir*. (Contains Otter's *Memoir*.) London, 1836.

MILLS, CLARENCE A. *Climate Makes the Man*, 1944.

NITTI, F. S. *Population and the Social System*. London, 1894.

PALEY, WILLIAM. *The Principles of Moral and Political Philosophy*. 1785.

PAUL, C. KEGAN. *William Godwin: His Friends and Contemporaries*. Two Volumes. London, 1876.

PEARL, RAYMOND. *The Biology of Population Growth*. 1926.

—— *The Natural History of Population*. 1939.

PLACE, FRANCIS. *Illustrations and Proofs of the Principle of Population: including an examination of the proposed remedies of Mr. Malthus, and a Reply to the objections of Mr. Godwin and others*. London, 1822. (Reprint edited by Norman E. Himes, London, 1930.)

PRICE, RICHARD. *An Essay on the Population of England, from the Revolution to the Present Time*. Second Edition. London, 1780.

PURVES, GEORGE. *Gray versus Malthus. The Principles of Population and Production Investigated, etc*. London, 1818.

RALEGH, SIR WALTER. *The Historie of the World*, 1652.

—— *The Works of Sir Walter Ralegh, Kt*. Oxford, 1829.

RAVENSTONE, PIERCY. *A Few Doubts as to the correctness of some opinions generally entertained on the subjects of Population and Political Economy*. London, 1821.

ROGERS, THOROLD. *Six Centuries of Work and Wages*.

SADLER, M. T. *The Law of Population: A Treatise, in Six Books; in disproof of the Superfecundity of Human Beings, and developing the Real Principle of their Increase*. Two volumes. London, 1830.

SENIOR, N. W. *Two Lectures on Population, delivered before the University of Oxford, in Easter Term, 1828*. (*To which is added, a Correspondence between the Author and the Rev. T. R. Malthus*.) London, 1831.

—— *Outline of the Science of Political Economy*. 1836.

SMART, W. *Economic Annals of the Nineteenth Century, 1801–1820.* London, 1910.

SMITH, ADAM. *An Inquiry into the Nature and Causes of the Wealth of Nations.* 1776.

STANGELAND, E. *Pre-Malthusian Doctrines of Population.* 1904.

STARK, W. *The Ideal Foundations of Economic Thought.* (Kegan Paul.)

STEUART, JAMES. *An Inquiry into the Principles of Political Economy: being an Essay on the Science of Domestic Policy in Free Nations, in which are particularly considered Population, Agriculture, Trade, Industry, Money, Coin, Interest, Circulation, Banks, Exchange, Public Credit and Taxes.* Two volumes. London, 1767.

SÜSSMILCH, JOHANN. *Die Göttliche Ordnung.* Berlin, 1775.

THOMPSON, WILLIAM. *An Inquiry into the Principles of the Distribution of Wealth most conducive to Human Happiness; applied to the newly proposed system of Voluntary Equality of Wealth.* London, 1824.

TOOKE, THOMAS. *A History of Prices, and of the State of the Circulation, from 1793 to 1837; preceded by a brief sketch of the state of the corn trade in the last two centuries.* Two volumes. London, 1838.

TOWNSEND, JOSEPH. *A Dissertation on the Poor Laws (by a Well-Wisher to Mankind).* London, 1786. (Reprinted in McCulloch's Collection of Scarce Tracts—see above.)

—— *A Journey through Spain in the Years 1786 and 1787.* Second Edition. 1792.

WALES, WILLIAM. *An Inquiry into the Present State of Population in England and Wales, etc.* London, 1781.

WALLACE, ROBERT. *A Dissertation on the Numbers of Mankind, in Ancient and Modern Times.* Edinburgh, 1809. (First Edition, 1753.)

—— *Various Prospects of Mankind, Nature and Providence.* London, 1761.

WEBB, S. and B. *English Local Government—English Poor Law History.* Part II, Vol. I.

WEYLAND, JOHN (Jun.) *The Principles of Population and Production, as they are affected by the Progress of Society; with a view to Moral and Political Consequences.* London, 1816.

WHATELY, RICHARD. *Introductory Lectures on Political Economy, delivered in Easter Term, 1831. Second Edition, including Lecture IX, and other additions.* London, 1832.

BIBLIOGRAPHY

[illegible]

INDEX OF NAMES

INDEX OF NAMES

INDEX

INDEX

INDEX

INDEX

INDEX